13/32/Hc

SCHOOLS IN WALES 1500-1900

Map showing the pre-1974 counties of Wales from Kenneth O. Morgan, *Rebirth of a Nation: Wales 1880-1980* (Clarendon Press, 1981), by permission of Oxford University Press.

SCHOOLS IN WALES

1500 - 1900

A Social and Architectural History

by

MALCOLM SEABORNE

GEE & SON LIMITED
DENBIGH

*This volume is published with the support of the
Leverhulme Trust*

Printed and Published by
GEE & SON LIMITED, DENBIGH, CLWYD, WALES

For my grandchildren:
JAMES
TOM
BEN
HATTIE

Preface

This book owes its origin to the encouragement which I received from Professor Robert Steel, the former Principal of Swansea University College, and its completion to the help and advice given by Professor Glanmor Williams of the same College. Professor Williams very generously read each section of my typescript as it was written and suggested many improvements in the text, as well as saving me from a number of errors. I owe much to his kindness, and such deficiences as remain should be put down to my account.

My second major debt is to the Leverhulme Trust, who awarded me an Emeritus Fellowship, thus enabling me to visit schools and archive collections in every part of Wales. The support of the Trust has also made it possible to include the numerous illustrations printed in this book.

I am also very glad to express my appreciation of the head teachers of schools and the staffs of local record offices in Wales, who gave me every assistance. Similar help was willingly given by the staff of the National Library of Wales, the National Monuments Record for Wales, the Welsh Folk Museum, the Welsh Library at the University College of North Wales, and Clwyd County Library. The staff of the central reference libraries at Newport and Swansea, and of the British Architectural Library in London, were equally helpful.

I should particularly like to thank the architects, archivists, librarians and curators who have given permission to reproduce many of the illustrations included in this book, as detailed in the Lists of Figures and Plates. I am also grateful to my son, Michael, who printed the negatives of the photographs taken in the course of my field-work, and to Elena Williams and Angela Hughes, who re-lettered my plans. Christine Lynas typed successive drafts of the book with great skill and patience, while Emlyn Evans, the Managing Director of Gee & Son (Denbigh) Ltd., took a keen personal interest in the production of the book, for which I am very grateful.

I also wish to acknowledge the help and encouragement given by Vernon Hughes of Abergele in Denbighshire, and by Thomas Lloyd of Cresselly in Pembrokeshire. To have had the advice of two such experienced architectural historians in north and south Wales was, indeed, a great boon.

Finally, I thank my wife for her constant support and practical help. She also helped me to locate old school buildings in remote rural parts of Wales, as well as fearlessly negotiating the congested roads of the conurbations of south Wales. The subject of this book, in the last analysis, is the children who were educated in the schools I have tried to describe, and my interest in young children has been refreshed by my four grandchildren, to whom this book is dedicated.

Pantymwyn, Mold.   M.S.
20 July 1992.

Contents

Abbreviations

Aberdare Report	*Report of the Committee appointed to Inquire into the Condition of Intermediate and Higher Education in Wales* (1881)
Ang.	Anglesey
Blue Books	*Reports of the Commissioners on the State of Education in Wales* (1847)
Brecs.	Breconshire
CADW	Welsh Historic Monuments
Caerns.	Caernarfonshire
Cards.	Cardiganshire
Carms.	Carmarthenshire
CCR	*Charity Commissioners' Reports* (1833-7)
CRO	County Record Office
CWB	Central Welsh Board
Denbs.	Denbighshire
Flints.	Flintshire
Glam.	Glamorgan
HMSO	Her Majesty's Stationery Office
Mer.	Merioneth
Mon.	Monmouthshire
Mont.	Montgomeryshire
n.d.	no date
NLW	National Library of Wales
Pembs.	Pembrokeshire
Rads.	Radnorshire
RCAHM(W)	Royal Commission on Ancient and Historical Monuments in Wales
RIBA	Royal Institute of British Architects
SEW	*Reports of the Commissioners on the State of Education in Wales* (1847)
SIC	Schools Inquiry Commission (1868)
SPCK	Society for Promoting Christian Knowledge

List of Figures in Text

List of Plates

19. Abergavenny, Mon., grammar school held in former St. John's Church (from Gwyn Jones, *Medieval Abergavenny*).

20. Ruthin, Denbs., headmaster's house, 1742.

21. Beaumaris, Ang., grammar school (L) 1603, and headmaster's house (R), later enlarged.

22. Deuddwr, Mont., school, eighteenth/nineteenth century.

23. Llandeilo Gresynni (Llantilio Crossenny), Mon., school built in 1820 at Brynderi.

24. Wrexham, Denbs., grammar school, painting by Moses Griffith c.1780. (National Library of Wales).

25. Bowl showing Edward Jones, schoolmaster, 1751. (Welsh Folk Museum).

26. Amlwch, Anglesey, National school, 1821.

27. Nolton, Pembs., Grant's school, 1810.

28. Trelleck, Mon., endowed school, rebuilt 1820.

29. Penley, Flints., Madras school, 1811.

30. Llangasty Tal-y-llyn, Brecs., 1850, church school and master's house designed by J. L. Pearson.

31. Chirk, Denbs., school and teacher's house designed by Thomas Penson, 1844.

32. Trelawnyd, Flints., church school designed by Lloyd Williams & Underwood, 1860.

33. Magor, Mon., church school designed by Prichard & Seddon, 1856.

34. Llangollen, Denbs., British school, 1846.

35. Aberystwyth, Skinner Street, British school, 1846 (and later?).

36. Bangor Normal College by John Barnett, 1858-62.

37. Aberdare, Glam., British school by Evan Griffiths, 1866. (Welsh Folk Museum).

38. Blaenafon, Mon., school founded by Sarah Hopkins, 1816.

39. Llandygai, Caerns., school founded by Douglas Pennant, 1843.

40. Dowlais, Glam., Lady Guest in the school designed by Sir Charles Barry in 1855. (Glamorgan CRO, Cardiff).

41. Bala, Mer., grammar school, 1851, by Wigg & Pownall, later extended (R) in similar style.

42. Cowbridge, Glam., grammar school by John Prichard, 1849-52. (Welsh Folk Museum).

43. Swansea, new grammar school by Thomas Taylor, 1853. (National Museum of Wales).

44. Carmarthen, grammar school, c.1844. (National Monuments Record for Wales).

45. Llandovery College, Carms., by Fuller & Gingell, 1851 and later. (National Library of Wales).

46. Cardigan, guild hall, including a grammar school (ground floor, L), by R. J. Withers, 1858-60.

47. Monmouth School, rebuilt by W. Snooke, 1865-95. (Monmouth Museum).

48. Llandaff, Glam., Howell's school by Herbert Williams, 1860. (Welsh Folk Museum).

49. Welshpool, Mont., grammar school by George Gilbert Scott, 1853.

50. Holt Academy, Denbs.. 1855 and later.

51. Whitland, Carms., board school by George Morgan, 1877.

52. Roath Park, Cardiff, board school by E. W. M. Corbett, 1894.

53. Manselton Board School, Swansea, by G. E. T. Laurence, 1900. (Swansea City Archives).

54. Acrefair, Denbs., board school interior, 1905. (Clwyd CRO, Ruthin).

55. Pentre Rhondda, Glam., board school interior, c1900. (Welsh Folk Museum).

56. Cardigan, county intermediate school, official opening ceremony, 1898. (Aberystwyth Public Library).

57. Abergavenny, Mon., new grammar school building nearing completion, 1898. (Abergavenny Museum).

58. Carmarthen, Queen Elizabeth grammar (intermediate) school, science laboratory, c.1909. (Welsh Folk Museum).

59. Llanfyllin, Mont., county intermediate school by Harry Teather, 1900.

60. Bangor, Friars School by John Douglas, 1900.

61. Denbigh, county intermediate school by James Hughes, 1902.

List of Tables

Introduction

The history of education in Wales has often been written with the emphasis on the controversies which accompanied many of the changes which took place. The present study takes account of the political and religious background, which is particularly important in Wales, but it is mainly an attempt to assess, after each phase of development, what of permanent value had been achieved when the dust of conflict had cleared away. Attention is focused on the changes which took place in the internal organization and external architecture of the schools built in Wales at successive stages from the Reformation to the end of Victoria's reign.

In this book, the architectural character of the schools mentioned is fully considered, but the buildings are viewed primarily as social documents. Documentary material relating to the history of education in Wales is often fragmentary, and the evidence provided by school buildings constitutes a valuable additional source of information. Even those schools with little or no architectural merit are often important from the educational and social points of view. A detailed examination of the earliest purpose-built schools in Wales shows that they were an accurate reflection of contemporary developments, both in education and architecture, and provide insights not available from other sources.

A further pressing reason for attempting this survey is that the number of old and often interesting school buildings which survive is being reduced year by year and, as redevelopment schemes increase in scale, the physical evidence of the history of education in Wales is rapidly disappearing; there is therefore an urgent need to record what is left before it is too late. A study of surviving school buildings shows that schools have been in a constant state of change, and that the proponents of new developments in education have never hesitated to alter the buildings which they inherited. New schools expressing new ideas were also built, only to be radically altered or replaced by succeeding generations. It is hoped that the searching out of what is left of earlier school buildings, supplemented by contemporary illustrations and modern photography, will draw attention to unfamiliar and, in some cases, aesthetically pleasing examples which have survived down to our own time. In the process, it is also hoped that readers will have obtained a fuller picture of an important aspect of the social history of Wales.

Finally, the development of schools in Wales may be regarded as a case-study in what historians of education call 'cultural transfer'.[1] As formal education continues to spread throughout the world, there is currently much discussion about the impact of schooling on minority cultures. Welsh culture has proved to be highly resilient, and the extent to which education in Wales was influenced by, but differed from, the situation in England is exemplified in the following pages. It should be added that, throughout this book, the historic (pre-1974) counties of Wales, as shown on the adjoining map (see frontispiece), are used as the basis for all geographical references.

[1] See the *International Newsletter for the History of Education*, No. 16, November 1991 (ISSN 0 254-8569).

CHAPTER I

Tudor and Stuart Schools

Wales shared in the movement for founding or re-founding grammar schools which was a notable feature of Tudor activity in educational matters. Well-educated men were needed for maintaining the reformed Church and for staffing the legal and administrative system, both in London and in the localities, and the new grammar schools of Wales, often founded by expatriate Welshmen, played an important part in sending Welsh boys to Oxford or Cambridge and to the Inns of Court, and so to careers both inside and outside Wales.[1] Although the physical remains of sixteenth-century school buildings in Wales have almost wholly disappeared, some evidence can still be gleaned about them.

The grammar school at Abergavenny, which was founded in 1543 from the revenues of a suppressed monastery, met in the parish church in the traditional manner and did not have a purpose-built school.[2] At Carmarthen, a grammar school

---

[1] For a detailed account, see W. P. Griffith, 'Schooling and Society' in J. G. Jones (ed.), *Class, Community and Culture in Tudor Wales* (Cardiff, University of Wales Press, 1989), ch. 3 and, more generally, Glanmor Williams, *Recovery, Reorientation and Reformation. Wales c.1415-1642* (Oxford, Clarendon Press, 1987), ch. 18.

[2] L. S. Knight, *Welsh Independent Grammar Schools to 1600* (Newtown, Welsh Outlook Press, 1926), 17. When the grammar school at Abergavenny occupied St John's church, the former priory church of St Mary became the parish church (Gwyn Jones, *Medieval Abergavenny* (Abergavenny, Seargeant Brothers, n.d.)).

was also founded in 1543, but had to be re-founded in 1576; a separate school building did not appear until 1622. This was a single-storey limestone building, situated on the site of the present hospital in Priory Street.[3] Redundant ecclesiastical buildings were sometimes used for the new grammar schools. For example, the former collegiate church at Abergwili was transferred in 1541 to the suppressed Dominican friary at Brecon, some of whose buildings, much enlarged in the nineteenth century, are still used by Christ College, which is now an independent school.[4] The grammar school at Bangor, founded in 1557, similarly occupied part of the former premises of a Dominican friary. It retained its name of Friars School but nothing survives of the original building, apart from a few carved stones.[5] At Llandaff, St Asaph and St David's, the schools (probably choristers' schools, rather than grammar schools as such) appear to have survived the upheavals of the Reformation changes but very little is known about them during this period. At St David's, the choristers' school was held in a building to the south-west of the west front of the cathedral and, below it, was a workshop used for repair work in connection with the cathedral: this was on the site of the new chapter house built by Nash in the 1790s and is shown on a plan included in Edward Yardley's *Menevia Sacra* (1739-61).[6]

Several new grammar schools were founded in Wales in the Elizabethan period. At Presteigne, the grammar school established by John Beddoes in 1565 had a school and house for the master, either in the same building or immediately

[3] M. Evans, *An Early History of Queen Elizabeth Grammar School, Carmarthen, 1576-1800* (Carmarthen, The School, n.d.), 50f. For the illustration of the 1622 school, see Fig. 4(a) below. For the earlier school, see *Carmarthen Antiquary*, X (1974), 49-63.

[4] The former friary buildings at Brecon are described in R. Haslam, *The Buildings of Wales. Powys* (Harmondsworth, Penguin Books, 1979), 293f. For Barlow's transfer of the college at Abergwili to Brecon, see *Bulletin of the Board of Celtic Studies*, XV (1953), 222.

[5] RCAHM (Wales), *An Inventory of the Ancient Monuments in Caernarfonshire*, II (London, HMSO, 1960), 13.

[6] F. Green (ed.), *Menevia Sacra by Edward Yardley* (London, The Bedford Press, 1927), plan facing p. 5 and description p. 7; references I owe to Canon Wyn Evans.

adjoining it, in St David's Street facing the churchyard, but they were destroyed in a fire which damaged much of Presteigne in 1681.[7] At Caernarfon, a school founded or re-founded in the sixteenth century appears to have had an Elizabethan building, and Speed's map of the town made in 1610 shows 'The Free Schole' at the castle end of 'Shire-hall Strete' on the site now occupied by the County Hall.[8] The only sixteenth-century school which still provides some evidence of a purpose-built structure is at Ruthin, which was re-founded in 1574 by Gabriel Goodman, a native of the town and Dean of Westminster from 1561 to 1601. The school building near the parish church (Plate 1),* though extensively restored in 1700 and further altered in the nineteenth century, probably retains its original lay-out. The school's historian says that the original building consisted of one large room on the ground floor, with the master at one end and the assistant master or usher at the other (which was the usual arrange-ment in the larger schools), and with accommodation for the master and boarders in the attic rooms above. He adds that 'in the nineteenth century it was scorned as a building, but in 1574 it was a model of the new Reformation school'.[9] Other schools, or at least schoolmasters, are mentioned in other places in the sixteenth century — as at Margam (1558), Harlech (1590), Caerleon (1592), Welshpool (1595) and elsewhere.[10] There were also private tutors employed in gentry households who sometimes also taught local children, the best-known example being the household school of the Wynn family at Gwydir probably attended by William Morgan before he went on to Westminster School and St John's College, Cambridge, and subsequently to make his classic translation of the Bible into Welsh.[11] It would certainly be a

[7] W. H. Howse, *School and Bell* (Halesowen, Parkes, 1956), 15.
[8] L. S. Knight, op. cit., 11-12 and Appendix XXI.
* The Plates are reproduced following p. 216.
[9] Keith M. Thompson, *Ruthin School* (Ruthin, The School), 77. 91.
[10] For early schools in Glamorgan, see *Glamorgan County History*, IV (1974), 115.
[11] Glanmor Williams, 'William Morgan's Bible and the Cambridge Con-nection' in *Welsh History Review*, XIV (1989), 363f.

mistake to underestimate the importance of informal schools and of private education in the sixteenth century and later, but the setting up of formally constituted schools with their own endowments and buildings was relatively rare before 1600. By the early nineteenth century, the Charity Commissioners were able to discover only seven endowed schools in Wales of pre-1600 foundation which had survived (usually in later buildings), as set out in Table I.

TABLE I — PRE-1600 SCHOOL ENDOWMENTS

Date	Place	Former County	Founder	Comment
Not known	St Asaph	Flint	Cathedral (Dean and Chapter)	Permitted to continue in 1549
1541*	Brecon	Brecon	William Barlow (Bishop of St David's)	Transferred from Abergwili (Dyfed)
1543	Abergavenny	Monmouth	Henry VIII	Allocated the tithes of Usk Abbey
1557	Bangor	Caernarfon	Geoffrey Glynne (Brother of Bishop of Bangor, lawyer)	Rebuilt
1565	Presteigne	Radnor	John Beddoes (Merchant clothier)	Rebuilt
1574*	Ruthin	Denbigh	Gabriel Goodman (Dean of Westminster)	Elizabethan building restored
1576*	Carmarthen	Carmarthen	Queen Elizabeth & Earl of Essex	Rebuilt

* Refoundations

The seventeenth century saw a considerable increase in the number of schools established in Wales, and this reflected several important new developments, the seeds of which may be detected in the previous century but which did not come to fruition until the Stuart period. A useful starting point is provided by the reports of the Charity Commissioners, who thoroughly investigated school charities in the 1830s, but a number of limitations in this source need to be recognized.[12] In the first place, the Commissioners were concerned only with schools endowed with property, which produced the income necessary for maintaining the schoolmaster and a limited number of free scholars, to whose number it was usually permitted to add fee-paying pupils. A few endowments escaped the Charity Commissioners' net and there were many other more ephemeral 'schools' — in the sense of schoolmasters (often parish priests or fee-charging private individuals) teaching small groups of children — which were not endowed and so did not come within the purview of the Commission. In some parts of England, the subscription books in which schoolmasters were required to certify their religious orthodoxy have revealed a host of such teachers,[13] and in Wales W. P. Griffith has shown for the period up to about 1640 how much data on this subject can be accumulated from a variety of sources, especially the admission registers of Oxford and Cambridge colleges. Since the main focus of the present study is the development of school buildings, there is some justification for concentrating on the endowed schools, which were the schools most likely to have had their own buildings. Even within the limited sphere of the endowed schools, however, the Commissioners' reports make abundantly clear the perils arising from inadequate endowments and from legal disputes over the entitlements to property, as well as from the failures of trustees, who tended to become more lazy or negligent with the passage of time. Continuity in school provision was still relatively rare.

Another major difficulty is that of determining the educational character of most of the lesser-known schools. The terms of an endowment were often vague on the question of

---

[12] The Charity Commissioners' *Reports* (hereafter cited as *CCR*) covered Wales as follows: 26th Report (1833) Anglesey; 28th Report (1834) Caernarvon, Cardigan, Carmarthen, Merioneth and Pembroke; 32nd Report (1837) Brecon, Denbigh, Flint, Glamorgan, Montgomery and Radnor. The Report on Monmouth (27th Report, 1833) formed part of the English series.

[13] E.g., E. H. Carter, *The Norwich Subscription Books* (London, Nelson, 1937).

curriculum: much obviously depended on local demand and on the qualifications of the teacher. The most prestigious schools were the major grammar schools, but it is unlikely that their imitators always pursued the complete classical curriculum. John Brinsley, the leading Puritan educationalist of the early seventeenth century, complained that even in the grammar schools it was often necessary to admit 'petties' or little boys who had not learnt English grammar, let alone Latin.[14] And here it may be noted that the Welsh grammar schools followed those in England in using English or, in the higher forms, Latin, as the medium of instruction. Some seventeenth-century founders clearly set out to provide schools to prepare the pupils for further education at other schools. Thus, at Llanrwst in 1676, Thomas Wynne settled property for a curate 'to read divine service and keep school', and to teach ten children gratis, 'such children to continue in the school till they . . . should be capable of a higher school'.[15] This was very much in the tradition of the chantry and guild schools of the previous century, where one of the very few records surviving for this type of school (a guild school at Montgomery in 1549) declared its aim to teach 'young beginners only to write and sing, and to read so far as the Accidence Rules, but no grammar'.[16] Other seventeenth-century foundations provided for curates to say prayers and to teach children, by implication in elementary subjects only. At Llanfair Dyffryn Clwyd, Mr Rice (Rhys) Williams built a chapel of ease, called Jesus Chapel, in 1619, and in 1623 endowed it with a stipend for a curate 'to read evening prayers in the said chapel on Sundays and morning prayers on holy days, and Wednesdays and Fridays in Lent, and to teach a school therein'.[17] Similarly, the will of the Reverend John Ellis, the incumbent at Dolgellau (1665), provided the income for a schoolmaster to read prayers three times a day

---

[14] J. Brinsley, *Ludus Literarius* (1627), reprinted by Liverpool University Press, 1917, 12-13.
[15] *CCR*, 32, 61.
[16] Quoted by W. P. Griffith, op. cit., 83, spelling modernized.
[17] *CCR*, 32, 69. This school/chapel, as rebuilt in 1787, still survives near Llanfair Dyffryn Clwyd.

and to teach twelve children in Harlech up to the age of sixteen, which was below the usual age for completing the full grammar-school course.[18] He made exactly the same provision for Dolgellau, yet the Charity Commissioners classified the Harlech school as 'non-classical' and the Dolgellau school as 'grammar', presumably because by the 1830s there were eight pay-scholars at Dolgellau learning the classics.

The converse process may also be observed, that is, schools which may well have been founded as grammar schools but were classified as non-classical by the Commissioners because of later developments. One example of this was the school founded at Northop in Flintshire in 1606 which was teaching wholly elementary subjects by 1837. It is true that this school (as was not unusual) had no statutes, but it was founded by the Reverend George Smith, chancellor of the diocese of St Asaph, whose bishop was one of the trustees. Provision was also made for a master and later an usher, and, as we shall see, for a school building; and in 1678 it was mentioned in a list which included the grammar schools at Bangor, Ruthin and others in North Wales.[19] No doubt it later succumbed to the more successful schools at Hawarden and St Asaph. Similarly, the Free School at Hanmer, endowed in 1625 under the will of Roger Billinge and classified as a non-classical school in 1837, had a graduate master at the time of endowment, one of a line stretching back to the previous century.[20] There is no doubt that the Charity Commissioners made genuine efforts to ascertain the original intentions of the founders of all the schools they examined but it was, and is, often impossible to determine with certainty the standing of local schools in the seventeenth century. Nevertheless, it is probable that most of the post-1650 schools described as non-classical by the Commissioners were teaching elementary rather than classical subjects, even in the seventeenth century. This was mainly because a

---

[18] For Harlech (Llandanwg) see *CCR* 28, 530 and for Dolgellau, 561.
[19] T. W. Pritchard, 'Northop Grammar School', *Flints. Hist. Soc. J.,* XXIX (1979-80), 3-17.
[20] D. Pratt, *Clwyd Historian,* No. 23 (1989), 10.

considerable number of grammar schools had been founded during the first thirty years of the century, and they, along with the earlier foundations in Wales and the grammar schools in England frequently attended by the sons of the gentry, may well have satisfied the demand for a classical education.

The list of thirty-eight schools with seventeenth-century endowments set out in Table II shows impressive progress. Grammar schools were established in most of the market towns and followed the lines laid down in the previous century. Ecclesiastical foundations continued; but more significant were those made by laymen, including members of the gentry and merchants like William Jones at Monmouth and Thomas Nevitt or Ednyfed, a citizen and draper of London, who made a bequest towards a grammar school in his native Ruabon.[21] The first thirty years of the century were a veritable golden age of grammar-school foundations, both in Wales and England. This was followed by a notable gap in the 1630s and 1640s, no doubt resulting from the uncertainties of the Civil War period. The Act for the Better Propagation of the Gospel in Wales, passed in 1650, set up no fewer than 60 free schools throughout Wales, but by 1660 only 21 of them appear to have survived, and these seem to have withered away soon afterwards: only Cardigan Grammar School continued as a major foundation, chiefly because it was taken over by the town council.[22]

After the Restoration, the endowment of schools, particularly non-classical schools, continued at a steady pace. The non-classical or elementary schools were founded mainly by minor gentry or yeomen, all of whom appear to have been members of the Established Church; there seems to be no evidence, such as one finds in some Puritan areas in England, of schools endowed by Dissenters in the Restoration period, though they did make provision for theological training in Dissenting academies. The charity schools set up by the

[21] A. H. Williams, 'The origins of the old endowed grammar schools of Denbighshire', *Trans. Den. Hist. Soc.*, II (1953), 48-9.
[22] *CCR,* 28, 593.

TABLE II — SEVENTEENTH-CENTURY ENDOWED SCHOOLS

Date of Endowment*	Place	Former County	First endowed by	Charity Comm'n category**
1603	Wrexham	Denbigh	V. Broughton	Grammar
1605	Chepstow	Monmouth	R. Cleyton	Non-classical
1606	Northop	Flint	Revd. G. Smith	Non-classical
1606	Hawarden	Flint	G. Ledsham	Grammar
1609	Cowbridge	Glamorgan	Sir E. Stradling	Grammar
1609	Beaumaris	Anglesey	D. Hughes	Grammar
1612	Llanrwst	Denbigh	Sir J. Wynn	Grammar
1614	Monmouth	Monmouth	W. Jones	Grammar
1614	Haverfordwest	Pembroke	T. Lloyd	Grammar
1616	Botwnnog	Caernarfon	Bishop H. Rowlands	Grammar
1621	Carmarthen	Carmarthen	Lord Chichester	Non-classical
1621	Usk	Monmouth	R. Edwards	Grammar
1623	Llanfair Dyffryn Clwyd	Denbigh	R. Williams	Non-classical
1624	Defynnog	Brecon	Sir J. Davy	Non-classical
1625	Hanmer	Flint	R. Billinge	Non-classical
1632	Ruabon	Denbigh	T. Nevitt	Grammar
1650	Llanegryn	Merioneth	H. Owen	Grammar
1652	Berriew	Montgomery	H. Jones	Non-classical
1653	Cardigan	Cardigan	Act for Propagation of Gospel	Grammar
1654	Llantilio Crossenny†	Monmouth	J. Powell	Grammar
1660	Rhayader	Radnor	J. Davies	Non-classical
1664	Treuddyn	Flint	G. Roberts	Non-classical
1664	Nercwys	Flint	G. Roberts	Non-classical
1664	Holt	Denbigh	G. Roberts	Non-classical
1665	Dolgellau	Merioneth	Revd. J. Ellis	Grammar
1665	Llandanwg (Harlech)	Merioneth	Revd. J. Ellis	Non-classical
1670	Hay-on-Wye	Brecon	W. Pennoyer	Non-classical
1675	Llanasa	Flint	Thomas ap Hugh	Non-classical
1675	Bassaleg	Monmouth	R. & F. Morgan	Non-classical
1676	Llanrwst	Denbigh	T. Wynne	Non-classical

* The date of endowment is sometimes later than the date of foundation.
** The categorization of schools is further discussed in the text.
† This is the anglicized name of the parish hereafter referred to as Llandeilo Gresynni.

Date of Endowment	Place	Former County	First endowed by	Charity Comm'n category
1682	Swansea	Glamorgan	Bishop H. Gore	Grammar
1684	Haverfordwest	Pembroke	M. Tasker	Non-classical
1686	Brecon	Brecon	R. Powell	Non-classical
1689	Penallt	Monmouth	Revd. Z. Babington	Non-classical
1690	Deytheur (Deuddwr)	Montgomery	A. Newport	Grammar
1691	Trelleck	Monmouth	Revd. Z. Babington	Non-classical
1691	Pembroke	Pembroke	G. Dawes	Grammar
1695	Deneio (Pwllheli)	Caernarfon	Revd. H. Jones	Grammar

Welsh Trust and the marked increase in the number of books published after 1660 laid the foundations for the work of the SPCK and the Circulating Schools in the following century, but the Trust schools did not occupy purpose-built premises and the terms of the endowments of the non-classical schools about which information is available made provision for the teaching of English rather than Welsh; they were in any event set up mainly on the eastern borders of Wales, where English was widely used. It should be added that, although the grammar schools were a male preserve, it is likely that some girls attended the endowed elementary schools. The terms of these endowments usually refer to 'children' rather than to 'scholars' or 'boys' mentioned in grammar-school statutes, though the formal provision for a school mistress made at Woollaston in Monmouthshire by Margaret Cleyton, the executrix of her husband's will, for a school at Chepstow, was exceptional.[23] There is plenty of evidence of privately educated gentlewomen in Tudor and Stuart Wales, but little seems to have been done for the education of girls below gentry or merchant rank until the eighteenth century.

The geographical distribution of seventeenth-century endowed schools is also worthy of comment. As one would expect, they were situated mainly in the more fertile and populous areas along the coasts of north and south Wales

[23] CCR, 27, 394.

and along the boundary with England. No less than half of the total number of endowments were in Monmouthshire (7), Denbighshire (6) and Flintshire (6). The Act of Union of 1536 had designated Caernarfon, Denbigh, Carmarthen and Brecon as the administrative centres for chanceries and exchequers and there were, as we have seen, sixteenth-century grammar schools at Brecon and Carmarthen. The school at Caernarfon seems to have been overtaken by the major grammar schools at Bangor and Beaumaris, and, although Denbigh certainly had its schoolmasters in the seventeenth century, a grammar school was not formally instituted there until 1727.[24] This may be accounted for by the emergence of Wrexham (which had a grammar school from 1603) as a more important centre.[25] It has been calculated from the Hearth Tax returns that by 1670 the main Welsh towns, in decreasing order the size, were Wrexham, Brecon, Carmarthen, Haverfordwest, Cardiff and Caernarfon.[26] All but the last two had permanent schools well before 1670, and by 1700 every county in Wales may be said to have benefited in some degree from the endowment of schools.

If one begins in the north-west and moves anti-clockwise around the central massif of Wales, it may be noted that in Anglesey an important grammar school had been founded in 1603 at Beaumaris (endowed 1609), and in Caernarfon-shire the Friars School at Bangor continued to flourish and was joined later in the century by grammar schools at Botwnnog and Pwllheli. Merioneth had endowed schools at Llanegryn, Dolgellau and Harlech, while Cardiganshire had its own grammar school in the county town. In Pembroke-shire there were two schools at Haverfordwest and another at Pembroke. Carmarthen had its sixteenth-century grammar school, with a non-classical school in the same town, while Glamorgan had grammar-school foundations at Cowbridge

[24] W. A. Evans, 'The history of the Denbigh Grammar School', *Y Bych* (Denbigh County School Magazine), 1954, 588.
[25] D. H. Owen (ed.), *Settlement and Society in Wales* (Cardiff, University of Wales Press, 1989), 231.
[26] Ibid., 269. Swansea, which had its own grammar school from 1682, was probably larger than Caernarfon and Cardiff at this date.

and Swansea. Monmouthshire, in addition to the earlier foundation at Abergavenny, had seven other endowed schools, often formalizing previously informal teaching, at Chepstow, Monmouth, Usk, Llandeilo Gresynni, Bassaleg, Penallt and Trelleck. In Breconshire there was the school founded in Henry VIII's reign at Brecon, with a non-classical school in the same town and others at Defynnog and Hay-on-Wye. Radnorshire had its Elizabethan school at Presteigne and a later foundation at Rhayader, while Montgomeryshire acquired endowments at Berriew and Deuddwr, near Welshpool. In Denbighshire, already provided with a major foundation at Ruthin, there were grammar schools at Wrexham, Llanrwst and Ruabon, with non-classical schools at Llanfair Dyffryn Clwyd, Holt and Llanrwst. Flintshire, in addition to the cathedral school at St. Asaph, had by 1700 acquired endowed schools at Northop, Hawarden, Hanmer, Treuddyn, Nercwys and Llanasa. It is clear that in terms both of grammar-school and elementary education this was a period of considerable advance, and this list takes no account of the other more transitory schools which have left no firm record behind them, or were not endowed in the seventeenth century.

Even the endowed schools did not always have purpose-built schools (for example, the school established at Holt in 1664 met in a room underneath the town hall),[27] and relatively few original seventeenth-century school buildings have survived the vicissitudes of three centuries of building development. As one might expect, it is the major foundations which have left most evidence behind them about their original buildings and it also appears that more early school buildings survive in the north than in the south of Wales because of the extensive urban developments which later occurred in the south. The survival of seventeenth-century school buildings depended on many chance factors and it would be unwise to read too much into their present

[27] *CCR*, 32, 119

geographical distribution. The original siting of schools within particular communities, however, is often significant. The great majority of schools in Tudor and Stuart times were closely linked with the Church and many were built adjoining the parish church and often in part of the churchyard itself. This was true of Ruthin School and continued to be so for many schools founded in the seventeenth century and later. In the case of town schools supported by the local vestry or corporation, the market-place was a favoured position. The school at Brecon was neither near the church nor the centre of the town since its location was dictated by the position of the former friary buildings. At Llanrwst, however, a large site outside the town was intentionally selected. Richard Mulcaster, the leading Elizabethan writer on education, advocated that grammar schools should be 'planted in the skirts and suburbs of towns . . . for the benefit of the open fields for exercises of more range',[28] and it may be that Sir John Wynn had this in mind when in 1612 he drew up his statutes for Llanrwst School, which he ordered to be built at Cae Hullyn, some distance from the parish church. This piece of land was not to be ploughed or enclosed and the pupils were 'to have liberty to play all over it'; the benefit of the grass (i.e. for grazing or for hay) was to go to the usher who, like the master, was to have a house and garden near the school.[29] This was very generous provision and was actually carried out, though legal disputes about the tithes which formed the main part of the school endowment continued for many years after the school was built. The school building itself is discussed below.

As far as the external style and internal planning of school buildings were concerned, a specialized architecture for schools had hardly yet emerged and surviving buildings may most appropriately be compared with developments in contemporary domestic architecture. Peter Smith has shown that the eastern half of Wales formed part of an important

[28] R. Mulcaster, *Positions* (1581) ed. R. H. Quick (London, 1888). 222-31.
[29] R. J. Parry, *Llanrwst Grammar School 1610-1960* (The School, 1960), 7.

'intermediate zone' of building which incorporated features of both the lowland region to the south-east and the highland region to the west. In the highland region surviving farmsteads tend to be poorer and more recent and, as we have already noted, early school buildings were much more numerous on the eastern than the western side of Wales. He also distinguishes between a 'First Great Rebuilding' in the late medieval period, which saw the emergence of the single-storey hall-house, and a 'Second Great Rebuilding' of the Tudor and Stuart period, which marked the beginning of the replacement of hall-houses by 'sub-medieval' storeyed houses, particularly by the squire and yeoman class.[30] Many medieval hall-houses were converted into storeyed dwellings during the sixteenth and seventeenth centuries, but Smith notes that 'in a few aristocratic houses the social significance of the great hall was such as to preserve it little altered'.[31] Bearing in mind the universal practice of conducting all the teaching in a school in one room, usually under a single master, it is not surprising to find that the hall-house open to the roof was often taken as the model for school buildings at this period and indeed later. However, just as the desire for greater privacy and upstairs bedrooms led to the development of the sub-medieval storeyed house, so the need to provide accommodation for the master and, in a few places, boarding pupils, led to the provision of some $1\frac{1}{2}$ or 2-storey school buildings.

If we now consider the evidence provided by the few surviving buildings, the school at Beaumaris, founded in 1603 by David Hughes, has been extensively rebuilt in modern times but the foundations and possibly parts of the walls of the former schoolroom, which measures 66 by 18 feet, appear to be original. The original date-stone, with the founder's initials, has been reset in a later porch.[32] More

---

[30] The above points are taken from P. Smith, 'Houses and building styles' in D. H. Owen (ed.), op. cit., ch. 5.
[31] P. Smith, *Houses of the Welsh Countryside* (London, HMSO, 1975), plates 14 and 15.
[32] RCAHM (Wales), *An Inventory of the Ancient Monuments in Anglesey* (London, HMSO, 1937), 16 and plate 104.

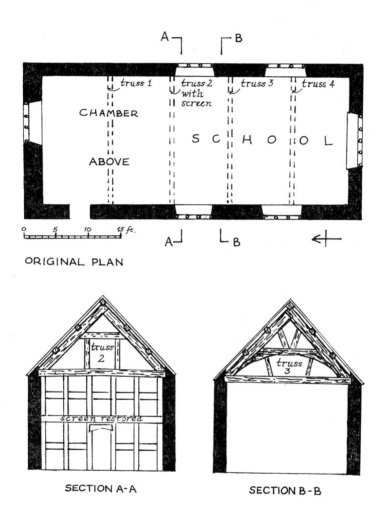

Fig. 1. Northop grammar school, Flints., 1608, original plan and sections.

complete evidence of the 'hall-house' type of school plan
survives from the school at Northop, which was probably
built in 1608. The original building at Northop was restored
in the 1970s and this provided the opportunity for a full
archaeological investigation (see Fig. 1 and Plate 2).[33] The
founder, the Reverend George Smith, made his bequest
conditional upon the parishioners of Northop erecting 'a
convenient school-house' and 'a convenient chamber or
lodging for the said schoolmaster', and he wisely provided
that, if such a school-house was not built within a year of
his death, his benefaction should be transferred to the parish
of St Asaph.[34] As a result, it appears likely that the school
was built during the summer immediately following his
death. The original stone building, which stands in the north
corner of the churchyard, consists of a rectangular room
measuring internally 48 by 19 feet and with four trusses
supporting the roof. A chamber for the master was created as
a loft over the north end and it is thought that the original
access to it was by means of a door in the north gable at
first-floor level, probably reached by an external stair. A
fireplace was built at first-floor level in the master's chamber,
but no evidence of heating was found in any other part of
the building. It may be noted that it was not unusual to omit
fireplaces in schools at this period: the original schoolroom at
Winchester College (1382) did not have one, and none was
provided in its new schoolroom of 1687. The original entrance
to the school at Northop was through a door at the northern
end of the front wall and there may have been a lobby
leading to the schoolroom, which may account for the off-
central position of the window in the north wall. The schoolroom itself was open to the roof and there was evidence of a
screen (later replaced with heavy furniture) separating the
master's quarters from the schoolroom. The original floor
appears to have been of compressed earth, later covered with

[33] The investigation was carried out by members of the Flintshire Historical
Society under the supervision of Peter Davey. His typescript, 'Interim
Summary' (1975), and copy plans on which Fig. 1 is partly based, are in
Clwyd Record Office, Hawarden, ref. NT 398.
[34] T. W. Pritchard, op. cit., 4-5.

sandstone flags. The roof trusses marked 1 and 2 on the plan defined the master's end and are of a different form to that of trusses 3 and 4, which defined the pupils' area. All the trusses came from earlier buildings elsewhere (a not uncommon practice) and it is considered that the first two are of sixteenth-century date, and the last two of the fifteenth century.

We noted earlier that a grammar school was founded at Llanrwst in about 1612 and the original schoolroom survives as part of a complex of later school buildings (Fig. 2).[35] What was the schoolroom is now a library (Plate 3) and was firmly in the hall-house tradition, since the master and usher were accommodated in separate buildings on the specific orders of the founder. The schoolroom measures internally 61 by 19 feet and its roof is supported by five trusses; the greater length of the schoolroom compared with that at Northop may be explained by the initial provision made at Llanrwst for both a master and usher, whose chairs would have been placed at opposite ends of the room, as was probably also the case at Beaumaris with its schoolroom of over 60 feet in length. There are several blocked and newly opened doors resulting from successive changes of use and it is impossible to be certain of the position of the original entrance or entrances. A few original windows survive and the remains of what might have been the original opening for a fireplace can also be seen on the south wall. The plan shows the living accommodation for the master and usher as it was before these rooms were converted to offices; much of the surviving structure of the domestic quarters could be of eighteenth-century date and later, including the former dormitory over the area marked on the plan as the lounge/drawing room.

The former grammar-school building also survives at Botwnnog (Plate 4). It was erected in the churchyard in about 1618, soon after the death of the founder, Henry Rowlands, Bishop of Bangor, whose will provided for a school to be

---

[35] I am grateful to the Architect of Gwynedd County Council (Caernarfon office) for providing plans upon which Fig. 2 is based, and to the Headmaster for showing me around the building.

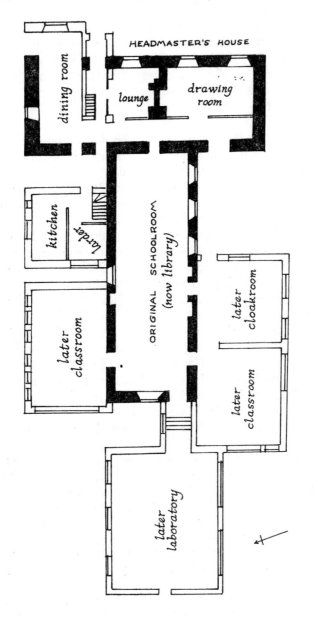

Fig. 2. Llanrwst grammar school, Denbs., 1612, ground plan.

built 'to the glory of God and the good of that country where he had his beginning' and 'as acknowledging that he had his preferment by learning and the ministry'.[36] It originally consisted of a schoolroom measuring 29 by 18½ feet, and a drawing by Moses Griffith made in 1774 shows that by that date, if not earlier, it also had an attic room, presumably for the master.[37] A small dwelling-house was built adjoining the school in about 1810 for an usher, who was appointed in that year to teach writing, navigation and arithmetic.[38] The Royal Commission on Ancient and Historical Monuments in Wales, whose officers examined the school and adjoining house in the early 1960s, stated that the former schoolroom had been heightened and re-roofed and a doorway inserted on the west, the original doorway in the north wall having been blocked up; they also considered that the three window openings on the south side were original.[39] It is now difficult to confirm these observations since the former school and usher's house have been converted into a private dwelling and the stone walls covered with pebble-dash.

We also noted previously that in 1632 Thomas Nevitt left a legacy of £2 a year to the schoolmaster at Ruabon, and a surviving letter of 1637 refers to 'a decent Schoolehouse' on the north side of the churchyard erected nineteen years earlier.[40] This building of 1618, constructed of rubble sandstone, still stands in Church Street. The Charity Commissioners wrote in 1837 that 'the school was built by the parish previous to 1632. It consisted of a school-room and a room over it, wherein the masters, being bachelors, used to dwell [i.e. successively] . . . In 1825 the master built, at his own expense, a kitchen and brewhouse, with two rooms over them, adjoining the school.'[41] The former kitchen and brew-

---

[36] *CCR*, 28, 457.
[37] Moses Griffith's drawing is reproduced as Plate XVIII in A. H. Dodd, *A History of Caernarvonshire* (Caerns. Hist. Soc., 1968).
[38] *CCR*, 28, 460.
[39] RCAHM (Wales), *An Inventory of the Ancient Monuments in Caernarvonshire*, III (London, HMSO, 1964), 24-5.
[40] T. W. Pritchard, 'A History of the Old Endowed Grammar School, Ruabon', *Trans. Den. Hist. Soc.*, XX (1971), 103.
[41] *CCR*, 32, 127.

NORTH

FIRST FLOOR

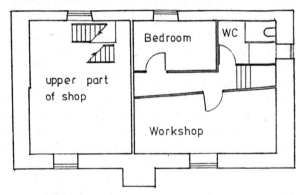

GROUND FLOOR

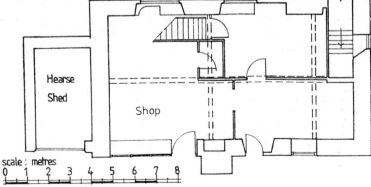

scale : metres
0 1 2 3 4 5 6 7 8

Fig. 3. Ruabon grammar school, Denbs., 1618, plan and elevation.

house with rooms over them also survive at right angles to the schoolroom, as does a hearse-shed subsequently built of stone adjoining the east gable of the school. The schoolroom itself is now a shop and has been extensively altered, but a survey of the building was made in 1983 (see Fig. 3) and some conclusions can be drawn from it.[42] In the first place, it seems probable that the school of 1618 was an adaptation of a sixteenth-century building: the rear wall is narrower at first-floor than at ground-floor level, and there are also the remains of a wooden mullioned window to the right of the front stack which could be of sixteenth-century date. This external stone stack (later heightened in brick) appears to be an early seventeenth-century feature and would have served a lateral fireplace inside. The best surviving internal features are the massive stop-chamfered cross-beams and lateral beam in the schoolroom which, it may be assumed, were inserted in 1618 to provide support for the master's rooms above. The interior of the building measures 36 by 18 feet, which is longer than the school at Botwnnog but shorter than the other grammar schools here being considered. The brick chimney stack on the east gable, together with the shop front and all the surviving windows, appear to be of nineteenth-century date, as do all the doors, apart from some in the upper rooms which have panels of eighteenth-century type. The stairs and partitions in the schoolroom are recent. One can conclude that this was a medieval hall-house converted into a sub-medieval two-storeyed school early in the seventeenth century.

The evidence to be derived from surviving school buildings of the second half of the seventeenth century is much more meagre. There were, as we have seen, fewer major foundations and it is probable that many of the non-classicel schools met in churches or pre-existing secular buildings. Some useful evidence is available from the line drawings included in the description by Thomas Dineley or Dingley of

---

[42] I am indebted to I. Hamilton for permitting me to examine the building and to David Lodge, Architect, for providing the drawings which appear as Fig. 3.

At the Entrance into Carmarthen from Golden Grove you have on the left hand the freeschole belonging to the Town, built of white hard stone:

Fig. 4. (a) Carmarthen grammar school, renovated 1666.

The free schoole not long since built of brick beareth this form in the Church yard.

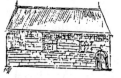

(b) Hanmer school, Flints., 1676.

(c) Hay-on-Wye school, Brecs., 1670.

the official progress of the Duke of Beaufort through Wales in 1684.[43] Three schools are illustrated, the earliest being the grammar school at Carmarthen, already noted as a sixteenth-century foundation with a school building of 1622. This was renovated by the corporation in 1666 and Dineley's drawing of it is reproduced as Fig. 4(a). He also illustrates the school at Hanmer which was endowed in 1625 but did not have a purpose-built school until 1676. This school was built of brick since Hanmer is some distance from the Carboniferous stone belt, and some of the original brickwork survives in the building still used as a primary school. What is now the infants' classroom was the original schoolroom, which retains its roof members including two fine arch-braced trusses with pierced balustrades (Plate 5). This clearly shows the influence of the persisting hall-house tradition, with attention focused on the ornate roof timbers. Thomas Dineley's drawing (Fig. 4(b)) confirms that this was a single-storey structure, with the entrance at one end of the front wall, as at Northop. The third school illustrated by Dineley is that at Hay-on-Wye, which was founded as a non-classical school in 1670 but has long since been demolished (Fig. 4(c)). This appears to show a single-storey building of stone or brick with some half-timbering in the gable end and it was located in the market square.

Another non-classical school of similar date formerly existed at Llanasa in Flintshire, and, although it was demolished in about 1960, there are photographs of it in the National Monuments Record at Aberystwyth, one of which is reproduced as Plate 6. This school was built in 1675 and had an inscribed stone reading 'Thomas ap Hugh hanc scholam fundavit legato 30 librarum Anno Domini 1675'. In his will Thomas ap Hugh described himself as a 'yeoman' and he left £30 'towards erecting a school-house'. The Charity Commissioners described the building as 'a house and school

[43] *The Account of the Official Progress of His Grace Henry the First Duke of Beaufort Through Wales in 1684*, the original MS of Thomas Dineley reproduced by photolithography (London, Blades, 1888), illustrations on pp. 100, 191, 238.

. . . from time to time repaired by the parish', and they noted that 'it has been the custom for the master to teach six poor children, in consideration of the house in which he lives. The other scholars are paid for by voluntary subscription.'[44] It may be remarked that it was common practice for the parishioners to take over the maintenance of local schools, or even, as we have seen at Northop and Ruabon, actually to raise the money for the buildings. A description of the school at Llanasa, written shortly before it was demolished, spoke of it as a sandstone rubble, rectangular building of about 36 by 20 feet, with a later addition in the same range to the north (left on the photograph). A number of three-light mullioned windows remained but two of the three chimney stacks were modern. The interior was thought to have consisted originally of one room on each floor and the only remaining internal original features were a wide fireplace at the north end, and a number of floor and roof timbers, which were 'rough and poor'.[45] It seems safe to infer that this school was built on the model of a sub-medieval storeyed house.

In concluding this review of pre-1700 school buildings, it should be mentioned that, when the population (particularly of south Wales) greatly increased in the nineteenth century, some buildings of earlier date and designed for other purposes were pressed into service as schools. Among surviving examples, though no longer used as schools, may be mentioned the fifteenth-century Prior's Lodging at Monmouth, which became a National school, and the Presbytery at Llantwit Major, which was used as a Board school and still retains some medieval features. Smaller domestic buildings of Tudor and Stuart date were also sometimes adapted as schools in the eighteenth and nineteenth centuries, as at Colwinston in Glamorgan, originally a lobby-entry house,[46] and the half-timbered house (now known as School Bank) which was used as an estate school by the

[44] CCR, 32, 213.
[45] P. Smith, 'The Old School House, Llanasa'. in Flints Hist. Soc. J., XVIII (1960), 163.
[46] RCAHM (Wales), An Inventory of Ancient Monuments in Glamorgan, IV, part 2 (London, HMSO, 1988), 276.

Godsal family of Iscoed Hall in Flintshire. The later adaptation for school purposes of the 'Church Houses' of Tudor and early Stuart date in the Vale of Glamorgan is commented on in the following chapter, and the relationship between older buildings and the new demands for education will be a continuing theme in the present study.

CHAPTER II

Schools for the poor in the Eighteenth Century

Mention was made in the last chapter of the difficulty of distinguishing between some of the classical and non-classical schools founded during the seventeenth century, but in the course of the eighteenth century a differentiation based both on curriculum and social class became more pronounced. Social stratification was, however, no new phenomenon and recent research has also considerably modified the view of some earlier historians that the eighteenth century in Wales was a time of tepid Anglicanism and arid Dissent. There was a good deal of activity in education and a veritable renaissance of publications in Welsh, which had begun after the Restoration and continued into the eighteenth century.[1] Behind the educational developments which were taking place may be seen a fundamental change of outlook. Many of the radical alterations made by the Reformation and the Civil War had been imposed on the Welsh people from above, and it may be argued that it was only in the late seventeenth and eighteenth centuries that the new religious outlook penetrated

[1] The modern approach is exemplified by G. H. Jenkins, *Literature, Religion and Society in Wales 1660-1730* (Cardiff, University of Wales Press, 1978).

into the lives of the general population. The forces of Puritanism influenced not only the relatively small groups of Dissenters, but also the Established Church, and nowhere was this more noticeable than in the provision made for schools.

The initial impulse had come from the Welsh Trust (1674-81) and from the Society for Promoting Christian Knowledge. This Society was founded in 1699 and four of the five founding members had Welsh connections. 'It is manifest', stated an SPCK circular of 1705, 'that a Christian and useful education for the children of the poor is absolutely necessary to their piety, virtue and honest livelihood.'[2] This was the driving force behind the setting up of the so-called 'charity' schools, though there is a sense in which all the endowments for education since the Middle Ages had been works of charity. David Owen, the modern historian of philanthropy during this period, writes of 'the amazing outpouring of wealth for public purposes that marked the first four decades of the [eighteenth] century', and this was true of Wales no less than England.[3] Mary Clement, in her study of the Welsh charity schools, noted 157 schools in Wales, mentioned in SPCK and other records during the period from 1699 to 1740, with the largest concentrations in the counties of Pembroke (33), Carmarthen (24) and Denbigh (20).[4] It has been shown from more recent research into the charity school movement in England that the lists drawn up by the SPCK often included parish schools which had been founded well before the SPCK came on to the scene, and that the particular type of catechetical school advocated by the Society was by no means universally adopted.[5] In Wales, the SPCK urged that English-medium schools should be set up, but it was soon recognized that in Welsh-speaking areas there was

[2] *An Account of the Methods whereby the Charity-schools have been erected and managed* (London, Joseph Downing, 1705), 1.
[3] D. Owen, *English Philanthropy 1660-1960* (Harvard University Press, 1965), 71.
[4] M. Clement, *The S.P.C.K. and Wales 1699-1740* (London, SPCK, 1954), 158.
[5] B. Simon (ed.), *Education in Leicestershire 1540-1940* (Leicester University Press, 1968), ch. 3.

little hope of making any impact on popular education if instruction was confined to English. It therefore turned a blind eye to the adoption of Welsh, especially in the north Wales schools, and it later played a vitally important part in the success of the circulating schools established by Griffith Jones by publishing large quantities of Bibles and other religious works in Welsh.

The circulating schools associated with Griffith Jones of Llanddowror near Carmarthen have also attracted much attention from historians of Welsh education and it has often been pointed out that it was these short-term schools, which concentrated on the teaching of both children and adults to read the Bible and other pious literature in Welsh, which also prepared the ground for the later spread of Methodism in Wales. More generally, the contribution made by the circulating schools to the spread of literacy may justly be described as dramatic. It has been estimated that between 1737, when they began to be established, and the death of Griffith Jones in 1761, over 3,000 short-term schools had been set up all over Wales, and that during this period some 200,000 children and adults were taught to read Welsh, out of a total population of perhaps 400,000.[6]

Neither the SPCK nor the circulating schools required specially-designed buildings. Griffith Jones, in particular, always stressed the need for saving expense in the poorer agricultural districts, where the support of the local incumbents in putting the parish churches or other buildings at the disposal of the teachers was an important element in their success. It is instructive to look back on the situation in the eighteenth century as recorded by the Charity Commissioners in the 1830s, when the impact of the earlier religious and literary revival had been absorbed and when a new movement for popular education was about to begin under the stimulus of rapid economic change. A study of eighteenth-century endowments for elementary education

---

[6] Glanmor Williams, 'Griffith Jones, Llanddowror (1683-1761)', in C. E. Gittins (ed.), *Pioneers of Welsh Education* (Swansea, Faculty of Education, 1964), 20.

shows how considerably the ideas of the SPCK and of Griffith Jones influenced the founders of endowed schools, without, however, extinguishing the more traditional provision made for the poor in towns and parishes throughout Wales. A *Digest* of educational charities, based on the voluminous reports of the Charity Commissioners, was published in 1842 and provides a very useful summary from which some conclusions may be drawn.[7] It should, however, be noted that some minor or insecure endowments were omitted, perhaps because of the narrow legal criteria which seem to have been adopted by the Commissioners, or by the clerks who compiled the summary. Thus, for example, there is no mention in the *Digest* of the eighteenth-century endowments for education at Bishopston and Port Einon near Swansea, or of the early example of a 'works' school established in 1706 by Sir Humphrey Mackworth of the Company of Mines Adventurers at Neath.[8] There are also a few surviving eighteenth-century school buildings (probably representative of others which have now disappeared) which were not legally endowed and so find no mention in the reports of the Charity Commissioners, but which were clearly of local importance at the time they were built. The seventy-nine non-classical endowments of the eighteenth century which are included in the *Digest* for the Welsh counties nevertheless represent a good cross-section of the provision made for elementary education. They are listed in Appendix IA and analysed in Table III.

The distribution and dates of endowments were not purely the result of the chance existence of individuals or groups with sufficient resources to endow schools. As the Table shows, the first quarter of the century was the most fruitful for new elementary-school foundations, no doubt because of the influence of the SPCK, while the new endowments of the second quarter may well have reflected the success of the circulating school movement. The third quarter of the century

---

[7] *Digest of Schools and Charities for Education as reported on by the Commissioners of Inquiry into Charities* (London, 1842).
[8] Glanmor Williams (ed.), *Glamorgan County History*, IV (Cardiff, Glamorgan County History Trust, 1974), 454-6.

TABLE III

DISTRIBUTION AND DATES OF NON-CLASSICAL ENDOWMENTS
1700-1800

County	1700-24	1725-49	1750-74	1775-99	Un-specified	Total
Anglesey	3	2	—	—	—	5
Brecon	1	1	1	1	—	4
Caernarfon	3	1	—	3	—	7
Cardigan	—	—	1	2	—	3
Carmarthen	4	4	—	2	—	10
Denbigh	7	4	3	—	1	15
Flint	2	2	—	—	—	4
Glamorgan	3	1	—	—	—	4
Merioneth	1	—	—	—	1	2
Monmouth	1	3	—	—	—	4
Montgomery	5	2	1	4	—	12
Pembroke	1	—	1	1	—	3
Radnor	1	1	—	2	2	6
Totals	32	21	7	15	4	79

showed a marked fall in the number of endowments, coinciding with the decline of the circulating schools, while the partial revival in the last quarter of the century marks the beginning of a new wave of philanthropy which continued into the nineteenth century. The sample of schools recorded in the *Digest* is too small to make valid generalizations covering the whole of Wales, but, when supplemented by the further details given in the reports themselves and by local research, a number of salient points emerge. In the first place, as the list of founders given in Appendix IA shows, the great majority of the endowments were made by laymen (though clergymen continued to play a part), while a significant number were endowed by women. This was not only a reflection of contemporary feelings of 'benevolence', with women playing a leading role, but also of a much fuller recognition of the value of elementary education for girls. As we noted earlier, the Tudor and Stuart grammar schools catered for boys only, and, even among them, it has been observed that 'the children of the mass of labouring poor would effectively have been excluded in all but the rarest cases'.[9]

[9] J. G. Jones (ed.), *Class, Community and Culture in Tudor Wales* (Cardiff, University of Wales Press, 1989), 89-90.

The extension of education to the poorer classes, both male and female, during the eighteenth century marked a notable advance, and the motives of those who provided it may be variously assessed. The predominantly moral and religious basis of the SPCK and of the circulating schools has frequently been noted and the motivation of other founders of schools in this period was similarly circumscribed. At Llansadwrn in Carmarthenshire, Lititia Cornwallis's foundation of 1731 provided for the teaching of reading, writing and knitting, with the intention of training children to 'be qualified to make good and faithful servants', while at Berse Drelincourt near Wrexham, Mary Drelincourt in 1751 built an orphanage (now converted to a private house) where practical housewifery skills were taught.[10] A new church and vicarage were also built which, with the now-altered orphanage, form an interesting complex of buildings on the outskirts of Wrexham. Other schools also laid stress on vocational skills. At Meifod in Montgomeryshire, William Pugh's foundation of 1714 was for a schoolmaster to teach the considerable number of sixty 'poor children, of both sexes in reading, writing, and arithmetic, sufficient to enable them to take situations in shops' (for which there was probably a demand in the border towns); and, at Carmarthen, Powell's school of 1729 laid particular emphasis on arithmetic and navigation, no doubt to satisfy the demands of a busy port.[11]

Many schools, though only rarely confining the curriculum to reading alone, made the teaching of the Church catechism their central purpose. One such, whose much-altered building of 1728 survives as a community centre, was founded by Lady Jeffreys at Bangor Is-coed in Flintshire. The original inscription on the building states that Lady Jeffreys had bequeathed 'the sum of five hundred pounds for the teaching to read and write and instructing in the catechism of the Church of England and for putting out apprentices, poor children of the parish of Bangor'. Another leading supporter of the SPCK in

[10] *CCR*, 28, 662; 32, 146.
[11] Ibid. 32, 271; 28, 637.

north Wales was Dr John Jones, a native of Pentraeth in Anglesey and later Dean of Bangor. He established a fund in 1719 for setting up schools in Anglesey and Caernarfonshire for instructing 'poor children to read Welsh perfectly and for teaching them the principles of religion according to the catechism of the Church of England, and, if it might be, for training them up a little in writing and arithmetic'.[12] For most of the eighteenth century the schools founded by Dean Jones met in the church buildings, or in the vestries, and purpose-built schools were not provided for them until the early nineteenth century, under the pressure of increasing population.

Nor were purpose-built schools part of the plan adopted by Dr Williams, an eminent Presbyterian divine and a native of Wrexham, whose will of 1715 provided for the establishment of a public library in London and for the setting up of a number of schools for instructing the poor, chiefly in north Wales. The Charity Commissioners reported of the masters of these schools that 'being in almost every instance the ministers of dissenting congregations . . . the common practice has been to keep the school in the chapel, or in the vestry or other room attached to it; in some instances the masters have kept the school in their own dwelling-house'.[13] Part of Dr Williams' ministry had been in Ireland, where he advocated 'the practice of the Protestant religion among the Irish in their native language', but he stated that the schools to be established in Wales should be for poor children 'to read English and to study the Assembly's catechism'.[14] However, arithmetic was added later and it is known that Welsh classes were, for example, held in the Dr Williams' school at Llanuwchllyn in Merioneth, which from 1741 met in a small building (now a ruin) at Prys Bach.[15] It was from this seed

[12] Ibid. 26, 702. See also H. Ramage, *Portraits of an Island. Eighteenth Century Anglesey* (Anglesey Antiquarian Society, 1987), 188-91.
[13] *CCR*, 32, 17.
[14] Ibid. 32, 14-15.
[15] This school later moved to the old Independent chapel at Llanuwchllyn. I am grateful to Ifor Owen for information and a reference to R. T. Jenkins, *Hanes Cynulleidfa Hen Gapel Llanuwchllyn* (Evans, Bala, 1937).

that the Independent college at Bala eventually developed, and it was from the Dr Williams' foundation that a girls' secondary school was established at Dolgellau later in the nineteenth century.

The language to be used for instruction (whether English or Welsh) is not always stated in the terms of endowments, and, when it is, it cannot always be accepted at face value. It is, however, significant that the majority of the eighteenth-century endowed schools in north Wales provided for the teaching of Welsh, and in most cases for writing and arithmetic as well. In a few cases, English was specified even in Welsh-speaking areas, as at Penmachno in Caernarfonshire, where Roderick Lloyd endowed a school in 1729 for the children of poor parishioners 'to write and read English'.[16] Lloyd was a member of Lincoln's Inn in London and may have had in mind the possibility of others from his native area following in his footsteps. At Aberffraw in Anglesey, Sir Arthur Owen's will of 1735 prescribed 'a school for the teaching and instructing of youth in the Welsh language' but it is known that the first schoolmaster, John Beaver, was a Londoner and one-time tutor to Thomas Holland and his brother, heirs of Plas Berw.[17] The gravestone to John Beaver and his wife, Ellin, which survives in the churchyard at Aberffraw, is in English, and later the Charity Commissioners were to point out that the school was not using the language designated by the founder. A number of schools, including the one at Aberffraw, took pay-scholars, and this might have diverted them from the original intention of the founders to concentrate on the teaching of Welsh. In the endowed schools of south Wales the medium of instruction is only rarely mentioned, though one may note that at Llanfynydd in Carmarthenshire, the Reverend David Jones provided a school (1738) to teach children 'to read the Scriptures and write a legible hand' and he also left money for 'buying Welsh Bibles for the poor inhabitants of the said parish'.[18]

[16] CCR, 28, 172.
[17] Ibid. 26, 686. Information about J. Beaver is from notes provided by the Anglesey Coast Heritage Centre, Aberffraw.
[18] CCR, 28, 605.

Fig. 5. Trelech a'r Betws, Carms. Sketch of interior of school, 1804.

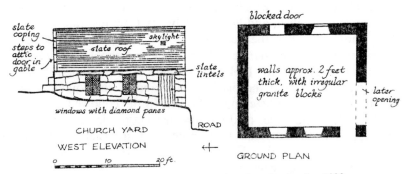

Fig. 6. Llanarmon, Llŷn, Caerns., churchyard school, c.1800.

It is also interesting to note the impact of the 'new philanthropy' of the late eighteenth and early nineteenth centuries, which replaced the earlier and harsher outlook which had tended to stress the importance of inuring the poor to a life of manual labour. At Tywyn in Merioneth, Lady Moyer in about 1760 increased the school endowment earlier made by Vincent Corbet since 'to promote the glory of Almighty God being my hearty desire', she did not know 'how better to please him who when on earth . . . showed so many favours to them [i.e. poor children]'.[19] To genuine piety was sometimes added a surprisingly liberal view of education, as when William Davies's will of 1788 provided for a school at Trelech a'r Betws in Carmarthenshire with a curriculum which was to consist not only of 'reading and writing English and arithmetic', but also 'such other things as would be most beneficial to spread knowledge in general among the poor inhabitants'. He also left money for candles to be used by 'occasional scholars' who might wish to study in the evenings.[20] The school building at Trelech was later replaced, but a painting of the interior of the original school of 1804 survives on a wall-board erected to William Davies's memory in the parish church. The church is at Pen-y-bont, two miles south of Trelech, and the wall-board, which is now covered in dark varnish, has proved impossible to photograph clearly. A sketch of it is given in Fig. 5 and shows that, as was still the usual arrangement, the 'school' consisted of a single room. In one half of the room the master, wearing a hat, sits on a chair at a table on which he is writing, with a pile of what may be exercise-books or slates in front of him. To the side of the master's table are three rows of desks, at each of which sit three boys with books in front of them, apparently writing. The boys' school is separated from the girls' by a bench on which five girls sit, wearing long dresses and hats; they face the mistress on the other side of the room and hold open books on their laps. The mistress, who does not wear a hat, is sitting on a chair with a table beside her and appears

[19] Ibid. 28, 573.
[20] Ibid. 28, 630.

to be helping a girl, standing in front of her, to read. Four
smaller children sit or kneel in the space between the
mistress and the older girls, and are presumably infants. The
only other furniture in the room is what appear to be shelves
with books in a recess in the wall and, in the corner of the
master's side of the room, a bookcase with two closed
drawers below, on which the boys seem to have laid their
caps.

Two other aspects of elementary education in Wales during
this period merit a brief mention: neither was new, but they
were given greater prominence in the eighteenth century.
The first was the association of schools with almshouses for
the elderly poor, which had begun with Gabriel Goodman's
Elizabethan foundation at Ruthin and had continued at
Monmouth and elsewhere in the seventeenth century. The
second was the provision sometimes made for clothing as
well as educating poor children. This had its origin at Christ's
Hospital in London in the reign of Edward VI and was widely
imitated in other places, including the school which was
founded by Mary Tasker at Haverfordwest in 1684, where the
boys received a suit of clothes every year, consisting of a
blue coat turned up with red, a waistcoat and breeches, and
the girls a jacket and petticoat, and a cape and hat. Grey
school uniform was provided at Caerleon in Monmouthshire in 1717 and blue at Llanfyllin in Mongomeryshire in
1720. Provision for clothing the children was also made by
Dame Strode at Gresford in Denbighshire, whose original
school building of 1725 survives virtually unaltered, together
with the adjoining almshouses (Plate 7). A few founders left
money for feeding as well as clothing the children, notably
at Kerry in Montgomeryshire, where Richard Jones, a retired
naval purser, made provision in 1785 for 'victualling' the
children, as recorded on a monument to him (for which he
also made provision in his will) in the parish church, which
shows him with a boy on one side and a girl on the other
(Plate 8). Most of the schools which gave clothing to the
children were located in the more prosperous districts of east
and south Wales, and it may be noted that the first official

Welsh society in London (the Ancient Britons) was founded in 1715 with the main object of establishing a Welsh charity school for the children of expatriate parents. This school was also supported by the Honourable Society of Cymmrodorion and school uniform was provided for the children.[21] A drawing made early in the following century shows the school uniform supplied to the girls (Plate 9).

Enough has perhaps been said to indicate the variety of provision made for elementary education in eighteenth-century Wales, and the buildings in which it took place equally followed no set pattern. Peter Smith has described the 'Third Great Rebuilding' which began after the Restoration and introduced the centralized plan with symmetrical, 'classical' façades.[22] He stresses that the rate of introducing this new style varied greatly both in time and place, and, as far as schools were concerned, only a few of the wealthier or later eighteenth century foundations adopted the classical plan; elsewhere, local vernacular traditions persisted into the nineteenth century. It is also necessary to recall that the great majority of elementary schools were for relatively small groups of children, and that the terms of endowments only rarely provided for purpose-built schools. We have already noted that neither Dean Jones nor Dr Williams made provision for separate school buildings, and the majority of references to buildings in the reports of the Charity Commissioners are to the use of the church or vestry, or to schools meeting in the house of the master, who was often the parish clerk. In the towns, schools sometimes met in the town hall or in part of the market-house. At Llanbrynmair in Montgomeryshire, the school was held in a portion of the church, which was boarded off and set apart for that purpose, and Haslam has noted structural evidence of the use of churches

---

[21] On the London school, see R. T. Jenkins and H. M. Ramage, *A History of the Honourable Society of Cymmrodorion* (London, the Society, 1951), 15, 47-9, 88, 191. See also Rachel Leighton, *Rise and Progress: the Story of the Welsh Girls' School* (Ashford, 1950).

[22] P. Smith, 'Houses and building styles' in D. H. Owen (ed.), *Settlement and Society in Wales* (Cardiff, University of Wales Press, 1989), 133f.

by schoolchildren at other places in Powys.[23] At Llanfyllin in Montgomeryshire, a girls' schoolroom was built on to the nave, though this was not until 1826, as the Regency windows confirm. (The boys at this period were meeting in the town hall.) At Bleddfa in Radnorshire, part of the nave was partitioned off, as also happened at Defynnog in Breconshire, which was a seventeenth-century foundation.

In places where the church building itself was not considered to be suitable for housing a school (and complaints about the damage caused by children using churches were beginning to appear in visitation records)[24] it was common practice to use some other parish building, or to build a schoolroom on the edge of the churchyard. Two good early examples of the latter may be seen at Gwyddelwern in Merioneth and Llanarmon in Llŷn (Caernarfonshire). At Gwyddelwern, a small, two-storey stone building, still known locally as Ysgol Bach, has been much altered at the front but retains the external stone stairs to the first floor and massive stone quoins at the rear (Plate 10). At Llanarmon, space for a small school building was carved out of the rising ground of the churchyard, and the former school may be entered either from the road below or from the churchyard above. It consists of a single room, with storage in the roof space reached by a door in the gable end. The walls are constructed of large igneous rocks, with massive irregular slate lintels to the doors and windows, and a heavy slate roof (see Fig. 6). Other small stone buildings which are known to have been used as schools in the eighteenth century, though altered in the nineteenth, also survive in the churchyard at Llanarmon-yn-Iâl (Denbighshire) and, just outside the churchyard, at Tremeirchion (Flintshire), while at Derwen in Denbighshire the stone lychgate was converted into a two-storey school, with the master and mistress accommodated on the ground floor and

---

[23] R. Haslam, *The Buildings of Wales, Powys* (Harmondsworth, Penguin Books, 1979), 119, 132, 222, 317.
[24] Graffiti, allegedly made by children, may still be seen in the church at Llandeilo Gresynni in Monmouthshire. For complaints of damage in Leicestershire churches, see B. Simon, *Education in Leicestershire*, op. cit., 86n, and other English examples in J. G. Davies, *The Secular Use of Church Buildings* (London, SCM Press, 1968), 188-91.

the children on the first floor, to which they gained access by stairs from the churchyard.

Perhaps the most interesting school building of this period which still survives in north Wales (though now converted to a private house) is the school founded by Sir Arthur Owen at Aberffraw in Anglesey, to which some reference has already been made. Although this school had an inscribed stone with the initials of the founder and the date 1729 (as recorded in the files of the Royal Commission on Ancient and Historical Monuments), this has now been covered up or removed, and a detailed examination of the building suggests that the school may have been formed from two pre-existing cottages. (As Fig. 7 shows, the walls meet at irregular angles and the wall thicknesses also vary.) Despite the alterations made to the building at various times since 1729, the original lay-out can be reconstructed, and the plan which appears to have been adopted was an ingenious one. On the ground floor, the boys' schoolroom was in one half of the building, and the kitchen and living-room for the master and mistress were in the other half. On the first floor, the part of the building above the boys' schoolroom was used by the teachers as bedrooms, with access to them from stairs which were partitioned off from the boys' schoolroom; the other half of the first floor was used as the girls' schoolroom, with access to it by external stone steps.[25] This building is still known as 'The Eagles', which is thought to be a corruption of 'Eglwys', since it was built on the reputed site of the palace chapel of the Princes of Gwynedd; an archaeological investigation however, carried out before the building was converted, failed to discover the remains of any structure dating from that period.[26]

[25] This is the lay-out according to local tradition. The Education Commissioners of 1847 noted that there were two schoolrooms, for boys and girls respectively, each measuring about 17 by 14 feet. It is quite possible that the measurements in the girls' school ignored the large chimney breast; alternatively, the girls may have been accommodated directly above the boys' schoolroom. This building was threatened with demolition in 1982 but was extensively restored by the Director of Housing, Llangefni. I am indebted to the present occupier, Janet Row, for help and information
[26] N. Edwards and A. Lane (eds.), *Early Medieval Settlements in Wales AD 400-1100* (Cardiff, University College Department of Archaeology, 1988), 20.

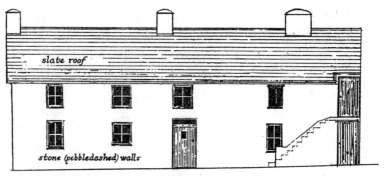

FRONT ELEVATION AFTER CONVERSION

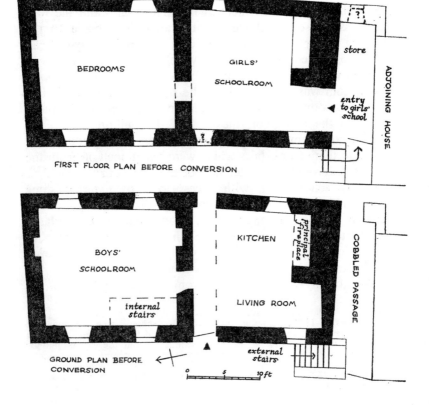

Fig. 7. Aberffraw, Anglesey, Sir Arthur Owen's school, 1729.

There is considerable evidence that two-storey buildings with external access to the first floor were also used as schools in Glamorgan in the eighteenth and early nineteenth centuries. The Education Commissioners of 1847 noted that the schoolroom at Penmark in the Vale of Glamorgan was in 'the upper room in the old church-house' and added that 'It appears that these buildings were originally places for holding courts leet. They are converted into schoolhouses very generally in this part of the county, e.g. at Porthkerry, Llancarvan, St Nicholas, and Penmark.'[27] The same development has been noted in Devon during this period, and M. W. Barley has suggested that the church-houses there were probably derived from the medieval concept of the first-floor hall.[28] At Penmark, the Education Commissioners stated that the lower floor was occupied by the master, and the room above was used by the children, while at St Nicholas the old poorhouse (i.e. the former church-house) was about to be fitted out with desks and benches for a National school. At Llancarvan, they noted that the upper storey of the church-house was used as a school and the ground floor as a poor-house, and at Porthkerry the lower room was used for the girls to sew in, with the schoolroom above. The building at Porthkerry appears to be the only former church-house (now called the 'Old Schoolhouse') which has survived in the Vale, and is shown on Plate 11. The plan of the building, the oldest part of which is thought to date from about 1600, is printed in the Inventory of Glamorgan compiled by the Royal Commission on Ancient and Historical Monuments.[29]

Another small eighteenth-century school building which formerly existed in Glamorgan (on the border with

[27] *Reports of the Commissioners of Inquiry into the State of Education in Wales* (London, 1847), I, 321. Courts leet were also held at 'The Eagles' in Aberffraw, mentioned above. It is probable that other lowland parishes had general-purpose buildings of this kind. (The so-called 'College' at Felindre Farchog, which survives near Nevern in Pembrokeshire, was used for courts leet, and not, apparently, as a school.)

[28] R. R. Sellman, *Devon Village Schools* (Newton Abbot, David and Charles, 1967), 19, 26-7; and M. W. Barley, *The English Farmhouse and Cottage* (London, Routledge, 1961), 7-8.

[29] RCAHM (Wales), *An Inventory of the Ancient Monuments in Glamorgan* (London, HMSO, 1988), IV. Part 2, 271.

Monmouthshire) is worth mentioning because it was one of the few schools in Wales whose endowment later greatly increased in value, making it possible to replace the old building with a major new one. (In this case, it was the mineral rights attached to the portions of the upland Blaenau given by the founder which increased the endowment.) This was the school at Gelli-gaer founded by Edward Lewis in 1715 to teach the three Rs. It was rebuilt at Pengam in 1851, and later became an important secondary school. The original school building was near the church at Gelli-gaer and was not actually opened until about 1760, owing to a dispute about the will. In this case, the schoolroom (measuring 22 by 16 feet) was on the ground floor and the master's residence was on the floor above; external stairs to the first floor were built in 1815.[30] This building was listed in 1959 as 'a plain cottage of no architectural merit, listed only for local historical interest'. Later the building was demolished, and stones taken from it were used to construct a cairn, which now stands, with a plaque depicting the original school, in the present school grounds at Pengam (Plate 12).

In the later eighteenth century, there is some surviving evidence of purpose-built schools of two storeys but with internal stairs, whose style followed the more formalized domestic architecture of the period. We may instance the school built by Catherine Jones in 1763 at Llanferres in Denbighshire, which retains its original inscription (Plate 13), and accommodated the teachers on the ground floor and the children above.[31] There is also the two-storey, cottage-like school at Cilcain in Flintshire, shown on Plate 14. The well-carved inscription reads: 'This Building was Erected on the Common by a Voluntary Subscription from the Landowners and Occupiers of Land in this Parish as a School for the use and Benefit of the Parishioners 1799'. A large space was left

---

[30] A. Wright, *The History of Lewis' School, Pengam* (Newtown, Welsh Outlook Press, 1929), 31-2. Although Edward Lewis made his will in 1715, it was not proved until 1729, which is the date from which the school claims its origin.

[31] There is an interesting short history of this school by T. W. Pritchard, *Llanferres Endowed School 1763-1976* (Mold, Centre for Educational Technology, 1976).

below this inscription, presumably in the hope that further gifts would be received, but the school remained a 'private-adventure', i.e. fee-paying, school until in 1842 a new National school was built alongside it and it became the teachers' house. Since the 1799 school was built by subscription and was not endowed, it is an example of a school which does not appear in the reports of the Charity Commissioners. Two schools of similar date have also survived in Montgomery-shire. The school at Kerry, which had been in existence as a parish school before it was endowed by the ex-naval purser Richard Jones, mentioned above, was subsequently extended but retains its basically Georgian façade.[32] In the adjoining village of Churchstoke, an endowment made by William Downes in 1790 provided accommodation for the teachers and children in a building which is an almost exact replica of the school at Cilcain. This is the part shown on the left-hand side of Plate 15, the part on the right being the later National school.[33]

We can conclude this account of elementary-school building in the eighteenth century by referring to two major surviving schools, which were both situated in rich agricultural districts. Although they are separated in date by nearly a century they both adopted a 'classical' plan of centrally-placed schoolrooms, with 'pavilions' at each end for the accommodation of the teachers or for subsidiary teaching spaces. This type of lay-out was widely imitated in the following century, as we shall see. The first, which is shown on Plate 16, was built at Caerleon in 1724 under the will of Charles Williams who had made his fortune in London. His declared aim was to found a school in Caerleon 'in the nature of those schools which of late years had been erected and settled in the city of London and Westminster . . . called by the name of

---

[32] Further details in H. N. Jerman, *Kerry. The Church and the Village* (Aberystwyth, Cambrian News, 1976), 30-33. Plans of this building are in the National Library (ref. KPR 40). These show that a three-bay brick building of eighteenth century date was extended to five bays in 1817 and remodelled in 1848 by J. W. Poundley, the Kerry architect who later designed the National school (1868) which is still in use.

[33] Plans of this school are in the National Library (Greg. Box 20.5).

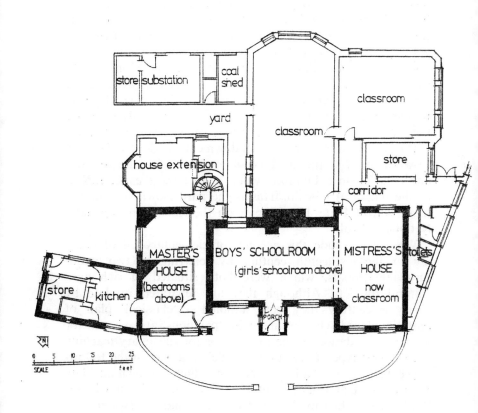

Fig. 8. Caerleon, Mon., Charles Williams' school, 1724, plan showing original building in black.

charity schools' and he endowed his school with the very considerable sum of £4,000.[34] The school building, which is still in use as part of a primary school, was described by the Charity Commissioners as containing 'in the centre a lofty school-room for the boys, with another above for the girls; a residence for the mistress in one wing, and in the other the master's house, attached to which are a coach-house and stable, with a large garden and a meadow of about an acre'.[35] The plan reproduced as Fig. 8 shows the building as it was in 1964, with the original part indicated.[36] It is possible that the spiral staircase shown in the master's house was originally matched by one for the mistress. The school was extended at the rear in the nineteenth and twentieth centuries and further classrooms were built in what was originally the master's garden and meadow.[37] An equally impressive school was planned for Berriew in Montgomeryshire towards the end of the eighteenth century, though it was not built until 1819.[38] It still stands on the edge of the churchyard in Berriew, but since there was no further space for later development, a new school was subsequently built on another site and the old school has been converted into a community centre. This is illustrated on Plate 17.

Although the surviving architectural evidence of elementary schools in the eighteenth century is fragmentary and incomplete, they nevertheless reflect an important educational change: formal education was now beginning to be offered to girls as well as to boys, and not only in the market towns but also in relatively isolated rural communities. And, although English may have been regarded in some places as the language necessary for social advancement, Welsh remained for most people in Wales the language of the home and, increasingly, of religion.

[34] CCR, 27, 450.
[35] Ibid. 27, 459.
[36] I am indebted to Arthur Beer, B Arch, FRIBA, for kindly providing the plan upon which Fig. 8 is based, and to Peter Smith, FRICS, for redrawing it in a form suitable for publication.
[37] A full history of this school is given in T. M. Morgan, Caerleon Endowed Schools 1724-1983 (Risca, Starling Press, 1983).
[38] As the Latin inscription on the building states, this school was founded in 1652, and rebuilt in 1819. Details in CCR, 32, 299.

CHAPTER III

Classical Schools in the Eighteenth Century

The great age of grammar school foundations was over by the end of the seventeenth century and only eight endowed grammar schools were established in Wales during the eighteenth century, compared with twenty-four in the period from 1540 to 1700. It is, however, important to note that most of the grammar schools founded earlier continued to play an active role. Historians of education have been too prone to anticipate the strictures of the reformers of the early nineteenth century and to condemn practices which arose from the social conditions of a pre-industrial age. English was widely used in the law courts and French was the language of diplomacy, but Latin continued to be required for entry to the major professions, especially the Church, and was still the language of international scholarship. Pennant, the eminent Flintshire naturalist and topographer, corresponded with Linnaeus in Latin, which he had learnt at grammar schools in Wrexham and London before going first to Queen's and then to Oriel College, Oxford.[1] Many future clergymen pro-

---

[1] R. P. Evans, 'A sketch of the life of Thomas Pennant', prefacing the reprint of Pennant's *The History of the Parishes of Whiteford and Holywell* (London, 1796, reprinted by Clwyd Library Service, 1988), 2.

ceeded from grammar schools in Wales to Jesus College, Oxford, which during this period reinforced the links which it already had with several Welsh grammar schools. (St John's College, Cambridge, had similar links with a number of Welsh schools.) Both in the private schools for boys frequently kept by clergymen in their own houses, and in the dissenting academies, Latin was regarded as an essential part of the curriculum.

The grammar schools in Wales, therefore, continued to develop, though admittedly in directions not altogether envisaged by their founders. School statutes usually permitted the masters to admit fee-paying pupils in addition to the 'free' scholars. The knowledge of Latin and the ability to enter the learned professions were normally confined to those social classes who could afford to pay their sons' tuition fees, and who could also, if necessary, afford the boarding fees. In response to what appears to have been a growing demand, the grammar school buildings were altered, usually by considerably enlarging the accommodation for boarders. In sparsely-populated areas, schools which aspired to gain any sort of academic reputation were obliged to make such provision. There was also some development in the curriculum, with more attention being paid to non-classical subjects, not originally foreseen by the founders and requiring the employment of additional tutors, who sometimes had their own teaching rooms on or near the school site. It has been aptly remarked that 'the education of the middle-classes in modern subjects was first advocated by the Puritans and attempted by the tutors of the Nonconformist Academies',[2] but the new spirit of enquiry was far from being wholly absent from the grammar schools of this period. The dissenting academies sometimes admitted Anglicans, and only later became exclusively concerned with preparation of candidates for the ministry; equally, the grammar schools were not exclusively Anglican, and it was James Owen (1654-1706), who, having

---

[2] H. P. Roberts, 'Nonconformist academies in Wales (1662-1862)', in *Transactions of the Honourable Society of Cymmrodorion*, 1928-9, 9.

attended the Queen Elizabeth grammar school in Carmarthen, went on to open a dissenting academy at Oswestry and later at Shrewsbury, where he defended the practice of 'occasional conformity'.[3]

The limited number of new grammar schools founded in the eighteenth century, as detailed in the reports of the Charity Commissioners, form an interesting group and are listed in date order in Table IV.

TABLE IV

NEW GRAMMAR SCHOOL FOUNDATIONS IN THE
EIGHTEENTH CENTURY

Date of First Endowment	Place	Former County	Name of Benefactor
1712	Bala (Llanycil)	Merioneth	Revd Edmund Meyricke
1713	Trelawnyd (Newmarket)	Flint	John Wynne
c.1718	Welshpool	Montgomery	Richard Tudor
1719	Cwmdeuddwr	Radnor	Revd Charles Price
1726	Denbigh	Denbigh	A group of yeomen and gentry including W. W. Wynn of Wynnstay
1746	Lledrod	Cardigan	Thomas Oliver
1757	Ystradmeurig	Cardigan	Edward Richard
pre-1762	Holywell	Flint	Origin unknown

The first two foundations of the eighteenth century had strongly contrasting origins. The school at Bala was established for thirty poor boys to be taught 'grammar learning', though this school was clearly not regarded by its founder as likely to provide the full grammar-school course since he stated in his will that the older pupils were, if considered suitable, to be 'removed to other schools'.[4] The founder Edmund Meyricke, was born near Bala and later became a

[3] Ibid., 44-5.
[4] CCR, 28, 553.

fellow of Jesus College, Oxford, after which he held numerous livings in Wales. He died at Carmarthen in 1713 and not only founded the school at Bala but left considerable property to Jesus College.[5] Although this school had no obvious competitors in the surrounding area, it drew on a very scattered population and appears not to have risen much above the elementary level until the nineteenth century. By contrast, the school at Trelawnyd in Flintshire was in a developing area, because of the lead mines which were being opened up there. Its founder, John Wynne (1650-1714), had attended Jesus College and Gray's Inn and later became an industrial pioneer with strong Nonconformist sympathies. His ideas about the curriculum to be taught at Trelawnyd represented the height of 'enlightenment', though he rightly judged that there might be obstacles in the way of its full implementation. He established a Presbyterian chapel in Trelawnyd and, in his will of 1713, gave a house to the minister, Thomas Parrott or Perrot, a Carmarthenshire man, for use as 'a public grammar-school with Latin and Greek authors'; but he added that 'in case the same be obstructed and hindered by law, for want of conformity in matters of religion, then [the master was] to teach and instruct all persons, both young and old, in order to enable them to write, and cast accounts, and speak languages, particularly the French, and to teach them the mathematics, and all in order to fit persons for travel, for trade, and for navigation'.[6] In the event, the school never succeeded, more through lack of support than because of its innovatory curriculum. Perrot moved to Carmarthen, possibly as early as 1718, where he took charge of a dissenting academy which had been established there in 1704. During Perrot's time it was said to have been attended by 150 Nonconformist and Anglican students, but it appears that the numbers were beyond his disciplinary powers and, on his death in 1733, the students transferred to two other academies, at Maes-gwyn in the parish of Beguildy in Radnorshire and Llwyn-llwyd in

[5] See J. N. L. Baker, 'Edmund Meyricke and his benefaction', in *Jesus College Record*, 1966, 19-28.
[6] *CCR*, 32, 216.

Breconshire. Later, following a dispute between the Presbyterian and Congregational boards, the Presbyterian academy moved back to Carmarthen (1751) and a separate Congregational academy was established at Abergavenny (1757).[7] In the meantime, Wynne's school at Trelawnyd became defunct and, by an ironic twist of events, what was left of his endowment subsequently went towards the cost of building a Church elementary school in 1860, which is still in use as a primary school.

As for the other grammar school foundations of the eighteenth century, the school at Cwmdeuddwr seems to have been too remotely situated to become established as a classical school, though it was provided with a new building in the churchyard in 1794 (replaced later in the nineteenth century by an elementary school).[8] The 'Latin school' at Welshpool suffered from the proximity of the earlier (and larger) foundations at Oswestry and Shrewsbury. During the eighteenth century it met in a room over the church porch, and the classical side ceased in about 1790.[9] The grammar school at Denbigh was similarly affected by the competition of the schools at Ruthin and Wrexham, and also met in improvised accommodation, in this case the vestry-room underneath the chancel of St Hilary's church, of which only the west wall and tower now remain.[10] At Holywell, a grammar school of obscure origin occupied the early Tudor chapel built by Margaret, Countess of Richmond, now known as St Winefride's Chapel.[11] Although Holywell, like Welshpool, was an important market town, its grammar school remained a small one, probably because of its proximity to the earlier schools at St Asaph and Hawarden. Only the school at Ystradmeurig, to which the small endowment in the neighbouring parish of

[7] Roberts, 'Nonconformist academies', op. cit., 15-21, 89.
[8] *CCR*, 32, 466.
[9] *Montgomeryshire Collections* (Powysland Club), xv (1882), 320-22. Richard Tudor was noted as bailiff in 1718, 1730, and 1749 (his will was undated).
[10] *CCR*, 32, 6; and 'The history of the Denbigh grammar school' in *Y Bych* (Denbigh County School magazine, July 1954), 589.
[11] *CCR*, 32, 177-8. The first mention of a school in this chapel is in the general vestry book for 1762.

Lledrod was sensibly united, acquired a purpose-built school, and that was some years after the death of the founder. This school was in a relatively remote part of Cardiganshire and will be referred to again later in this chapter.

Two of the oldest grammar schools in Wales had an architectural history in the eighteenth century which re-emphasized their medieval roots. At St David's, we noted in chapter I that the grammar school used a building which was demolished in the 1790s to make way for the new chapter house designed by John Nash. The school was accordingly moved to the older chapter house (now the library) in the cathedral itself, and this is the picture entitled 'Grammar School at St Davids' which appeared in J. C. Buckler's *Sixty Views of Endowed Grammar Schools* in 1827 (Plate 18).[12] At Abergavenny, the grammar school continued to occupy the former parish church of St John, and its constitution had been placed on a new footing when in 1664 the endowment was leased to the principal, fellows and scholars of Jesus College, Oxford, on condition that they admitted and maintained one fellow and one scholar elected from the pupils of the school. In 1689 the members of the corporation of Abergavenny, who were entrusted with the management of the school, refused to act because of their hostility to William III, and the school charter was forfeited. The school was, however, reinstated by Act of Parliament in 1760, on the petition of Jesus College and the corporation. As a result of this, the former tower and nave of St John's church were renovated and a two-storey annexe, consisting of a study for the master on the first floor, with a writing school below, was built alongside it (Plate 19).[13] This group of buildings was used by the school until 1898, and still remains in the centre

---

[12] See also Wyn Evans and Roger Worsley, *St. Davids Cathedral 1181-1981* (St. Davids, Yr Oriel Fach Press, 1981), 154.
[13] *CCR*, 27, 363f. See also E. C. Thompson, 'The grammar school of Abergavenny' in *Jesus College Record*, 1966, 17-19; and Gwyn Jones, *Medieval Abergavenny* (Pontypool, Seargeant Brothers. n.d.), 10-11, from which plate 19 is reproduced with permission. The eighteenth-century buildings are described in N. Carlisle, *A Concise Description of Endowed Grammar Schools in England and Wales* (London, Baldwin, Cradock and Joy, 1818), II, 168.

of Abergavenny as an interesting island site, surrounded by shops and with a later public house attached to it. This part of the town centre gives perhaps the best surviving impression in Wales of the hurly-burly which typically surrounded the urban grammar schools of an earlier age.

In the more rural areas, and in the smaller towns, the development of the boarding side has left behind some architectural record. The typical pattern was to enlarge the headmaster's house and, if necessary, also to permit boarders to lodge in private houses in the locality. This was a marked feature of grammar school development throughout the eighteenth century and gave rise (more in England than in Wales) to the modern conception of a 'public school'. The expansion of the number of 'commoners', while the number of foundation scholars remained fixed, was already well established at Winchester, Eton, Westminster and Shrewsbury in the seventeenth century, and was followed by Harrow and Rugby in the eighteenth. On the architectural side, the need for this development had been clearly recognized by Sir Christopher Wren when in 1693 he was called upon to design a new school in rural Leicestershire. 'If you have room for boarders', he wrote, 'it is no great addition of charge, in regard it is but a floor over the hall . . . and I should think that a less salary with advantage of room for boarders is more considerable than a large allowance without it, and to have gentlemen's sons well accommodated is what will bring reputation to the school and a good interest to the master.'[14]

As far as Wales is concerned, two of the best surviving examples of this development may still be seen at Ruthin and Beaumaris. We noted in chapter I that the Elizabethan school building at Ruthin was remodelled in 1700, probably to provide accommodation for boarders on the first floor above the schoolroom. Then in 1742 a separate house, nearly as large as the original school, was built for the headmaster and his boarders at right angles to the schoolroom. The school-room was, as we saw, a stone building of traditional design,

[14] Wren Sociey, XI, 88 (spelling modernized).

but the new headmaster's house was built of more fashionable brick and was given regularly-spaced, sash windows and classical proportions (Plate 20). Under the notable head-mastership of Thomas Hughes (1739-68), full advantage was taken of the links, initially established by Gabriel Goodman, between the school and St John's College at Cambridge. A contemporary diarist noted that during Hughes's time, 'most of the young gentlemen of the country [were] under his care', and it appears that the catchment area of the school extended as far west as Dolgellau and as far south as Llangollen. Among the boarders was Lloyd (later the first Lord) Kenyon, whose letters home give a vivid picture of schoolboy life in the middle of the eighteenth century and he also mentions that French was taught at the school in addition to the classics.[15] Later members of the Kenyon family went to Harrow and Thomas Hughes's great-grandson was at Rugby, as a result of which *Tom Brown's School Days* came to be written.

At Beaumaris, the former grammar school building of 1603 survives as a community centre (Plate 21). The single-storey schoolroom was remodelled during the eighteenth century and the roof timbers ceiled over, though the teaching of classical authors continued to take place in the one large room, where a surviving bookcase, which may be of eighteenth-century date, is a reminder of its original use as a grammar school. Important curricular developments took place at Beaumaris during the eighteenth century, for in 1710 the feoffees made an allowance for a 'scrivener' which gradually took the form of a fixed salary for a writing master, in addition to the master and usher provided for by the founder. Traditionally, the writing masters taught arithmetic as well as penmanship, and one finds that something approaching a 'modern' side, distinct from the classical, developed at Beaumaris, as in other major grammar schools in the eighteenth century. It was also becoming usual for the parents of better-off boys to enter into private contracts for

---

[15] Keith M. Thompson, *Ruthin School* (The School, 1974), 92-8.

instruction in French, mathematics and music.[16] The boarders, who seem to have been recruited from a wide geographical area, were either boarded in the master's house or in lodgings in Beaumaris, and the successive enlargements to the school house (shown on the right of the photograph) provide a striking architectural commentary on this development.

Somewhat similar developments were taking place at the Friars School in Bangor, which still occupied the former friary buildings. A writing master was appointed by virtue of a bequest made in 1690 by Thomas Jones, a native of Llŷn and an officer of the Customs House in London, who probably appreciated the value of learning the skills of clear writing and arithmetic. In 1731 there is also a reference to a dancing master, and a later historian has remarked that 'at this period there was in Friars more than at any previous time since the foundation of the school, a clique of rich boys who enjoyed special tuition and privileges denied to the poorer scholars'.[17] In 1721 there were seventy-six boys in the school, of whom only thirteen were scholarship boys. The rest were the sons of small squires and clergy, well-to-do farmers and merchants, who came from all parts of Anglesey and Caernarfonshire. At any rate, the school continued to flourish, and a new school building was erected on an adjoining site in 1789. This was in turn demolished when the Friars School moved to a new site on the outskirts of the town at the end of the nineteenth century; the foundation stone of the 1789 school survives in the present building in Ffriddoedd Road, together with a few stones from the old friary.

Comparable changes were taking place in south Wales during this period, but the architectural evidence has largely disappeared. The grammar school at Monmouth, founded in 1614, had the major advantage of being linked with the Worshipful Company of Haberdashers in London, who

[16] J. Williams, *David Hughes and his Free Grammar School at Beaumaris* (Bangor, Douglas, 1864), 22.
[17] W. O. Williams, 'Friars School from its foundation to the year 1789' in *The Dominican, Fourth Centenary Number*, (school magazine), no. 66, 1957, 37-8. Williams is shocked by the mention of a dancing master at Bangor; one was also employed at Cardigan during this period.

provided both financial support and continuity. The development of non-classical teaching took place somewhat later than at Beaumaris and Bangor. In 1793, however, it was decided that the usher should teach writing and arithmetic, and in 1802 there were sixty-four boarders, including many sons of county families, apparently all accommodated in the masters' houses. Classical instruction was given by the master in the 'upper school', while in the 'lower school' the usher taught writing, arithmetic, English grammar and geography. The upper school (which had the smaller number of pupils) consisted simply of an upstairs gallery boarded up at one end of the schoolroom.[18] The emphasis on residential accommodation, the associated almshouses, and the existence on the foundation not only of a master and usher, but also of a 'lecturer' (all of whom were Anglican clergymen), must have made Monmouth at this period a veritable Barchester. A description of the buildings in 1818, written by Nicholas Carlisle, reads as follows:

> The ground at Monmouth upon which the present Buildings are erected, is situate on the South-East side of the Town, near the bank of the river Wye, and forms a Square of nearly two acres in extent. At the Upper end, are the Houses of the Lecturer and School-master; and at the Lower end, is the Usher's: on the North-west side, are the Alms-Houses: and, on the South East, is the Lecturer's garden. The School is placed between the Master's House, and the Alms-Houses. The Lecturer's House is a very desirable residence, having lately undergone considerable alterations: to which belongs an extensive garden, laid out in great taste, and running parallel with the river Wye . . .[19]

The later growth and rebuilding of the school have considerably modified, if not wholly destroyed, this idyllic picture.

At Swansea, the grammar school founded by Bishop Gore in 1682 continued to use the original school building in Goat Street. In about 1766, during the mastership of the Reverend

---

[18] *CCR*, 27, 439. See also H. A. Ward, *Monmouth School 1614-1964* (London, Haberdashers' Company, 1964), 13-14.
[19] Carlisle, *Endowed Grammar Schools*, op. cit., II, 173.

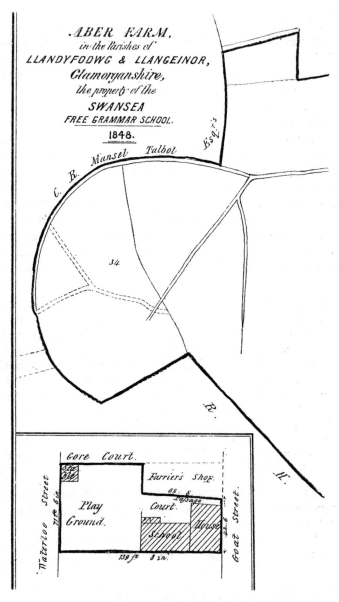

Fig. 9. Swansea, plan of the school endowment at Aber Farm, and of the school and master's house in Goat Street, Swansea, 1848.

Jenkin Williams, there were some seventy pupils, and the sons of many leading families in Glamorgan and Carmarthenshire were said to have been educated under him. In about 1787, the corporation increased the stipend of the master and, seven years later, it was reported that 'a large number of boys of the middle and upper classes from the town and the surrounding country were educated there'.[20] In 1837 the Charity Commissioners stated that 'the chief dependence of the master appears to be upon pay scholars, whom he is at liberty to receive without limitation; and the house in which he now resides is calculated, both from its situation and appearance, rather for the boarders than the free boys'.[21] The Commissioners included in their report a small plan which shows that the school building measured 41 by 23 feet, while the master's house was 36 by 24 feet and occupied the main frontage to Goat Street. The grammar school was given an impressive new building in 1852 and the old buildings were demolished, but a plan of the original buildings was made in 1848 and is reproduced as Fig. 9.[22]

Of the other grammar schools in south Wales, those at Cowbridge and Carmarthen are the best documented for the eighteenth century. The school at Cowbridge had been re-founded in 1685 by Sir Leoline Jenkins, an eminent civil lawyer and former principal of Jesus College, Oxford, which now took over the government of the school. It flourished, particularly under the mastership of Daniel Durel between 1721 and 1763. Again one finds that the main syllabus consisted of Latin and Greek, but a writing master and a drawing master are mentioned at this period, and additional subjects were taught, including English, French and geography. The pupils also seem to have had the use of the town library and it is possible that the writing master was also the master of the Eagle Academy, a flourishing private school which existed

[20] G. G. Francis, *The Free Grammar School, Swansea* (Swansea, Ivey and Pearse, 1849), 13-14.
[21] *CCR*, 32, 385.
[22] G. G. Francis, op. cit., facing p. 18, which also has a plan of Aber Farm, the school endowment.

at Cowbridge from about 1730 and met in the town's assembly rooms.[23] It was during Durel's time that the seventeenth-century grammar school building was extensively repaired, including the provision of a fireplace in the school-room, which had not previously had one. In the 1730s a new extension was erected consisting of a room measuring 24 by 14 feet for the boarders to dine in, with two chambers and a garret over it.[24] When the old school was rebuilt on the same site in 1849, the 1730s extension was left standing and survives between the Victorian school and the town wall; it was later used as a changing room for school games and is still known as the 'Boot House'. This building is plain and utilitarian in appearance but it appropriately fills a gap between the town wall and the south gate, and has rightly been listed on that account.

Equally active in the eighteenth century was the Queen Elizabeth grammar school at Carmarthen, whose seventeenth-century building was illustrated in chapter I. Here the school benefited from the support of the corporation, which allocated some of the town rents to keep the building in good repair and also helped to finance a total rebuild in 1797. The build-ing of 1797 was described as 'a long, low building in Priory Street, attached to the [former] Archdeacon's house where the master lived'. There were desks and benches on raised plat-forms, with the master's and usher's seats opposite the front door. A former pupil wrote that the pupils' seats were arranged on both sides of the room and that the school was 'like a college chapel'.[25] This was an entirely traditional arrangement for a grammar school of this period and, we may safely infer, of the school which it replaced. As with the other schools already mentioned, it was supported by the local gentry and clergy, as well as by the burgesses of the town. This was the school attended by Moses Williams (1685-1742), the leading Welsh scholar, as well as by James Owen,

---

[23] Iolo Davies, *'A Certaine Schoole'. A History of the Grammar School at Cowbridge* (Cowbridge, Brown and Sons, 1967), 33n.
[24] Ibid., 54.
[25] M. Evans, *An Early History of Queen Elizabeth Grammar School, Carmarthen, 1576-1800* (The School, n.d.), 78.

the tutor of the dissenting academy at Shrewsbury, mentioned earlier. Another former pupil was Griffith Jones, the founder of the circulating schools.

There was also in Carmarthen a non-classical school founded in 1729 under the will of Sir Thomas Powell for the teaching of arithmetic and navigation, and, like the grammar school, it was actively supported by the corporation. In 1795 the Common Council appointed David Peter as master of this school and, by so doing, linked this charity with the Presbyterian academy which had returned to the town in 1751; indeed, it appears that this link had been established somewhat earlier.[26] David Peter had himself been a student at the academy and became the minister of Lammas Street chapel in Carmarthen in 1791. From 1795 to 1835 he held both the senior tutorship of the Presbyterian academy and the mastership of the Sir Thomas Powell school, which seems to have acted as a preparatory school for the academy. David Peter and his assistant preached, and may have taught, in Welsh, and the academy at Carmarthen was attended by many students of the Independent persuasion, notwithstanding the rival academy at Abergavenny.[27] The Charity Commissioners, who reported on Powell's school in 1834, noted that the master was a Presbyterian minister, but stated that 'no boys were excluded on account of religious opinions'. At that date there were six boys being taught free, and thirty-five pay-scholars.[28] This is another interesting early example of the influence of Nonconformist opinion on officially-provided education in some parts of Wales, which had begun with the schools of Dr. Williams. It may be noted that virtually all schools at this period depended on fee-paying pupils to sustain endowments which were wholly inadequate for the growing demand for what would nowadays be called secondary education. We shall see that, later in the nineteenth

---

[26] Roberts, 'Nonconformist academies', op. cit., 21. The link was between Powell's school and Lammas Street chapel, whose ministers taught in the academy. (The academy migrated to Swansea in 1784 but returned to Carmarthen in 1795.)

[27] Ibid., 26-7.

[28] CCR, 28, 637-8.

century, the grammar school at Carmarthen and Sir Thomas Powell's school were amalgamated under a Court of Chancery scheme, and acquired a new school building in the process.

There can be little doubt that the Church authorities in south Wales were influenced by the example set by the dissenting academies in preparing boys for the ministry. The value of Welsh livings was notoriously low and pluralism was was widely practised. Much of the work was done by poorly-paid curates who could never have afforded to attend a college at Oxford or Cambridge. *De facto*, they were in the same position as the Nonconformists, who were debarred from entry to the ancient universities on legal grounds. In this situation, Thomas Burgess, who became Bishop of St David's in 1803, licensed certain grammar schools to train young men who could be directly ordained into Welsh parishes, without having attended a university.[29] This led to the revival of several grammar schools in south Wales, including the one at Carmarthen, and eventually to the opening of Lampeter College in 1827.

These developments had to some extent been anticipated at the remarkably successful school established by Edward Richard at Ystradmeurig, near Aberystwyth. The lack of well-educated, Welsh-speaking clergy was nowhere more keenly felt than in the rural parts of Cardiganshire. Edward Richard, a native of Ystradmeurig and a former pupil of the Queen Elizabeth grammar school in Carmarthen, decided in 1757 to set up a grammar school for educating twelve poor boys of the parish in the principles of the Church of England and the rudiments of grammar; by further indentures of 1771 and 1774 he increased the number of boys to thirty-two and settled property to finance a 'perpetual grammar school'.[30] During his life-time (he died in 1777), the school was held in the parish church, where Richard's considerable library of 700 books was also housed. He was well aware of the evils

[29] D. T. W. Price, *Bishop Burgess and Lampeter College* (Cardiff, University of Wales Press, 1987), 51f.
[30] *CCR*, 28, 587-9.

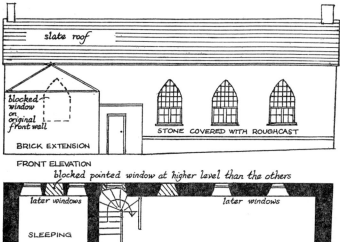

FRONT ELEVATION
blocked pointed window at higher level than the others

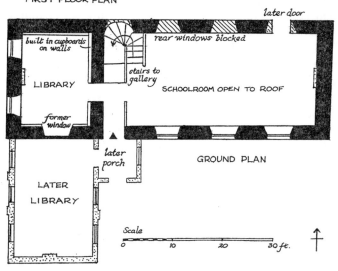

Fig. 10. Ystradmeurig grammar school, Cards., 1812.

of non-residence and, in his will, solemnly enjoined his successors as master to note that:

> This School is not to be a Sinecure; you must attend, and get your bread by labour and industry. This is my will, and I hope it will be observed; discharge, therefore, your Trust faithfully, as knowing that you are accountable for your behaviour, not only to the Trustees, but also to THE ALMIGHTY.[31]

The endowment of the school at Ystradmeurig was augmented, soon after Richard's death, by one made in 1746 by Thomas Oliver in the neighbouring parish of Lledrod, which was linked with it, and in 1812 the trustees raised a subscription to erect a school building which still survives near the parish church at Ystradmeuring. This building, which is shown in Fig. 10, is interesting architectually as an example of the use of the early neo-Gothic style for a Welsh school. It consisted of a large schoolroom, with a small library at one end of the building, over which was a sleeping room for boarders,[32] though there was a tradition which lasted until the present century, of pupils being boarded in local farmhouses. This school played an important part in preparing candidates for the ministry, and had a subsequent history not so much as a grammar school as a seminary for ordinands.[33] Apart from Richard's work for education in its more formal sense, he was also a leading member of the 'Augustan' circle of Welsh scholars, who studied ancient Welsh, and contemporary English, literary forms and corresponded with each other about the future of Welsh literature at a critical point in its development.[34]

[31] Quoted in N. Carlisle, *Endowed Grammar Schools,* op. cit., II, 966.
[32] *CCR,* 28, 590. The sleeping room was unoccupied at this date (1837); in 1847, it was reported that the master occupied a study at the end of the schoolroom, whether the sleeping room or the library is not clear. Later students dubbed the upper room 'The Vatican', which suggests that the master's study was there.
[33] For a fuller history, see D. G. Osborne-Jones, *Edward Richard of Ystradmeurig* (Carmarthen, Spurrell, 1934).
[34] See Saunders Lewis, *A School of Welsh Augustans* (first published in 1924, reprinted by Firecrest Publishing, Bath, 1969), ch. 3.

This account has concentrated on the major foundations, but similar changes were taking place, to a greater or lesser degree, in the other grammar schools of this period. We noted earlier that the new foundations of the eighteenth century had varied fortunes depending on their location, the strength of local demand, and other factors such as the value of the endowment and the proximity of rival schools. The schools which had been established in the Tudor and Stuart period tended during the eighteenth century to sort themselves into a kind of rank order, and some of them proved to be ill-fitted to meet the challenge of the new industrial age which was about to be born. Paradoxically, it is sometimes the schools which were least successful as grammar schools whose buildings have survived, whereas it is the successful ones whose buildings were demolished to make way for larger replacements. This point is well illustrated by two surviving buildings (no longer in use as schools) situated in relatively remote rural districts in Montgomeryshire and Monmouthshire.

The first is the school founded in 1690 at Deuddwr (the name of a scattered hamlet about seven miles north of Welshpool which was anglicized to 'Deytheur' in official records and on modern maps). The founder was Andrew Newport, the lord of the manor, and the school was built, or rebuilt, during the eighteenth century.[35] The accommodation used by the master was enlarged, perhaps more than once, and it is clear that he regarded the mastership as a sinecure, to which was also attached the nearby chapelry of Penrhos. It came to epitomize the worst excesses of contemporary pluralism, and the Education Commissioners, who visited the school in 1847, found that the whole of the building was occupied by the master as a residence, while the school, with twenty-two boys in attendance, was held in 'an outbuilding adjoining the master's stable' and was taught by a young usher, twenty years of age, who had previously been an agricultural

---

[35] *CCR*, 32, 256. The full name of the parish is Llansanffraid Deuddwr.

labourer.[36] Although this school was later reformed, it never succeeded as a viable school, and after closure and subsequent dilapidation, it has been converted into a private house (Plate 22). The building itself is of brick and was extended on each side during the eighteenth or nineteenth centuries; the pattern of the roof slates may indicate that the roof was originally hipped.

Another grammar school in a remote rural area which suffered during the eighteenth century from having a nominal schoolmaster, who employed an assistant at a lower rate of pay, was that founded by James Powell in 1654 at Brynderi, which is about two miles north of Llandeilo Gresynni and about eight miles east of Abergavenny. The master occupied a farmhouse, which, to judge from the stone building which has survived as a private house, was a very large one. Then in 1820 the school was rebuilt nearby in brick, and a strict classical style was adopted for it (see Plate 23). In spite of this rebuilding, and its continuance as a small grammar school which produced a number of notable pupils during the nineteenth century, the school later ceased to be a grammar school and was taken over by the County Council as an elementary school in 1902.[37] It was, sadly, due for closure as a primary school in 1991.

External architectural style is not always a safe guide to the development of school planning, and the grammar school at Wrexham, for example, which Moses Griffith's painting shows in the elegant classical dress given to it when 'repairs' were carried out in 1717 (see Plate 24), was still basically a seventeenth-century building containing one large schoolroom, without any residential accommodation for the master.[38] The early nineteenth-century buildings at Ystradmeurig and

---

[36] *Reports of the Commissioners of Inquiry into the State of Education in Wales* (London, 1847), III, 147. The later history of this school is given in *Y Cymmrodor*, xliii (1932), 43 f.

[37] See Sir Joseph Bradney, *A History of the Free Grammar School in the parish of Llantilio Crossenny* (London, Mitchell Hughes and Clarke, 1924). The master's former residence at Ty-gwyn is illustrated on p. 27.

[38] A. F. Palmer, *History of the Town of Wrexham* (Wrexham, Woodall, Minshall and Thomas, 1893), 106-9.

Llandeilo Gresynni were also planned in accordance with the traditional concept of the single-storey school building; by contrast, the purpose-built schools of the eighteenth century were invariably of two storeys and domestic in character since they combined the teaching and residential accommodation in the same building. The grammar school at Deuddwr, mentioned above, was planned in this way and, when the grammar school at St Asaph left the cathedral close in 1780, it occupied a small two-storey building at Roegau which is indistinguishable from an ordinary house, to which purpose it has now reverted.[39] This was also true, as we noted in chapter II, of some of the non-classical schools of this period. The use of a farmhouse near Llandeilo Gresynni for school purposes, before the school of 1820 was built, also reminds us that most of the private (unendowed) classical schools and academies met during the eighteenth century in the masters' own houses. These could, of course, have been of any earlier date and architectural style. The records of the numerous private schools and academies are, as one would expect, scattered and incomplete, but an interesting, though unprovenanced, piece of evidence of their internal appearance has survived in the form of a bowl of Delft ware inscribed to 'Edward Jones Scoole Master 1751', now in the St Fagans Folk Museum (see Plate 25). The single master with his small group of pupils was probably the most characteristic feature of the education of the middle classes during this period.

The multiplication of private educational establishments in the eighteenth century is nowhere better illustrated than by the numerous and often migratory dissenting academies, to which some reference has already been made. It is clear that during the eighteenth century they all met in houses or other buildings belonging to chapels or to private individuals, and not in purpose-built schools. The academy at Llwyn-llwyd in Breconshire, at which both Howel Harris and William Williams were students, was held in a barn near the tutor's

---

[39] D. R. Thomas, *The History of the Diocese of St. Asaph* (Oswestry, Caxton Press, 1908), I, 388.

house,[40] as was that at Pentwyn in the parish of Llan-non in Carmarthenshire, where Richard Price the philosopher was a pupil.[41] Lady Huntingdon's academy at Trefecca in Breconshire, which opened in 1768, occupied an Elizabethan house known as 'College Farm', close to the better-known 'College', which Howel Harris built for his 'family' between 1752 and 1772 in the neo-Gothic style made famous by Horace Walpole's house at Strawberry Hill in London.[42] The first purpose-built academy established by the Independents was at Ffrwd-fâl (Ffrwd Vale) near Llandovery in Carmarthenshire, and was not built until 1835.[43] The Baptists had a small academy in a succession of houses at Trosnant near Pontypool between 1732 and 1770, but a purpose-built academy was not opened at Pontypool until 1836. Later on the scene were the Calvinistic Methodists, who held an academy in various buildings in Bala from 1837 and opened a new college there in 1865.[44] By this time, the dissenting academies had become theological colleges, outside the main stream of school education.

However inadequate the premises used for educational purposes in the eighteenth century, there can be no doubt that the majority of the tutors, both in the endowed grammar schools and the private academies, were competent Latinists. Many of them also made significant contributions to learning, including the study of local history, as evidenced by the history of Anglesey written by John Thomas, schoolmaster at Beaumaris, and the first guide to Swansea written by John

[40] Roberts, 'Nonconformist academies', op. cit., 20.
[41] Ibid., 55. See also Gwilym Evans, 'Pentwyn Academy' in *The Carmarthenshire Historian* (Dyfed Rural Council, 1976), 67-77. Pentwyn Farm is about 1½ miles east of Llan-non.
[42] Roberts, 65. For an architectural description of the buildings at Trefecca, see R. Haslam, *The Buildings of Wales. Powys* (Harmondsworth, Penguin Books, 1979), 376-7. For College Farm, see *Capel Newsletter*, No. 12 (1990), on its 'deplorable state of disrepair'.
[43] Roberts, 52-3. There is an interesting description of this academy in *Reports of the Commissioners*, op. cit., I, 227-8, where the date of opening is given as 1834.
[44] Roberts, 57-9 (Trosnant); 70-75 (Bala). The 1865 academy building at Bala survives on the Trawsfynydd road.

Jones, the master at the grammar school.[45] There is also the memoir of the parish of Hawarden in Flintshire, written by Richard Willett after his retirement from the headmastership of Hawarden school.[46] Looking more generally at the provision made for post-primary education in eighteenth-century Wales, it would be easy to criticize its concentration on Latin and Greek authors, and its limitation to only a small section of society. But the products of these schools and academies — who included country gentlemen with antiquarian tastes, as well as Anglican parsons and Dissenting ministers with scholarly interests — were not hidebound by their knowledge of the classical languages. Some of them also contributed to the growing understanding of the ancient language and history of Wales and, by so doing, influenced the development of modern Welsh literature and learning.

[45] The authorship of *A History of Anglesey* (1775) is given in H. Ramage, *Portraits of an Island* (Anglesey Antiquarian Society, 1987), 321. *Swansea Guide* was published anonymously in 1802 (printer, Z. Morris, Swansea); the attribution to John Jones is by G. G. Francis, op. cit., 15.

[46] *A Memoir of Hawarden Parish* was published at Chester in 1822. It was written by Richard Willett, headmaster of Hawarden grammar school 1778-1814, and was reprinted by Clwyd Library Service in 1990.

CHAPTER IV

Church Schools and the National Society, 1800-1875

Although in 1833 the central Government began to make grants towards the cost of building schools sponsored by the National and British School Societies, and later by the Catholic Poor Schools Committee, the numerous schools established in the first seventy-five years of the nineteenth century remained under the control of their founding bodies and were —considered as a whole — a very remarkable manifestation of voluntary effort. This great movement for providing elementary schools for the poorer sections of the community had been stimulated by the unprecedented growth of population following rapid industrialization, particularly in south Wales. Merthyr Tydfil was the archetypal settlement of the new industrial age and soon grew to become the largest town in the whole of Wales. But there were few places, even in the remoter rural areas, which were not affected by this first attempt to provide elementary education on a mass scale. It is true that this major educational change has been widely studied by historians, but very little attention has hitherto been given to the changes in the physical environment of education and to the school buildings which constitute a considerable social and architectural legacy. In this and the following chapter an attempt is made to survey and assess this period of intense educational activity, mainly through a study of the school buildings which have survived down to the present day. The period under consideration falls naturally into two parts, with the dividing point at about 1840. During the first forty years of the century the need for something approaching mass elementary education was widely recognized but the organization of it was haphazard and piecemeal. There is much information about the organization of early British and National schools in the archives of their parent Societies, but relatively little attention was paid by school promoters to the form of the school buildings, and only a few schools, chiefly in London, were designed by professional architects.[1] The proponents of the monitorial method of teaching adopted by both the British and National School Societies were mainly concerned to show that very large numbers of poor children could be educated at a low cost, for the system was based on the children teaching each other, using step-by-step questioning on a predetermined pattern. In 1811, Joseph Lancaster's *Hints and directions for building, fitting up and arranging school-rooms on the British system of education* was published, and this recommended that schoolrooms should measure 70 by 32 feet, each accommodating 320 pupils; the children should be seated on long benches with desks facing the master, but there should be aisles on both sides, so that the children, when not at their desks, could stand in semi-circles facing the side walls, upon which lesson-boards should be hung. The master's job was to supervise the monitors who drilled the children in rote-learning. This basic plan continued to be recommended in the *Manuals* of the British School

---

[1] The National Society's archives at Church House, Westminster, contain many references to schools in Wales. The British and Foreign School Society's records are now housed at Lancaster House, part of the West London Institute of Higher Education, Borough Road, Isleworth, but their series of school plans was largely destroyed by bombing during the war: the only Welsh example to have survived is the British school at Goytrey (Mon.), which is also among the Building Grant Plans listed in Appendix III.

Society down to the 1830s and '40s, but how far theory was put into practice in Wales it is hard to say.

Andrew Bell, whose ideas were taken up by the Anglican National Society, was notably vague on the question of the buildings needed for children in elementary schools. 'The chief and great expense', he wrote, 'consists in a roof to cover them. The rest, under the Madras [i.e monitorial] system of tuition, is quite inconsiderable.'[2] In 1816, a sub-committee of the National Society 'appointed to propose a plan for building schools, so as to unite the greatest possible convenience with the least possible expense' stated that 'a barn furnishes no bad model, and a good one may be easily converted into a school', a statement which was to be repeated right through to the 1830s.[3] Some barns were in fact used as schools in Wales at this time, among which may be cited the tithe barns at Hawarden in Flintshire and Llanbedrog in Caernarfonshire. However, very few large purpose-built schools on the Lancasterian model seem to have been built during the early years of the century. Most of the school buildings in Wales which survive from the first forty years of the last century have the traditional single-storey schoolroom, with stone walls and slate roofs. Traditional practice was also followed in providing living accommodation for the master, either in the same building, using the attic space in the roof as a bedroom,[4] or in a two-storey annexe with sufficient space for a married master and his family. In other cases, a separate house or cottage (often a pre-existing one) was occupied by the master. Where the number of children was exceptionally large, it was usual to have two schoolrooms built end to end but often under one roof, a good example of which may be seen in the former National school at Beaumaris in Anglesey (1816), now converted into private houses.

[2] A. Bell, *The Madras School* (London, Bensley, 1808), 116.
[3] National Society, *Fifth Annual Report* (1816), 185-90.
[4] See, for example, the photograph and plan of the parish school at Llanycil (Merioneth, 1838) in J. Lowe, *Welsh Country Workers' Housing 1775-1875* (Cardiff, National Museum of Wales, 1985), 31. Compare the school of 1847 at Cadoxton, near Barry, Glamorgan, which survives in Coldbrook Road East.

It adds greatly to the interest of studying these early school buildings if the social and economic setting of the districts in which they were built is also studied. For example, the National school at Amlwch, also in Anglesey, which was built in 1821 and consisted of two separate schoolrooms linked by the teachers' accommodation, owed its existence to the great increase of population which followed the opening of the Parys copper mine (Plate 26). The building of separate schoolrooms for boys and girls seems usually to have been preferred to the construction of two-storey buildings. The endowed elementary school at Nolton in Pembrokeshire, built in 1810, was of two storeys, but followed the plan which we noted elsewhere in the eighteenth century, of providing the master's living accommodation on the ground floor and the children's schoolroom above; in this case, however, the stone stairs leading to the schoolroom are protected by a two-storey porch (Plate 27). The only other surviving example of a two-storey school of this period which has been located is at Northop in Flintshire, where boys were accommodated on one floor and girls on the other, in a new National school built in 1823.

When studying school buildings of the early nineteenth century, a useful starting point is provided by the details of new endowments given in the reports of the Charity Commissioners published in the 1830s. Twenty such endowments are listed for Wales and are summarized in Appendix IB. In at least two cases these were not so much new endowments as older ones recycled. For example, the National school at Northop was allocated the endowment of the defunct grammar school described in chapter I, and there are examples elsewhere of older charities being diverted to elementary education. The two endowments made by E. Goff, at Hay-on-Wye in Breconshire and Raglan in Monmouthshire, show that Nonconformist interests were not neglected: it was reported that at Hay the master was an Independent minister, while at Raglan the master was a Baptist. It is necessary to bear in mind that church/chapel animosity was much less intense before the publication of the Report on the State of

Education in Wales in 1847, which aroused such strong feelings that it has become known in Welsh history as 'The Treason of the Blue Books'. The school built in 1835 at Eglwysbach in Denbighshire, which is still in use as a primary school, had its endowment supplemented by voluntary subscriptions and became a National school. It was at about this time that the National Society began to make the teaching of the Church catechism a condition of financial help, which did not improve relationships with Nonconformist parents. On the other hand, the endowed school in the Merioneth parish of Llangelynnin (the building, which still survives, is in the village of Llwyngwril), is inscribed 'Church of England School 1831', so it may not have been affiliated to the National Society; similarly, at Whitton in Radnorshire, where an endowment made in the early eighteenth century by Dame Child was reorganized to finance a new school building in 1834, no such condition seems to have been imposed. Even today, the trustees of Whitton school, which is still in use, represent the whole community and, although it is a voluntary aided school, the Church in Wales has only a minority representation on the body of trustees.

The other endowed schools of the early nineteenth century whose buildings have survived have had varied histories. The original school at Llanystumdwy (1812) in Caernarfonshire was converted into the master's house and a new schoolroom was built alongside it in 1851; this was the schoolroom in which Lloyd George later led his famous schoolboy rebellion against the teaching of the Church catechism. At Gwyddelwern in Merioneth, the endowment of 1806 appears to have been used to supply a regular teacher for the small school in the churchyard which we noted in chapter II, while the school endowed in 1810 at Grosmont in Monmouthshire was held in an annexe to the master's house, which still survives with its external flight of stairs. The school endowed at Nolton in Pembrokeshire in 1806 was actually built in 1810, as described above, and is notable for its early use of pointed neo-Gothic windows, similar to those used at Ystradmeurig grammar school at about the same date. Other schools of this period continued to have round-headed windows of Georgian type. The fashion for neo-Gothic pointed windows for schools was gradually supplanted by the use of straight-headed 'Tudoresque' windows and doors, characterized by label-moulding with dropped and returned ends. An early example of this may be seen on the former school at Trelleck in Monmouthshire, which was a seventeenth-century endowed school given a new building in 1820 (Plate 28). This form of window was used on many schools in the 1830s and later.

The endowed schools represent only a small fraction of the schools actually built at this time. It is clear that private philanthropy, though of continuing importance, was no longer sufficient to meet demand, and the method of financing new school buildings which was increasingly being used was that of voluntary subscriptions, without an endowment. The charging of fees for attendance (usually a penny a week) was also a form of voluntary subscription and helped to pay for the teacher. A good indication of the various types of school being built at this period may be obtained by considering some of the fifty or so purpose-built schools of the period 1800-1840 which have survived in different parts of Wales (though only rarely still in use as schools). These are listed in Appendix II, with details of their location. It should be emphasized that the distribution of these schools is the result of chance survival, and this list, which does not claim to be complete, certainly under-represents schools in the industrial parts of south Wales, where the later growth of major conurbations has largely obliterated the remains of early nineteenth-century schools.

The first purpose-built monitorial school in Wales was erected in 1811 and survives at Penley in the Maelor district of Flintshire. It is called the 'Madras' school after the school in India where Andrew Bell first experimented with the monitorial system. The building originally consisted of two schoolrooms under a single roof covered with thatch, which has been renewed ever since (Plate 29). This was a vernacular feature, but in this instance was more in the *cottage orné* style of estate cottages, since the school was built for his estate workers by the second Lord Kenyon, a close friend and keen supporter of Andrew Bell. The only other thatched school which has been located in Wales is also in an estate village, at Merthyr Mawr in Glamorgan. This is an attractive L-shaped building erected in 1837 and originally consisted of a schoolroom and teacher's house. It was built by an unknown architect for the Right Honourable John Nicholl, M.P., and is now converted into two private dwellings.[5] Early estate schools survive in other parts of Wales, as at Llan-rhos, near Llandudno (Caernarfonshire), where in 1822 Miss Frances Mostyn founded a school which consists of a central single-storey schoolroom with hipped wings of two storeys at each end, presumably to accommodate the teachers. The tradition established in the eighteenth century of wealthy ladies taking the lead in founding schools may also be noted at Llandegfan in Anglesey, where the original inscribed stone on the former National school building records that the Duchess of Kent, who visited Anglesey with her daughter, the future Queen Victoria, in 1832, contributed £50 towards the cost of the building. In Monmouthshire, a particularly interesting example of female patronage survives at Blaenafon, where Sarah Hopkins founded a school in 1816 in memory of her brother, who was the co-proprietor of the local ironworks. The building is described in more detail in the following chapter on the 'works schools' built in the industrial areas of Wales.

Other early nineteenth-century schools may best be regarded as continuing the well-established practice of providing parish schools financed from the parish rates or from small legacies for the poor, examples of which have been noticed in previous chapters. The small stone building with round-headed windows which stands in the churchyard at Llanrhystud in Cardiganshire seems to have been built as a parish school in 1806, before the founding of the National Society. It probably owed its existence to the initiative of the

---

[5] The school as built at Merthyr Mawr differs somewhat from the illustration given in *Plans and Prospects* (Cardiff, Welsh Arts Council, 1975), 62.

local incumbent, as also with the plain rubble-stone building which still survives near the bridge in Llanfihangel Cwm Du in Breconshire which is said to have been the school built in the 1830s by the Reverend Thomas Price (*Carnhuanawc*), the noted antiquary and Welsh scholar; while accepting the need for the children to learn English, he insisted that the Welsh Bible should be read every evening in the school.[6] Other former school buildings of similar single-cell plan and built of local stone (in these cases with pointed Gothic windows) may also be seen at Llandderfel in Merioneth (1828), Llandre in north Cardiganshire (c. 1830), and at Mynytho on the Llŷn peninsula (1833). The same design was also adopted for the small school built in the churchyard at Kidwelly in Carmarthenshire in 1833, which has recently been restored for use as a church room. Most elementary schools of this period were sited close to the parish church, but at Llandderfel the school is in the middle of the village, while the school at Mynytho (still used as a school) is in the centre of the large upland parish of Llangian and has one of the most beautiful school sites in Wales, overlooking Abersoch Bay.

The close association between the parish schools and the parish churches continued throughout the nineteenth century and, since the majority of them eventually became affiliated to the National Society, it is difficult to distinguish between parish and National schools, especially in the earlier part of the century. The first National school in Anglesey was built at Llandyfrydog in 1815 and is now a private house. This school was associated with the Reverend J. H. Cotton, who did much to promote National schools in the diocese of Bangor when he later became dean of the cathedral.[7] At Conwy, the National school of 1838 was later enlarged and is now used as a visitors' centre, while one of the earliest National schools to have survived in Denbighshire forms part

[6] *Reports of the Commissioners on the State of Education in Wales* (London, HMSO, 1847), II, 33n. These Reports are hereafter cited as *SEW*. See also II, 137, where it is stated that English was taught at the school in the morning, and Welsh in the afternoon.

[7] D. A. Pretty, *Two Centuries of Anglesey Schools* (Anglesey Antiquarian Society, 1977), 49-50.

of the present primary school at Llanddoged (1827). In Montgomeryshire, the former National school of 1832 at Llanfechain survives as the village shop. Moving further south, one of the earliest National schools in Pembrokeshire forms part of the present primary school at Cresselly, erected in 1835. In Carmarthenshire, the former National school at Marros is now a roofless ruin but retains its original slate date-stone and inscription of 1840. In the Vale of Glamorgan, it appears that the adaptation of church houses as schools, mentioned in a previous chapter, resulted at first in fewer purpose-built National schools and the earliest located is at Cadoxton near Barry (1847). It is good to know that the local community in Cadoxton had not been disrupted by religious differences: it was reported that 'the Dissenters had assisted in haulage for the new school, and would send their children'.[8] Finally, in Monmouthshire, if one excludes the part of the medieval priory building in Monmouth which was used as a National school from 1814, the earliest surviving National school is probably that at Penallt, originally endowed in 1689 and rebuilt in 1834 near to what the inscription on the school calls a 'school church'. The latter was built because the old parish church was some miles from the new settlement, and schools were frequently used for church services in the out-lying parts of large parishes, of which there were many in Wales.[9]

In contrast to the Established Church, very few purpose-built day schools were erected by the Nonconformists during the first forty years of the nineteenth century. This was a reflection not of lack of interest but of resources. During this period Nonconformist effort and voluntary contributions went into the construction of purpose-built chapels to replace the farm and other buildings in which their earliest meetings

---

[8] *SEW*, I, 318.
[9] The original heart-shaped plaque on the former National school at Borth (Cards.) states that it is the 'National School House, built and licensed for divine service A.D. 1842'. At Gwernymynydd (Flints.) the National school of 1867 (now a private house) had a small chancel at one end, while the former National school at Belan (Denbs.) had an apse added to it in 1868.

were often held. It was natural that the chapel buildings themselves should have been used as Sunday schools and, for a time and in some places, as day schools as well. Purpose-built day schools in association with chapels appeared mainly after 1840 and will be considered in the next chapter. Until British schools developed, many chapel-goers would have sent their children to the parish or National schools for want of any alternative, and a study of local sources often suggests that the amount of animosity this caused, at any rate before the Blue Books of 1847, has been exaggerated by some later historians.

The Report on the State of Education in Wales, which appeared in 1847, was justly criticized for its lack of sympathy for Nonconformity and its misunderstanding of an ancient indigenous culture. The statistical data which it produced are nevertheless of value in assessing the amount of elementary school provision which had been made by this date. The rapid growth of the population as a whole, and of Nonconformity in its various forms, meant that the Established Church could no longer satisfy the demand for elementary education. This is apparent from the figures for attendance at day schools published in the Report, when compared with the population figures given in the 1841 census. The figures for school attendance are somewhat inflated because the statistical tables given in the Report state the number of children 'on the books', whereas it is clear from the reports on individual schools that actual attendance was often considerably lower; in addition, the population had continued to increase between 1841 and 1847. One can, however, obtain a general indication of the provision for day-school education from the percentages calculated from the data available, as set out in Table V. It will be seen that Church schools accounted for only about half of the total school population. In Glamorgan, the most populous of the counties, the inadequacy of Church school provision is especially striking; quite simply, the traditional resources for education could not cope with the massive demand. Much of the deficiency was made up by private-adventure elementary schools, of which there were no less than thirty-two in Merthyr Tydfil alone.[10] Many of these private elementary schools seem to have been undenominational in character and provided little more than what today would be called child-minding facilities. The schools noted as 'Other' were a miscellaneous group: they included some purpose-built British schools and many more day schools meeting in chapels or other buildings rented by Nonconformist congregations.

TABLE V — PUPILS IN DAY SCHOOLS IN 1847

Source: *Report on the State of Education in Wales (1847)*
Calculated from the figures in I, 59; II, 16 and III, 2-3.

County with population in 1841 in order of size	Day pupils as a percentage of county population %	Percentage of day pupils in:		
		Church schools %	Private schools %	Other %
Glamorgan 171,188	9	33	32	35
Monmouth 134,355	See note below			
Carmarthen 106,864	7	44	30	26
Denbigh 88,866	8	52	11	37
Pembroke 87,506	9	50	30	20
Caernarfon 81,093	7	68	13	19
Montgomery 69,219	7	54	27	19
Cardigan 68,766	6	42	42	16
Flint 66,919	11	65	16	19
Brecon 55,603	7	47	31	22
Anglesey 50,891	7	55	26	19
Merioneth 39,332	8	51	12	37
Radnor 25,356	5	73	25	2
Total excl. Monmouth 911,603	8	49	25	26

NOTE: The 1847 Report included only the industrial part of Monmouth-shire and comparable day school figures for the whole of the county are not available.

[10] *SEW*, I, 38-42. The great majority were dame schools.

The need for additional schools was well known to those working in education in Wales long before the Report of 1847 was published. In 1839 the National Society decided to redouble its efforts in Wales and it was supported by a number of reforming bishops and clergy, and by several prominent laymen. We shall see that in the 1840s Hugh Owen also revived the influence of the British School Society, especially in north Wales. The result of these combined efforts was that the years between 1840 and 1875 constituted something of a golden age of voluntary school building in Wales. Indeed, it can be argued that it was during this period that elementary education, in terms of buildings, reached its furthest geographical limit, from which it has gradually retreated since. Few areas, even in mountainous country, were without their small school buildings, many of which were subsequently abandoned as a result of rural depopulation and improved road transport, which has made it easier for children to attend new, strategically-placed schools serving groups of villages.

The part played by the central Government in accelerating the rate of school building in the Victorian period was of crucial importance. In 1833 Exchequer funds became available to make fifty per cent grants towards the cost of new schools supported by the National or British School Societies, and after 1839 the total amount available was increased annually. A Committee of Council on Education was formed in 1839 and asserted its right to approve the plans of schools which received grants. In the following year, the Committee issued a lengthy 'minute explanatory of the plans of school-houses', to which was attached a series of plans 'to enable the promoters of schools to avoid considerable expenses in the erection of school-houses, and to diffuse an acquaintance with the arrangements which have been sanctioned by extensive experience, as best adapted to the different systems of instruction'.[11] The Committee included specimen plans of

[11] *Minutes of the Committee of Council on Education*, 1839-40, 46-92, with 16 plans bound in at the end of the volume.

National and British schools, and of those recommended by David Stow, whose very influential book, *The training system adopted in the model schools of the Glasgow Educational Society*, had been published in 1836. The Lancasterian plan was mentioned at the beginning of this chapter. The plan which had come to be adopted by the National Society was also based on one large schoolroom, but differed from the Lancasterian plan in arranging for the children to sit on short benches arranged in 'hollow squares', each controlled by a monitor; writing was done at long desks fixed to the side walls. David Stow, by contrast, advocated the greater use of trained adult teachers, who should provide 'simultaneous instruction' to large groups of children sitting on galleries, or raised steps at the end of the schoolroom. A gallery was considered to be especially necessary for infants, who would thus clearly see the teacher and the 'visual aids' which Stow recommended. He also considered that a classroom, leading off the large schoolroom, was desirable for teaching smaller groups of children. Some of these ideas were taken up by the National Society, which published J. J. H. Harris's *The school-room: its arrangements and organization* in 1848. Harris later became the headmaster of St. Asaph grammar school and his book would have been known at least to the diocesan building committees which were now being formed.[12]

It was not only in educational theory that the 1840s marked a turning point. Pugin's *True principles of Pointed or Christian architecture* appeared in 1841 at the height of the controversy aroused by the Oxford Movement. The Ecclesiological Society, which took a keen interest in the architecture of schools as well as churches, was formed in 1845 and the High Victorian phase of the Gothic Revival was soon under way. The modern architectural profession was also in process of formation, and school buildings became an important part of its repertoire. In 1847 Henry Kendall (whose father had been one of the founders of the Institute of British Architects

---

[12] See the advertisement at the end of William Davis, *Handbook of the Vale of Clwyd* (Ruthin, Isaac Clarke, 1856).

in 1834) published his *Designs for schools and school houses, parochial and National;* five years later Joseph Clarke's illustrated book on *Schools and school houses* also appeared. These books would certainly have been known to some of the architects who designed schools in Wales and we shall see that the Gothic Revival had a notable effect on the schools built in Wales during this period.

In 1860 Harry Chester, the recently-retired assistant secretary to the Committee of Council on Education, wrote that 'When the Committee of Council on Education was first created in 1839, so little attention had been given to the planning of schools, that they were very commonly erected by the village brick-layer and carpenter, by rule of thumb, without any plans at all'. But now all this had changed: 'Educational societies vie with each other in architectural exploits, and the land is adorned with schools. The most celebrated architects undertake to design these buildings, and give their minds to the design. No one now thinks that a school can be built anyhow, without any reference to the uses to which the building is to be applied."[13]

Harry Chester was in a very good position to make this comment because he had inspected many of the plans submitted by school promoters with their applications for grant aid. The building grant plans submitted by school promoters in Wales were deposited in county record offices or the National Library after the second world war and form a very interesting and virtually unused source of information about schools in Wales. They are particularly valuable because they show the internal lay-outs which have now completely disappeared, even when the buildings themselves have survived. Knowledge of these lay-outs is essential for understanding the internal organization and teaching methods originally adopted. The building grant plans also show the external architectural form of the buildings as originally built, and, as we shall see, the great majority of them have now been altered, often drastically.

[13] *The Builder,* 1860, 461-2.

The building grant plans which survive relate to 434 schools in every part of Wales and date from about 1840 to 1875 (see Table VI). These drawings usually include elevations and sections as well as ground plans, but the amount of detail given varies considerably. Taking an average of four or five drawings per school, about 2,000 original documents have survived, some of considerable artistic merit and others in a fragmentary condition. Especially interesting are the often crude drawings of the earliest schools, and those of older buildings which were sent to the Committee of Council to illustrate improvements which were later needed. (This followed an administrative decision taken in about 1850, which made grants available not only for new schools but also for alterations to existing buildings.) Many of these early plans were drawn by 'the village brick-layer and carpenter' of the kind referred to by Harry Chester, but in Wales for 'brick-layer' one should read 'stone-mason'. These early plans form what might be termed the archaeological substratum of school building in Wales.

Before discussing a selection of individual schools, two more general questions need to be considered. First, how representative of the schools actually built are the plans which survive? There are certainly some schools which are known from other sources to have been built with Committee of Council grants but which do not appear in the collections of plans as we now have them. It is also known that the promoters of a number of schools whose buildings still survive did not apply for grant at all. It was not only the members of some Nonconformist denominations in south Wales who were opposed to State aid on principle, for some notable Anglican schools were erected without grant, especially after a Government decision in 1861 that any school receiving a grant must have a conscience clause permitting Nonconformist children to opt out of Anglican religious instruction: for a few High Churchmen this was, regrettably, unacceptable. Despite these deficiencies, Table VI shows that the proportions of schools with building grant plans in each county broadly corresponds to the relative size of the county

TABLE VI

THE NUMBER AND TYPE OF SCHOOLS WHICH APPLIED FOR
GOVERNMENT BUILDING GRANTS c. 1840-1875

NOTE. The architectural plans which accompanied applications to the
Committee of Council on Education were returned to county
record offices after the second world war. The Glamorgan plans
were divided between Cardiff and Swansea, and those for Brecon,
Cardigan, Montgomery and Radnor were deposited in the National
Library of Wales; the rest are in the area record offices noted in
Appendix III. The applications themselves are in the Public
Record Office (ref. Ed. 103). For the names of schools, architects,
etc., see Appendix III.

Counties, with population in 1861	Total no. of schools applying for grant*	National & Parochial	British & Nondenom- inational	Roman Catholic
Glamorgan 317, 752	73	57	12	4
Monmouth 174,633	49	45	3	1
Carmarthen 111,796	38	22	16	—
Denbigh 100,778	42	32	10	—
Pembroke 96,278	32	25	7	—
Caernarfon 95,694	43	28	15	—
Cardigan 72,245	13	11	2	—
Flint 69,737	28	22	5	1
Montgomery 66,919	26	18	8	—
Brecon 61,627	27	21	6	—
Anglesey 54,609	25	13	12	—
Merioneth 38,963	23	9	14	—
Radnor 25,382	15	15	—	—
TOTALS 1,286,413	434	318	110	6

population, so that, if plans have been lost, they have been
lost on a consistent basis. The main exception is Cardiganshire, which was the seventh most populous county in 1861

* The building grants paid to each school are listed in the *Report of the
Committee of Counci on Education, 1870-71,* 559-568, which also lists
schools existing in 1870 which had not received grants. The overall
numbers correspond closely with those given in this Table.

but has the lowest number of plans. The near-absence of grant-aided British schools in Cardiganshire might be explained not so much by opposition to State aid, which other strongly Nonconformist counties had given up by about 1860, as by an unusually high reliance on private elementary schools, as indicated in Table V. Since this collection of plans appears to be complete, Cardiganshire remains something of a puzzle. Possibly local economic conditions made it unusually difficult to raise the fifty per cent contribution required from local sources, or doubts about receiving State aid persisted longest in this part of Wales.

The second question is: how many of these schools still survive so that their buildings can be studied and an opinion formed about their architectural quality? An intensive survey of schools in Clwyd (the former Flintshire and Denbighshire) suggests that about two-thirds of the buildings with grant plans survive but that at least half of these have been so much altered as to have lost their original character. The same seems to apply to most other counties, but in the large conurbations in south Wales the more rapid pace of development has left relatively few examples of mid-Victorian school buildings. Details of the location of the schools with building grant plans are given in Appendix III, together with the names of the architects when stated on the plans; some indication is also given of which schools have survived.

It is possible within the scope of this book to describe in detail only a small selection of the schools for which plans survive, and no more can be attempted than to illustrate some of the main changes in internal planning and external architecture which took place during this period. The rest of this chapter continues with the National and parochial schools and the next with the British and non-denominational schools.

One of the earliest building grant plans is that of Llangollen National school in Denbighshire, dated 1840 (Fig. 11). (This building survives next to the Hand Hotel in Llangollen and retains its original name and date plaque.) The drawing was signed by 'Ellis Davies, Builder', for we are still in the

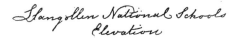

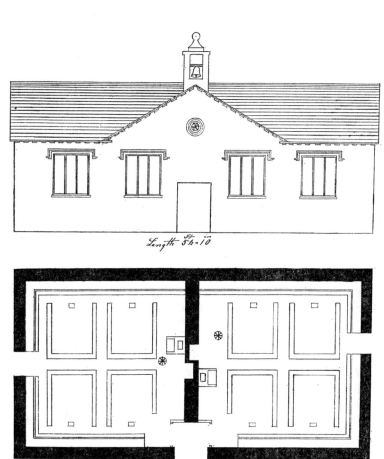

Fig. 11. Llangollen National school, Denbs., 1840. Ellis Davies, builder.

period before professional architects were generally employed for elementary schools; however, he knows enough to have given the school Tudoresque windows. The internal lay-out shows the fully-developed National school plan of this date. There are separate schoolrooms for boys and girls, and each room is set out with benches forming hollow squares, with a seat in each for the monitor. Writing desks are fixed around the walls, and the desks for the master and mistress are placed near the fireplaces. (The star-like objects near the teachers' desks are ventilating grills to the sub-floor.) This school was visited by one of the assistant commissioners at the time of the 1847 Report on the State of Education in Wales. He reported that the syllabus consisted of the usual subjects of the Scriptures and Catechism, reading, writing and arithmetic, with sewing for the girls. His comments on the teaching methods used make abundantly clear the deficiencies of the monitorial system. 'When examined in the Church Catechism', he wrote, 'out of 21 who professed to know it, 16 could repeat it fluently by rote; but when questioned irregularly, or in equivalent words, only two could answer, and they did not know the meaning of the terms which they repeated . . . Monitors are employed, but if the master's attention is withdrawn for an instant, the business of the school is at a stand."[14]

In 1845 the Committee of Council issued a further series of model plans which suggested modifications to the standard National and British school lay-outs, and in 1846 grants were made available for the employment of pupil-teachers, who were to be former pupils given extra training by the heads of the schools. The employment of pupil-teachers involved a greater use of desks and benches for group teaching, but there was still some use of benches arranged in squares for one-to-one drilling by monitors. Professional architects were also coming to be employed for the larger schools. This intermediate stage of planning may be illustrated by the National school at Llandovery in Carmarthenshire, which was

[14] *SEW*, III, 64.

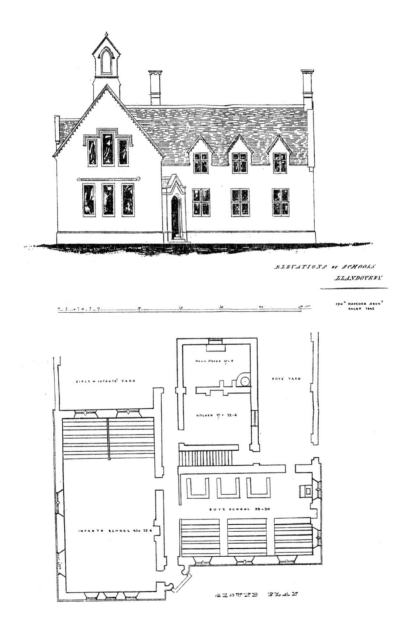

Fig. 12. Llandovery National school, Carms., 1845. E. Haycock, architect.

designed in 1845 by Edward Haycock of Shrewsbury. The building still stands in Garden Lane at Llandovery, but the only surviving original feature is the porch placed in the angle between the schoolrooms. The plan reproduced as Fig. 12, shows a two-storey building with some minimal Tudoresque decoration. The ground floor is occupied by the infants' schoolroom, with a gallery at one end, and by the boys' schoolroom, which has three groups of desks and benches, and three groups of benches only. The girls' schoolroom, with the same lay-out as the boys', was on the first floor above the infants' room, while the teachers' living accommodation was provided partly on the ground floor and partly on the first floor above the boys' schoolroom. This school cost £800 and was designed for 340 pupils.[15]

Further progress depended not only on adequate funding but also on the supply and training of teaching staff, which slowly improved as 'normal' schools, providing a norm or model, were set up and developed into teacher training colleges. In 1851 the Committee of Council issued an important minute which advocated the adoption of a type of plan which influenced the design of all grant-aided schools for the next twenty years, and also led to the alteration of many earlier buildings.[16] The optimum size of a schoolroom was considered to be 65 by 18 feet, with three rows of parallel desks and benches arranged on the long side of the room; each group of desks should be sub-divided by curtains, so that the teachers (who were now assumed to be pupil-teachers or qualified assistants) were given defined areas in which to work. The master or mistress could supervise all the classes in turn or, when the curtains were drawn back, address the whole school. The traditional large schoolroom was retained but the physical sub-division into separate 'class-rooms' was now making its tentative beginning. It was also laid down that every infants' schoolroom should have a gallery, and that

[15] *SEW*, I, 234-5. Although completed in 1847, the school did not open immediately because of lack of funds. £300 had been raised locally but a further £100 was needed to cover the half of the total cost not provided by Government grant.
[16] *Minutes of the Committee of Council on Education*, 1851-2, 78-91.

there should be a classroom, with a gallery, attached to every schoolroom for older children. The classroom was intended for use by each class in turn, taken by the master or a qualified assistant.

The agreement which had now been reached about the internal planning of schools facilitated the development of a suitable external architecture, and the expanding architectural profession responded quickly. The development of both the educational and architectural aspects of school planning may be illustrated by S. S. Teulon's design of 1855 for the National school at Briton Ferry in Glamorgan, illustrated in Fig. 13. Here we have a very competent Gothic elevation, which skilfully gives variety to the long schoolroom wall, and a plan which combines the boys' and girls' schools in one room measuring 62 by 18 feet. The schoolrooms are provided with parallel desks sub-divided by curtains and there is also a shared galleried classroom. The infants' school is provided with a large and a small gallery, and the teachers' house is integrated into the design. Many of the drawings included in the building grant collections after 1851 are variations of these design elements. In larger schools, the schoolrooms for boys and girls may be formed into a T or L shape, and provided with a classroom each; separate houses for the master and mistress might also be included. In smaller schools, the length of the schoolroom may be reduced and the classroom omitted, and school promoters who were short of funds sometimes omitted the teacher's house.

Teulon was not the only major architect to design schools in Wales.[17] George Gilbert Scott had a hand (with W. B. Moffat) in the design of Cardigan National school, and he also designed the school which is still in use at Trefnant in Denbighshire. Trefnant has a notable parochial group of

[17] His brother, W. M. Teulon, designed the former school building which still stands in Carmarthen Street, Llandeilo (ex inf. T. Lloyd). Another leading architect, Benjamin Ferrey, designed Church schools at Acton, near Wrexham, and at Llanuwchllyn and Bala in Merioneth. The school at Llanuwchllyn, now a private house, was attended by O. M. Edwards, and that at Bala is still in use as a Church in Wales primary school. (Ferrey also designed the church at Bala.)

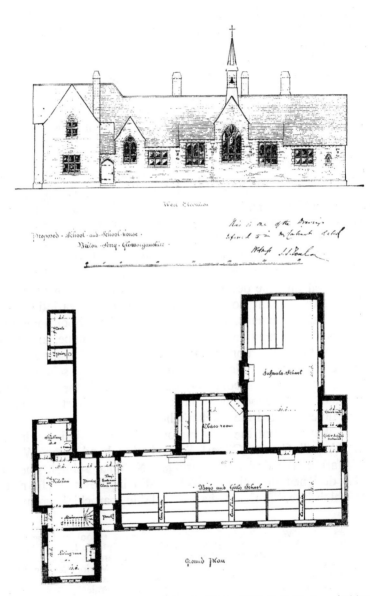

Fig. 13. Briton Ferry National school, Glam., 1855. S. S. Teulon, architect.

buildings, all designed by Scott between 1853 and 1860, and including the school, the rectory and the church itself.[18] Another outstanding parochial group may be seen at Tywyn (often spelt Towyn), also in Denbighshire, this time designed by G. E. Street and comprising the church of St Mary, a vicarage and school (1871-3). 'Few expressions of Victorian ecclesiology are more moving and evocative', wrote Edward Hubbard, 'than a complete parochial group by Street', and this comment remains true despite the traffic on the busy A548 road alongside which these buildings stand.[19] The quality of the stonework of the school is superb and the positioning of the windows on the master's house is extremely subtle. No building grant plans survive for the school at Tywyn, since the whole group was paid for by Robert Hesketh of Gwrych Castle. In south Wales, there is a very attractive parochial group at Llangasty Tal-y-Llyn in Breconshire, which, again, was privately financed. The church was rebuilt and a new school and master's house were erected alongside it in 1848-50 by the young J. L. Pearson, later architect of Truro Cathedral. He was engaged by Robert Raikes, kinsman of the founder of Sunday schools in England and an ardent supporter of the Oxford Movement.[20] The church has many Tractarian features, and the school and master's house blend perfectly with it (Plate 30).

Another London-based architect was R. J. Withers, who worked in south and west Wales, and was a very competent and imaginative practitioner. He restored many churches in Cardiganshire and designed, in a distinctive Gothic style, several schools for which building grant plans survive. His

---

[18] E. Hubbard, *The Buildings of Wales. Clwyd* (Harmondsworth, Penguin Books, 1986), 289-90 gives a full description. The National school in Cardigan (a two-storey, stone building in Tudor Gothic style of c.1850) survives opposite St Mary's church.
[19] Ibid., 286-7. Street also designed the school and master's house at Abergele (Denbs.), which still exist, but there are no building grant plans for them. Street's signed drawings of another school (still in use) at Llysfaen, near Abergele, are in the Caernarfonshire collection since Llysfaen was at this period linked with the diocese of Bangor.
[20] See the excellent leaflet available at the church.

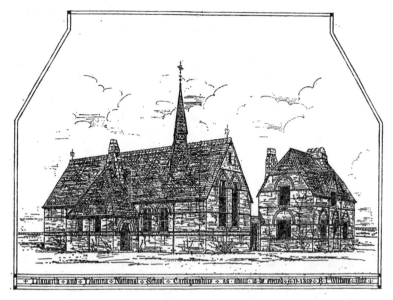

Fig. 14. Llanarth, Cards., 1859. R. J. Withers, architect.

Fig. 15. Llandaff, Glam., 1854-60. J. Prichard, architect.

school and master's house at Abergwili, near Carmarthen, which were designed in 1859, are still in use, but both have been marred by later alterations, especially the recent replacement of the roof slates by corrugated tiles. He also designed two schools in Cardiganshire: the one at Penbryn (1857) is now a drastically-altered private house, but the other at Llanarth (1859), though in a decaying condition at the time of writing, is well worth visiting for the many original details which remain. Withers' perspective drawing of the Llanarth school is included in the building grant plans and is reproduced as Fig. 14.

Of the architects who worked mainly in Wales, the Pensons must rate as among the most prolific. The elder Thomas Penson was the county surveyor employed by Flintshire quarter sessions until 1814. His son, also Thomas, practised in Wrexham and Oswestry and became county surveyor of Denbighshire and Montgomeryshire. Like many architects of the early Victorian period, he could adopt a variety of styles with equal facility. Probably his best surviving school buildings are the former girls' school at Chirk in Denbighshire, which was built in 1844 in a sophisticated Tudor style (Plate 31), and the former British school in Brook Street, Wrexham, which was built in 1843, without Government grant, in Jacobean style. His two sons, Richard Kyrke Penson and Thomas Mainwaring Penson, were also notable school architects, especially the former, who was appointed county surveyor for Carmarthenshire in 1853 and whose surviving schools include the Priory Street school in Carmarthen and the school at Ferryside. Other county surveyors who designed schools were John Lloyd, surveyor of Caernarfonshire (who is possibly not the builder/architect of the same name who designed a number of schools in the Mold area during this period), and H. John Fairclough, who practised from St. Asaph and later became county surveyor for Flintshire. John Lloyd's Tudor Gothic National school at Caernarfon (1842) was demolished to make way for the new by-pass, but his former British school in South Penrallt at Caernarfon, which was designed in Jacobean style in 1856 and later became a Board school, has survived. Fairclough's three schools in Flintshire, at Llanasa (1857), Bodfari (1858) and St Asaph (1862), have all survived and are built in a well-proportioned Gothic style. The school at St Asaph is still used as a school and has recently been listed, while the former school at Bodfari, which is now a private house, is a particularly attractive building.

The other main designers of National schools were the diocesan surveyors. In the diocese of Bangor, Henry Kennedy was responsible for many rather weak Gothic schools; curiously, his best school is probably the former Blue Coat school at Denbigh, designed early in his career (1845) in Jacobean style. This building has recently been restored to form the façade of new flats for the elderly. In St Asaph diocese, R. Lloyd Williams, who was based in Denbigh and later took Martin Underwood into partnership, designed many schools in a vigorous Gothic style, of which the best surviving example is probably at Trelawnyd in Flintshire (Plate 32). This building, which was completed in 1860 and is still in use as a school, seems to have been built without grant since Wynne's eighteenth-century endowment was used to cover much of the cost.[21] Another diocesan surveyor, Thomas Nicholson of Hereford, designed several good surviving Gothic schools in mid-Wales, as at Clyro (1859) and Knighton (1862) in Radnorshire. However, the outstanding diocesan architect in Wales during this period was John Prichard of Llandaff, who took John Seddon into partnership in 1852. These two were responsible for many excellent Gothic schools in Glamorgan and Monmouthshire. Prichard was among the very few architects in Wales whose designs for schools were illustrated in the architectural journals. *The Building News* published his designs for schools at Llandaff and Llandough, and his restoration of Llandaff Cathedral also gained much publicity in the architectural press. Prichard's preference for a variety of building materials was

---

[21] The school cost £1463, against a contract price of £930. The fees paid to Williams and Underwood are noted in the accounts of the Wynne Charity Trustees (Clwyd CRO., Hawarden, ref. P/64/1/18).

especially evident on his school at Llandaff: the dressings were of Bath stone and Bridgend sandstone, and the walls were of large river pebbles, banded with Pennant stone (Fig. 15).[22] Among the better-preserved of Prichard and Seddon's surviving schools are those at Magor (1856), Marshfield (1857) and Llanelen (1862), all in Gwent.[23] The school at Magor, now used by a private school, is illustrated on Plate 33.

It has not been possible to refer to all the church schools in Wales which have survived from this period of rapid change in education, but it is hoped that interested readers will be able to follow up the further details given in Appendix III. In any event, it is clear that the whole process of building schools had been transformed and that an equally radical transformation had taken place in the architectural style considered suitable for them.

---

[22] *The Building News,* 1867, 510, 513. The same journal also illustrated his school at Llandough (the village near Cowbridge, not the better-known Llandough near Cardiff), but captioned it wrongly as Llandaff (see *The Building News,* 1867, 340, 343). The school at Llandaff has been demolished, but Prichard's school at Llandough survives as a church hall on a minor road between St. Mary's Church and Llandough village.

[23] The building grant plan for the school at Marshfield has 'Prichard & Seddon' written on it. There is a perspective drawing of this school in the Seddon Collection at the Victoria and Albert Museum, reproduced in *Plans and Prospects* (Cardiff, Welsh Arts Council, 1975), No. 57. It is there suggested (p. 67) that Seddon did most of the work in Monmouthshire and Prichard in Glamorgan.

CHAPTER V

Chapel Schools and the Works School system, 1800-1875

Alan Everitt, in an essay on Nonconformity in the Victorian countryside, suggested that much of the explanation for its varying pattern lay in the diversity of rural economies.[1] Nonconformist chapels were, for example, more numerous in parishes where land was divided among small independent owners, and in new settlements in boundary areas between parishes. Referring to conditions in England, he noted that the differences between Methodism and the Church of England were not as great as those between Old Dissent and the Establishment, so that Methodism was sometimes able to take root in areas where Independent (Congregationalist) and Baptist communions had made little progress. He concluded his essay with the question: 'How far, one wonders, did these social and economic distinctions between different types of community also shape the history of education in the Victorian countryside?'

The answer, especially in Wales, is 'very considerably'. Ieuan Gwynedd Jones, the leading historian of the social and

[1] Alan Everitt, 'Nonconformity in the Victorian countryside', in T. G. Cook (ed.), *Local Studies and the History of Education* (London, Methuen, 1972), 37-62.

religious history of nineteenth-century Wales, has pointed out that, whereas in England and Wales as a whole the Church of England provided over half of the total seating accommodation recorded in the Religious Census of 1851, the proportion in Wales taken by itself was less than a third. The figures for attendance given in the Religious Census are much more difficult to interpret, but Jones suggests that, whereas in England and Wales as a whole attendances at Anglican services constituted 47 per cent of the total for all denominations, the figure in Wales may have been as low as 9 per cent, with 87 per cent in the Nonconformist chapels and the small remainder in Catholic and other churches.[2] Although it may be doubted whether much more than half of the adult population of Wales regularly attended any place of worship, Nonconformists were certainly in the majority of those who did.

It would go much beyond the scope of the present study to attempt to analyse the reasons for the preponderance of Nonconformity in Wales during this period, but no discussion of school provision can fail to mention the vital part played by the Sunday schools. In England, the Sunday schools, which began to appear towards the end of the eighteenth century, often owed their origin to philanthropists whose main desire was to make working-class children more literate (and, it was hoped, more aware of moral values) at a time when day schools were manifestly insufficient to cope with the rapidly-rising population, especially in the towns. In Wales, however, the origin of the Sunday schools was inextricably bound up with the Methodist Revival and with the concurrent increase in support for the older Nonconformist denominations. It was from the earliest Sunday schools, which were attended by both adults and children and were often held in farm buildings, that Calvinistic Methodist chapels developed in

[2] I. G. Jones, *Explorations and Explanations* (Llandysul, Gwasg Gomer, 1981), 227. He stresses that the figures varied greatly in different parts of Wales. Other methods of analysis suggest that Anglican attendances may have been nearer 20 per cent overall, which was still an abysmal figure from the Anglican point of view.

many parts of Wales, and from which the Independents and Baptists also drew much of their renewed strength.

In the last chapter, details were given of the overall provision for day school education at the time of the Report on the State of Education in Wales (1847). The provision for children in the Sunday schools at the same date, summarized in Table VII, gives a very different picture. The Church of England, which was responsible for 49 per cent of the day school provision, made only 20 per cent of the provision for children in Sunday schools. The Church Sunday schools were particularly weak in Anglesey, Caernarfonshire and Merioneth, where Calvinistic Methodists were much the largest providers of Sunday schools. The Baptist Sunday schools were strongest in the industrialized part of Monmouthshire and in Pembrokeshire, while the Independents were the leading providers in Breconshire, Carmarthenshire, Glamorgan and Pembrokeshire. Wesleyan Methodist Sunday schools were strongest in the more anglicized counties of Flint and Monmouth. It may also be noted that whereas in Wales as a whole pupils at day schools constituted eight per cent of the total population, the percentage of Sunday school pupils under the age of fifteen was nearly double this, at fourteen per cent.

The way in which the Nonconformist Sunday schools developed in Wales, often as precursors of chapels and then fully integrated with them, explains the surviving architectural evidence. Once chapels had been built, the Sunday schools met in them and there was no immediate need to provide separate Sunday school buildings, especially as the children who attended them were frequently accompanied by their parents. Most of the early nineteenth-century buildings noted as 'Sunday schools' on the older large-scale Ordnance Survey maps, and in the provisional lists of buildings of architectural or historic interest, usually turn out upon investigation to be former Church day schools, later used as Anglican Sunday schools and now either in occasional use as church halls, or abandoned. It was only when chapels in populous areas became fully established, and their supporters decided to rebuild them on ambitious lines, that separate Sunday school

TABLE VII

THE DENOMINATION OF SUNDAY SCHOOL PUPILS IN 1847

Source: Report on the State of Education in Wales (1847), calculated
from I, 60 (Carmarthenshire, Glamorgan and Pembrokeshire);
II, 49 (Breconshire, Cardiganshire and Radnorshire), 289 (the
industrialized part of Monmouthshire); and III, 56 (North Wales).
Only Sunday school pupils under 15 years of age are included.

County   Percentages of Sunday School Children by Denomination

	Church of England %	Baptist %	Calvin'c Methodist %	Indepen't %	Wesleyan Methodist %	Others %
Anglesey	8	9	59	16	8	—
Brecon	26	15	21	27	5	6
Caernarfon ...	9	5	63	15	8	—
Cardigan	22	7	48	16	7	—
Carmarthen ...	19	14	24	38	4	i
Denbigh	21	7	45	13	13	1
Flint	33	1	26	15	24	1
Glamorgan ...	23	16	22	27	6	6
Merioneth ...	9	4	58	18	11	—
Monmouth ... (part)	21	25	9	20	21	4
Montgomery	15	5	40	20	19	1
Pembroke	24	23	16	27	10	—
Radnor	56	11	10	11	7	5
Average ...... (excluding Monmouth)	20	11	36	22	9	2

buildings were sometimes provided. Often, in such cases, the
old chapel became the Sunday school and a larger new chapel
was built alongside.

One of the earliest references to the building of an
architect-designed chapel and associated schoolroom in the
periodical *The Builder* dates from 1855, when it was noted
that the architect R. G. Thomas of Newport had designed
a new Congregational chapel and schoolroom in Charles
Street, Cardiff, where it still stands.[3] This impressive new
chapel contained 530 sittings, with a schoolroom underneath
measuring 73 by 38 feet. It is possible that this was a day
school, but it is more likely to have been a Sunday school
since there were already two British schools and several

[3] *The Builder*, 1855, 333. The Early Decorated Gothic style was employed
for this building.

private schools in the town. One of the most thorough surveys of surviving chapel buildings in Wales was carried out in 1978 in Mid Glamorgan. Over 600 chapels were surveyed and the history of about two-thirds of them was fully investigated. The records of this survey are now in the Glamorgan Record Office in Cardiff and an examination of a sample of forty chapels surveyed in the Pentyrch and Llantrisant districts shows that fourteen had separate rooms for use by Sunday schools, but that only two of these date from before 1870, viz. Horeb at Pentyrch (1862) and Babell at Groesfaen (1866). Many other examples of Sunday school rooms, often provided after 1860 in connection with chapel rebuilding schemes, have survived in other parts of Wales.

The returns made by Sunday school supervisors to the Education Commissioners of 1847 make it clear that 'secular' subjects (which included writing and arithmetic) were hardly ever taught in the Sunday schools, which concentrated almost exclusively on the teaching of Biblical knowledge.[4] In addition, Welsh was noted as the medium of instruction in Sunday schools of all denominations in Welsh-speaking areas. If we now consider the development of the day schools, which traditionally taught the three Rs and often used English as the medium of instruction even in Welsh-speaking districts, it is apparent that such schools were introduced only very gradually by Nonconformist groups. During the first half of the nineteenth century Nonconformist effort, in terms of building, went mainly into providing purpose-built chapels, rather than buildings designed for use as day schools. In north Wales, where Calvinistic Methodists were particularly numerous, the rate of chapel-building greatly increased in the first quarter of the nineteenth century and accelerated further in the second quarter.[5] In south Wales, where the older dis-

---

[4] The 'Parochial Tables of Sunday-Schools' included in the appendices of the *Reports of the Commissioners on the State of Education in Wales* (London, HMSO, 1847), hereafter referred to as *SEW*, print the returns made by organizers of Sunday schools, including the place and date of establishment, the number of children and adults attending, the language of instruction, and the subjects taught.

[5] M. V. J. Seaborne, 'The Religious Census of 1851 and Early Chapel-building in North Wales', *The National Library of Wales Journal*, 26 No. 3 (1990), 281-310.

senting congregations were stronger, there were more eighteenth-century chapel buildings, but these, too, were frequently rebuilt during the first half of the nineteenth century. The concept of elementary day schools teaching secular subjects developed only with the consolidation of Nonconformity following the earlier period of rapid expansion.

The first Nonconformist day schools in Wales were often, but by no means always, affiliated to the British School Society in London, which from its inception in 1808 had adopted the principle that 'no Catechism, or other formulary peculiar to any religious denomination, shall be introduced or taught during the usual hours of instruction'.[6] The British School Society was initially supported by both Anglicans and Nonconformists, but it was not long before it came to be associated solely with Nonconformist interests, as distinct from the Anglican interests represented by the National Society. Partly because of this, the British Society made very little headway in Wales during the first forty years of the nineteenth century. The Society's initial lack of success has also been noted in industrial Lancashire during this period and the reasons were similar in both cases.[7] Briefly, the British Society did not have the resources or the diocesan organization which enabled the National Society to make increasingly rapid progress; school sites were also more difficult to obtain from sometimes unsympathetic landowners. It was not until the central Government, through the Committee of Council on Education, began to make grants for school buildings after 1833, with no doctrinal strings attached, that purpose-built British schools began to increase in number.

Many of the early Nonconformist day schools were held,

---

[6] This formulation is from the Society's *Plain Directions for the Establishment of Schools on the Plan and Principles of the British and Foreign School Society*, (London, 1847), 2. The Royal Lancasterian Society was founded in 1808 and took the title of the British and Foreign School Society in 1814.

[7] Michael Sanderson, 'The National and British School Societies in Lancashire 1803-1839', in T. G. Cook (ed.), *Local Studies, op.. cit*, 1-36.

like the Sunday schools, in the chapel buildings themselves. In this respect, they were following the precedent of the parish churches, in which, as we have noted in previous chapters, the earliest day schools were often held. Of the numerous surviving chapels in which day schools are known to have been held, two may be mentioned because of their historical interest. At Pen-y-bont-fawr in Montgomeryshire the former Bethania Independent chapel of 1824 still survives and was the building used for teaching day pupils by Evan Jones (*Ieuan Gwynedd*) in 1836. Evan Jones was later one of the leading critics of the Education Report of 1847 and a strong supporter of the voluntaryist principle, which rejected all interference in education by Church or State. His own school was very short-lived, but the principles which he supported had their long-term effects on the development of education in Wales. This building ceased to be used as a chapel when the present Bethania chapel was built in 1867, but a modern plaque commemorates its association with Ieuan Gwynedd. Another interesting surviving example is the Quaker meeting house built in 1717 at Pales near Llandrindod Wells in Radnorshire, part of which was used as a day school from 1867.[8] This is a charming, thatched building with a beautiful view over the surrounding countryside. The meeting house originally had two rooms so that men and women could meet separately for services and, with the abandonment of that practice, one of the rooms lay empty until it was brought into use as a day school for local children of any denomination, particularly those whose parents did not wish them to attend the Church school in the adjoining village of Llandeglau.

A closely-related category of early British schools consists of day schools which were held in former chapel buildings after the congregations had moved to larger chapels nearby. For example, the first British school in Cardigan opened in 1858 in the former Bethania Baptist chapel, which had

---

[8] Details from the interesting pamphlet 'Pales Meeting House', available in the meeting house, with additional information from Trevor Macpherson.

become available following the building of the new Bethania chapel in William Street in 1847.[9] Similarly, at Gronant in Flintshire the Calvinistic Methodists built a chapel for themselves in 1841 and, as a result of increasing numbers, moved to a larger new chapel in 1871; the 1841 chapel was thereupon converted into a British (later Board) school, with residential provision for the caretaker and a deacon in part of the old building. Other examples could be given of British schools meeting in former chapel buildings, and it is also not surprising that some of the earliest purpose-built British schools were very chapel-like in appearance. The building which still stands in Brook Street, Llangollen, has a large cast-iron plaque at the top of the front gable wall with the inscription '1846. BRITISH. SCHOOLS.' As with many early chapels in Clwyd which were 'improved' at about this time, the façade is of brick, while the other walls are of stone (Plate 34). Another interesting example is the small building which survives in Skinner Street, Aberystwyth, and is still known locally as 'Ysgol Skin'. This appears to have originated in 1846 as a British school established by the Calvinistic Methodists in the town,[10] and is in the style aptly called 'Victorian vernacular', in this case employing neo-classical pilasters and ball finials with gay abandon (Plate 35). It is often difficult to disentangle the building histories of of early British schools from the chapel improvements which were constantly taking place. Thus, the small stone building at Glanyrafon in Merioneth, which later became the Llawrbetws Board school, seems to have originated as a British school, but it has proved impossible to discover whether it was built when the adjoining chapel was improved in 1835, or when it was rebuilt in 1865, or at a date between the two.

Once the stage had been reached when Nonconformist groups considered that the provision of their own purpose-built day schools was both desirable and affordable, the problem of the identification of early British schools eases

[9] Donald Davies, *Those Were the Days* (Cardigan, The Cardigan and Tivy-Side Advertiser, 1991), 25.
[10] *SEW*, II, 153, 222.

considerably. The building grant plans of British schools (listed in Appendix III) certainly relate to purpose-built day schools, and the layout of the furniture shown on the plans would have made them unsuitable for holding normal chapel services. In the rural areas the first purpose-built day schools provided by Nonconformists were architectually extremely simple and devoid of ornamentation. As is well known, in 1843 Hugh Owen (himself a Calvinistic Methodist from Anglesey) wrote a public letter 'To the Welsh People', urging them to take advantage of Government grants to build new British schools. To this end, he distributed a number of model drawings to Nonconformist supporters in Wales and some of these have survived among the building grant plans. A 'Plan of a rural British School for 200 Boys and Girls, Together with a Residence for the Master' and noted as 'Prepared for Hugh Owen. London 1844' is included with the building grant plans for a new British school at Cemaes in Anglesey. In the following year, a similar plan 'Lithographed by S. P. Newcombe for H. Owen, London 1845' was issued and copies of it are among the building grant drawings for Ffestiniog Slate Quarries British School in Merioneth, and also for the proposed British school at Llwyndafydd in Cardiganshire. In fact, the promoters of the school at Llwyndafydd merely submitted Owen's plan, amended in ink (Fig. 16). It was probably due to Owen's influence that Anglesey and Merioneth, although among the least populous of the Welsh counties, had some of highest numbers of British schools built with grant aid (see Table VI on page 101).

Owen's model plan was for a mainly single-storey stone building, whose construction would have been well within the capacity of a local builder. The only distinctive external feature was that the master's house, which was attached to the schoolroom, was lit entirely from the side and presented a blank wall to the front (a good surviving example of this may be seen on the former British school at Marian-glas in Anglesey, built in 1845 and clearly based on Owen's model plan). No recommendations were made in Owen's plan con-

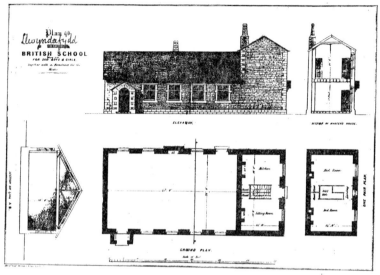

Fig. 16. Llwyndafydd, Cards. Hugh Owen's model plan, 1845.

CEMAES BRITISH SCHOOL
ANGLESEY

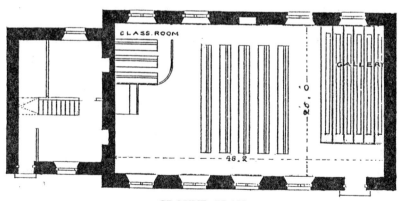

GROUND PLAN

Fig. 17. Cemaes, Anglesey, plan of British school, 1845.

cerning the internal layout, apart from ensuring that the schoolroom provided six square feet per child, which was the accepted norm at this date. No doubt, like Andrew Bell earlier in the century, Hugh Owen considered that the main need was for the children to have 'a roof to cover them'. By good fortune, the internal layout of the school actually built at Cemaes has also survived among the building grant plans and is reproduced as Fig. 17. This shows a schoolroom measuring 48 by 25 feet (compared with Owen's 47 by 26 feet), with a master's house attached to it. The schoolroom has five rows of desks and benches facing the master's desk, and a raised gallery behind them. A small 'class room' is shown in one corner, separated from the main room by a partition or curtain; since this is located immediately along-side the master's desk, it was probably intended for the older, more advanced pupils. It may be noted that this layout shows in its simplest form the arrangements generally adopted by British schools at this period. The earlier Lancasterian lay-out, with desks and benches occupying virtually the whole of the schoolroom, had been modified by the introduction of a gallery on the Stow model, and we shall see that this combin-ation of desks and galleries was further developed in some of the later British schools.

The school at Cemaes was visited in November 1846 by one of the assistant commissioners appointed to examine the state of education in Wales, and his report makes interesting reading.[11] It appears that the school building had been completed three months previously and, although designed for 200 children, only 128 were present on the day of inspection. Twelve monitors were employed and the subjects taught were the Holy Scriptures, reading, writing, arithmetic, and English grammar. The master, who had received six months' training at the British Society's model school at Borough Road in London, complained of the lack of books, slates, maps and other school apparatus which could not be procured for want of funds. The report states that the school had been

---

[11] *SEW* III, 8 (under Llanbadrig).

established by a few farmers and small tradesmen, who had subscribed to the cost of the building and had guaranteed the master's salary of £50 a year. The report adds that the labourers in the neighbourhood were very poor and, although some of the entrance fees had been paid by the promoters, the only source of income was the weekly payments made by the children, so that it was doubtful whether the school would be able to continue. It was evidence such as this which was leading the Committee of Council, step by step, to make grants not only towards the cost of providing new buildings and employing pupil-teachers, but also towards the running costs of schools which agreed to annual inspection. The school at Cemaes did in fact survive, until it was transferred to the local school board in 1897.

What appears to have been the only book written in English during this period which concerned itself with the design of Nonconformist schools (apart from the manuals of the British School Society) was F. J. Jobson's *Chapel and School Architecture* (London, 1850). Jobson states that he had studied ecclesiastical architecture under E. J. Willson of Lincoln before entering the Wesleyan ministry and becoming the secretary of the Wesleyan Building Committee. His main aim was to advocate the adoption of the Gothic style for chapels and their associated day schools. His hope was that Gothic architecture 'shall, with all its surpassing flexibility and unbounded power of adaptation, be again used in the service of God. It is now reviving, and is, more or less, employed by every Christian denomination'.[12] For schools he advocated not only the Gothic style but also the adoption of the Stow model, which provided galleries in every schoolroom. This book was reviewed in *The Builder* and would

---

[12] F. J. Jobson, *Chapel and School Architecture* (London, Hamilton, Adams & Co., 1850), 42. Jobson refers to the need for 'class-rooms' attached to chapels, but he was using the word 'class' in the Wesleyan sense of an adult devotional group: Wesleyan Sunday schools in England were clearly for children only and met in other premises. On chapel architecture in Wales, see A. Jones, *Welsh Chapels* (Cardiff, National Museum of Wales, 1984).

Fig. 18a. Elevation. Pembroke Dock British school.

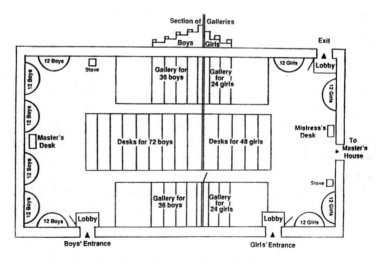

Fig. 18b. Plan, Pembroke Dock British school.

certainly have had its readers in Wales.[13] We shall see, however, that the Gothic style was by no means universally used for British schools in Wales, while the complete Stow plan, like the fully-developed Lancasterian plan, was adopted relatively rarely.

This intermediate phase of British school planning appears most clearly in the large schools in industrial areas, where British school supporters were often at their strongest. Fig. 18(a) reproduces an unsigned drawing dated 1846 of the front elevation of the British school at Pembroke Dock. This can only be described as a utilitarian building without architectural embellishments. This school actually opened in 1848, and some time later (possibly in about 1855) the promoters submitted a 'Plan for Estimate of Alterations to be made in Pembroke Dock British School', which bears the Committee of Council's seal of approval and must therefore have received grant. This plan is now in a fragmentary condition and has been re-drawn as Fig. 18(b). This shows one large room, divided by a partition into boys' and girls' schools, measuring 36 by 38 feet and 36 by 30 feet respectively. Each schoolroom has centrally-placed blocks of desks and benches facing the master or mistress in the Lancasterian manner, but there are also galleries, not at the back, as was usual in schools designed on the Stow model, but at the sides; reading circles, derived from Lancasterian practice, are marked out at each end. It is clear that in this school, as in most of the large British and National schools of this period, an 'interchange' system was in operation. Thus, in the boys' school, the 12 boys in each of the 6 reading circles would have exchanged places with the 72 boys in the desks, or with the 72 boys in the two galleries. The possible permutations of reading circles, desks and galleries are considerable and were justified in contemporary terms not only because such a system made full use of the building, but also because it satisfied one of the axioms of monitorial school organization, 'relief by change of position'. The plan shows

---

[13] *The Builder*, 1850, 469.

that this school accommodated 216 boys and 144 girls, at between six and seven square feet per child, which was within the accepted norm. Clearly this arrangement would have depended on the considerable use of monitors and pupil-teachers to assist the master and mistress, who would probably have been the only certificated teachers.

The Committee of Council's minute of 1851 referred to in the last chapter was an attempt to introduce a uniform system of school organization. It was an ingenious method of combining desks and galleries, while leaving sufficient open space for some monitorial teaching, and, as such, satisfied most contemporary requirements. However, the pressure of numbers in some districts, and the need to adapt to already-existing buildings, obliged the Committee of Council to approve layouts not fully in accord with their recommendations. Apart from layouts such as that at Pembroke Dock, a number of new schools with restricted sites were also approved and were permitted to have rows of desks and benches on both sides of the schoolroom; this meant that the width of the schoolroom was greater than that preferred by the Committee of Council, whose inspectors also disliked the arrangement by which the children faced each other across the room. Such plans were more usually approved in urban areas and in schools supported by the British and Catholic school societies (as for example, Bala British school, 1854, and St David's Catholic school, Cardiff, 1853). The preferred 'official' system took many years to be fully implemented throughout England and Wales, and it was only after about 1860 that the Committee of Council was able to insist on it for all new schools and for all proposed alterations to existing buildings. A few new schools, however, led the way, among which the British school at Pwllheli in Caernarfonshire, which opened in 1857, was a notable example.

It has often been remarked that Wales during this period lacked a strong middle class. While this may to some extent have been true of the heavily-industrialized districts and of some of the rural counties suffering from depopulation, it was less true of the ancient boroughs and the established market

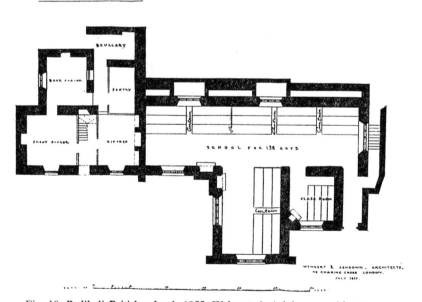

Fig. 19. Pwllheli British school, 1855. Wehnert & Ashdown, architects.

towns. It has recently been shown that Pwllheli was at the height of its prosperity in the period between 1835 and 1865 owing to its ship-building activity and extensive coastal trade, as well as on account of the internal market it provided for the Llŷn peninsula.[14] The town council was largely in the hands of relatively well-to-do Nonconformists, and it comes as no surprise to find that the British school erected in the town in 1857 was a large, two-storey building of ambitious design and was given the most up-to-date internal layout. As Fig. 19 shows, a Gothic style was adopted, designed by Wehnert and Ashdown, architects of London and Llandudno. It is likely that this partnership was chosen because of the town's traditional links with the Mostyn family, who employed these architects in the building of the newly-planned seaside resort of Llandudno. The plan shows the parallel desks and galleried classrooms recommended by the Committee of Council, with each of the groups of desks and benches accommodating eighteen or twenty children. Boys were accommodated on the ground floor, with the girls above, and a teachers' house was also built alongside. The only unusual feature was the additional wall at the rear of the ground floor, which was provided because the school was built into the side of a hill; this arrangement made it possible for light and air to reach the back of the boys' schoolroom, since the front was mainly occupied by an extension of the schoolroom and by a classroom. This school, which was built at Troed yr Allt, was extensively damaged by fire some years ago and has been partially rebuilt as flats. Originally, it must have been an impressive building, and (since the town's seventeenth-century grammar school had closed some years before) may best be regarded as serving the needs of a commercial, middle-class clientele. No provision was made in the new building for infant children, who presumably attended

---

[14] Lewis Lloyd, *Pwllheli. The Port and Mart of Llŷn* (Caernarfon, Gwasg Pantycelyn, 1991), passim.

the adjoining National school, whose building of 1843 survives with its Welsh inscription over the door.[15] Purpose-built British schools were provided in many other towns in Wales and professional architects were beginning to be employed to design them (see Appendix III). William Jenkins, a London architect presumably of Welsh origin, designed the first purpose-built British school at Carmarthen (now demolished) in a very competent Tudor Gothic style (1849), while James Wilson of Bath, who was well-known for his work on Nonconformist buildings in the west of England, also used the Tudor style for the first British school in Llanelli (1847). Thomas Mainwaring Penson designed the British school at Broughton in Denbighshire (1859), and his brother, Richard Kyrke Penson, the British school which formerly stood in Goat Street, Swansea (1861). Morriston British school was designed in a mixed Gothic style by John Humphreys (1865), who was also a notable builder of Nonconformist chapels. Another chapel architect, Richard Owens, a Liverpool Welshman, designed in a consciously non-ecclesiastical style the Undenominational School which survives in Well Lane at Ffynnongroyw in Flintshire (1869, built 1871). In the earlier part of this period, county surveyors like the Pensons and John Lloyd of Caernarfon were invited to design new British schools and, as the elementary school system came to be more fully established, certain architects may be said to have specialized in designing British schools. Owen Morris Roberts, whose drawings show him to have been a very competent architect, was responsible for several British schools in north-west Wales and his school buildings have survived in Chapel Street at Porthmadog in Caernarfonshire (1869) and at Corris in Merioneth (1870); he also designed a number of chapels. Many of the designers of British schools noted in Appendix III were builders rather

[15] The National school building survives at Penlleiniau, Pwllheli. In 1847 it was reported that the bilingual master declined to teach the catechism to the mainly Nonconformist children, and was supported by the incumbent, who did not think it right to 'compel them in matters of religion, merely because they pay 1d. a week for education in the National school' (*SEW*, III, 29).

than architects and are otherwise unknown, but it may be that the growing interest in Victorian buildings in Wales will produce further evidence of links between the designers of British schools and other buildings, especially chapels.

Most of the British schools were converted into Board schools following the passing of the Elementary Education Act of 1870 and their original buildings have either been considerably altered or demolished. Partial survivals and the evidence of the building grant plans, however, indicate that the Gothic style was not as widely used for British as for National schools. In the 1840s the Tudor style was adopted for schools of all types, but the more 'ecclesiastical' forms of Gothic, which were extensively used for the National schools, were much less in evidence for the British schools, or were used in such an attenuated form as not to be Gothic at all. Probably the most complete surviving British school building in the Gothic style was that built for the Wesleyans in Bangor to the design of John Lloyd of Caernarfon (1857). This is the former St Paul's school in Sackville Road (now part of Bangor college of further education), whose somewhat angular Gothic design is best viewed from the rear of the building. The Victorian taste for ornamented building was satisfied, at any rate in north Wales, by adopting the more secular 'Jacobean' style, with its tall, shaped gables, rather than the more elaborate Gothic designs with their Church associations. Thomas Penson employed this style on the British school in Brook Street, Wrexham, which was built without grant in 1843, as did John Lloyd of Caernarfon for the grant-aided British school in that town (Penrallt, 1856). Its most notable expression was in the normal school (later training college) at Bangor, which was designed by a London architect, John Barnett, in 1858-62 and is illustrated on Plate 36.

Few good surviving examples of British schools have been located in south Wales, but what evidence there is suggests that, for the larger schools in industrial areas, contemporary commercial or industrial buildings may have been taken as models. The school at Pembroke Dock mentioned earlier was a purely functional building, as was the British school at

Aberdare, which was designed by Evan Griffiths in 1866. This was built to accommodate 230 boys on the ground floor and 230 girls on the first floor and is illustrated from a contemporary engraving (Plate 37). This shows a large two-storey building, with regularly-spaced windows and the teachers' houses on each side. Its external appearance resembled that of the Glandare woollen mill at Aberdare, now demolished but recorded in an old photograph.[16] We shall see that, as larger schools came to be built following the introduction of compulsory elementary education, the problem of reconciling functional utility with suitable architectural form was one to which school architects gave increasing attention.

There is one further aspect of the building of British schools which needs to be considered. Bearing in mind the rapid growth of Nonconformity in Wales, why are only 110 British schools included in the collections of building grant plans, compared with 318 for the Church of England? Some recent writers have implied that the predominantly Welsh-speaking population disliked the day schools, whether National or British, because the medium of instruction was English and that there was therefore no enthusiasm to build more British schools. Greater weight, however, must be given to the economic circumstances of the time, to the disadvantages still suffered by Nonconformists, and to their lack of experience in planning schools and gaining financial help from the Government. It may be thought that the 'voluntaryist' movement, which was particularly strong among the older denominations and was opposed to State grants on principle, delayed the introduction of grant-aided schools, but this does not seem to have affected the rapid growth of day schools connected with the chapels. A list published by the British School Society in 1897 claimed a total of about 600

---

[16] *Aberdare. Pictures from the Past* (Aberdare, Cynon Valley History Society, 1986), plate 100. Evan Griffiths also designed Bethania chapel, Wind Street, Aberdare (1854), Hen Dy Cwrdd meeting house, Trecynon (1862), and Trinity church, Weatheral Street, Aberdare (1867), information I owe to the Director of Leisure Services, Cynon Valley Borough Council.

British schools established in Wales before 1875.[17] Many of
these schools were short-lived, or had only the most tenuous
links with the Society, but over 300 British schools were
actually in operation in Wales in 1870. It is, therefore,
clear that a considerable number of British schools were
established in rented premises, or in purpose-built schools
built without grants. A recent study of Victorian school
buildings in Flintshire brought to light two surviving purpose-
built British schools apparently financed entirely by voluntary
subscriptions, at Carmel near Holywell (1862) and at Rhuallt
near Prestatyn (1863), both adjoining Calvinistic Methodist
chapels.[18] Perhaps the current interest in Victorian chapels will
extend to a consideration of their associated buildings and
uncover other examples of British schools built without grant
in other parts of Wales.

Some of the disparity between the number of purpose-built
National and British schools was made good by the works
schools, which were especially numerous in south Wales and
were supported in part by contributions made by the workmen, many of whom were Nonconformists. Although very
little is now left of the works school buildings, their history
has been fully documented by Leslie Wynne Evans in his
book on *Education in Industrial Wales,* published in 1971.
He produced a list of 109 works schools, mainly connected
with iron works and collieries in Monmouthshire and
Glamorgan, copper and tin works in West Glamorgan and
Carmarthenshire, and slate quarries in Caernarfonshire and
Merioneth.[19] The school buildings were usually provided by
the owners, but some of the later schools were built with the

---

[17] This list was published with the *Annual Report* of the British and
Foreign School Society for 1897 (vol. 92). See also G. F. Bartle, 'The
Role of the British and Foreign School Society in Welsh Elementary
Education 1840-76', in *Journal of Educational Administration and
History,* 22 No. 1 (1990), 18-29. On British schools in Wales 1833-70, see
Idwal Jones, *Cymmrodorion Trans.* (1931-2), 72-164.

[18] M. Seaborne, 'Education and School Building in Flintshire during the
Early Victorian Period', *Flints. Hist. Soc. Journal,* 33 (1992). The inscriptions on the chapels are in Welsh, but those on the British schools
are in English.

[19] Leslie Wynne Evans, *Education in Industrial Wales 1700-1900* (Cardiff,
Avalon Books, 1971), 30-35.

help of government grant and are included in the building grant plans. The running costs were sometimes met by the employers, but many of them raised a small levy on the workmen's wages. In the course of time, most of these schools were recognized as inspected schools, so qualifying for Government grants towards their running costs. By about 1870, 40 of the 109 works schools were classified as National schools, 49 as British and 20 as 'neutral'; the last-named were wholly undenominational in character and were treated administratively as British schools.[20]

The works schools played a vital part in the development of elementary education in Wales because they provided schools in the newly-industrialized areas which were often far from the older centres of population in which the Church was the traditional provider. A few of the industrialists were convinced Anglicans, but many more were nominal Anglicans or came from a Nonconformist background. In general, therefore, there was less resistance to the idea of nondenominational education. Above all, the system under which deductions were made from the wages of the employees to help pay the running costs of the schools was a precursor of the compulsory school board rate, which was introduced by the Elementary Education Act of 1870, with the important difference that the school board rate was levied by elected bodies, which removed most of the objections of the voluntaryists.

A number of schools were built by industrialists, or by members of their families, before the State began to pay grants for new school buildings. Good surviving examples are the schools at Blaenafon in Monmouthshire and at Llandygai in Caernarfonshire. The former, which still stands (though derelict at the time of writing) in Church Road, Blaenafon, is thought to be the oldest ironworks school in Wales. Thomas Hill and Samuel Hopkins of Staffordshire had started the Blaenafon ironworks in 1789 and financed the

[20] Leslie Wynne Evans, 'Voluntary Education in the Industrial Areas of Wales', *The National Library of Wales Journal*, 14, No. 4 (1966), 417-9.

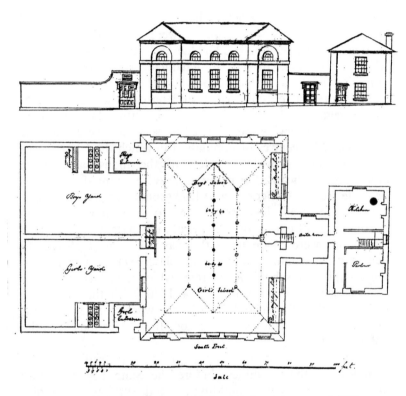

Fig. 20. Dowlais, Glam., plan of a school designed by Jones & Willcox,
architects of Bristol, 1819.

building of the parish church there in 1805. Eleven years later, the school was built by Sarah Hopkins in memory of her brother.[21] It was in the early neo-Gothic style used, as we have seen, for other schools of this date, and originally consisted of a long schoolroom subdivided for boys and girls and with the teachers' houses at each end (Plate 38). At Llandygai, Richard Pennant, later Baron Penrhyn, began to exploit the slate quarries on his estate from 1765 onwards. Soon after his death in 1808, his wife, Anne Susannah, built a school in his memory; this is a delightful neo-Gothic building which still stands near the church at Llandygai (the inscription on the school, dated 1816, was placed there on the death of the Baroness in that year). Another school, which is still in use, was built in 1843 on the other side of the churchyard at Llandygai by Douglas Pennant in memory of his wife, Juliana, and he also donated the land on which the British school in Bangor (whose building survives in the Garth) was erected in 1848.[22] The school of 1843 at Llandygai is in the Tudor Gothic style usual for its date and is worth seeing because both it and the master's house have, unusually, not been altered externally (Plate 39).

The most famous of the works schools were those built at Dowlais near Merthyr Tydfil by the ironmaster Sir John Guest. He became sole proprietor of the works at Dowlais in 1814 and an interesting plan of a proposed school dated 1819 has survived among the Guest papers in the Glamorgan Record Office. It is drawn on the back of a letter addressed to John Guest by the Bristol architects, Jones and Willcox, and since this is the earliest plan of a school in Wales known to have been designed by professional architects, it is reproduced as Fig. 20. It is wholly eighteenth-century in concept and its classical style is very reminiscent of some of the London charity schools built with lofty schoolrooms and clerestorey windows. The schoolroom is divided into boys'

[21] See the Latin inscription on the building, now very worn (a translation is provided by Evans, *Education in Industrial Wales*, 39 n.).
[22] See the inscriptions on the buildings at Llandygai (1843) and Bangor (1848).

and girls' schools, each measuring 60 by 40 feet. The only items of furniture shown are the 'pews' for the master and mistress and a shared 'cupboard for brushes'. A master's house is included in the design and provision is also made for a girls' yard with W.C.s, and a boys' yard with W.C.s and a 'watering place'. (Specifically-designed sanitary provision and playgrounds were only just beginning to be provided for elementary schools.) It is not certain that this design was ever executed, but it is evidence of John Guest's desire to obtain the best architectural advice available, which also showed itself in the very large schools later built at Dowlais.

Much of the impetus for building a comprehensive system of schools at Dowlais, including not only schools for boys, girls and infants but also adult schools for both men and women, came from Lady Charlotte Guest. After Sir John's death in 1852, she engaged Sir Charles Barry, the architect of the new Houses of Parliament, to design new central schools as a memorial to him, and these were opened in 1855. Barry's original plans do not appear to have survived, but a notice in *The Builder* stated that they were in the late Gothic style reminiscent of Tintern Abbey. There were seven schoolrooms, one for infants and three each for boys and girls, and the cost of the buildings amounted to £7,000.[23] These schools became British schools in 1855 and were later enlarged, but, having outlived their usefulness, have been demolished. A photograph of Lady Guest, taken in one of the schoolrooms later in the century, is reproduced as Plate 40. This shows the church-like character of the building, with the master at his desk and the assistant teachers sitting on the front row of a bank of desks set out on the long side of the room in the approved manner. One of the iron rods along which a curtain would have been run to separate the classes may be seen, and the decorations on the gas-brackets suggest that this photograph was taken at Christmas time.

This complete educational scheme was later imitated by Sir Titus Salt at Saltaire in Yorkshire, but it also had its

[23] *The Builder*, 1855, 462.

followers in Wales. The Monmouthshire collection of building grant plans includes those for the Pontypool Iron Works (National) School, which was designed in the Gothic style by R. G. Thomas of Newport in 1857. The boys' and girls' schoolrooms were arranged in the shape of a letter T, and each had its associated classroom. A significant advance was the inclusion of a reading room and a library, which were clearly intended to be available to adults as well as children. A very similar plan was reproduced in *The Builder* for the Melyn schools, near Neath in Glamorgan, which were built in Gothic style in 1874 at the sole expense of Leach, Flower and Company, the proprietors of the tinplate works which had opened there in 1863. The architect was John Norton of London and the cost £2,500.[24] In this case, the schoolrooms and reading room (which the report stressed was for the free use of employees) were formed around an open quadrangle.

The internal layouts of the works school buildings invariably followed the latest recommendations of the Committee of Council on Education and sometimes went beyond them in providing reading rooms and libraries for adults. The best available architects were employed to design them and the arrangements for heating, ventilation and lighting often used the latest technology. It is also important to note that the larger employers usually set up school management committees of workmen, deductions from whose wages were helping to finance the schools. Thus, although fewer British than National schools were built with Government building grants in Wales as a whole, Nonconformists in the most densely-populated parts of industrial south Wales were able to secure representation of their interests, especially in the provision of non-denominational religious instruction in the schools. In the run-up to the debates which led to the passing of the Education Act of 1870, the Committee of Council received the following enthusiastic report:

> It is much to the credit of a great majority of employers [in Wales] that they consulted the wishes of the workers in

[24] *The Builder*, 1874, 196 (illustration, 198).

the class of schools which they established, and wherever that was the case, the system produced excellent results . . . Large and well-organized schools, in which the religious teaching is based solely on the Bible, and is strictly neutral as between the different sects, have been established by means of a poundage on wages. All the schools give entire satisfaction to the workmen, whilst most of them are in admirable condition, and if a general system of compulsory education were introduced forthwith, these works schools would be prepared to meet the demand.[25]

This was written from the point of view of the employers rather than the employees, and the Liberal Government wisely made elected school boards responsible for the extension of elementary education throughout England and Wales. Nevertheless, the contribution made by the works schools to the development of education in Wales should not be underestimated.

A final word in this chapter should be said about the relatively few early schools built by the Roman Catholics with the help of Government grants (listed in Appendix III). Many Irish labourers were employed on the construction of the Chester to Holyhead railway and some of their families settled in Flint. In north Wales, however, Catholic educational activity was chiefly sponsored by aristocratic families. Viscount Feilding, later Earl of Denbigh, was converted to Roman Catholicism in 1850 and established a friary and convent at Pantasaph near Holywell: from these developed two elementary schools and a secondary school, as well as an orphanage. In 1857, Sir Pyers Mostyn, who belonged to the Catholic branch of the Mostyn family, sponsored a large Catholic school at Talacre, near Prestatyn, for which there are elaborate drawings in the Gothic style by J. Spencer of Liverpool among the building grant plans for Flintshire; this building survives but is no longer used as a school. In south Wales, there seem to have been fewer wealthy Catholics to finance schools, but Charles Hansom, a leading architect of

---

[25] *Minutes of the Committee of Council on Education*, 1868-9, 280.

Catholic schools and colleges, was engaged to design the infants' school which still stands with its inscription of 1857 alongside St Mary's Catholic Church on Stow Hill in Newport. He also designed St David's School in David Street, Cardiff (1853), but this building has disappeared under later development. Benjamin Bucknall designed Catholic schools in Bridgend and Swansea (1859), while E. Brigden, whose name frequently appears for projects mentioned in the Guest papers, designed a Catholic school at Dowlais in 1861. The internal planning of the Catholic schools shows no special features, apart from usually being adapted to restricted sites and consequently providing the maximum possible number of seats in the space available.

It is hoped that this account of the school building grant plans relating to the various denominations will have given form and substance to some of the generalizations made about education in Wales during this period, and that the buildings which have survived will be thought worthy of further study from both the social and architectural points of view.

CHAPTER VI

Middle Class Schools 1800-1880

The history of the endowed grammar schools in Wales
during the nineteenth century is very well documented,
almost excessively so in view of the fact that by 1880 there
was, on average, only one grammar-school place per
thousand of the population. The detailed reports of the
Charity Commissioners in the 1830s were followed by the
more selective descriptions included in the Blue Books of
1847; then came the comprehensive reports of the Schools
Inquiry Commission in the 1860s, and those of the Aberdare
Committee in 1880/81.[1]

The keen interest taken in the endowments for grammar
schools, whose earlier histories we have traced in previous
chapters, showed itself in the thorough investigation of how
far these older endowments were producing value for money
in Victorian terms. Reformers wanted to know exactly what
had become of ancient endowments for education, the extent
to which the classical languages were still being taught, and

[1] Most of the figures of numbers of pupils etc. in the following chapter
are taken from *The Schools Inquiry Commission, Special Reports of
Assistant Commissioners*, vol. XX, *Monmouthshire and Wales* (London,
HMSO, 1870), referred to hereafter as *SIC*. Other figures are taken from
the *Report of the Committee appointed to Inquire into the Condition of
Intermediate and Higher Education in Wales* (London, HMSO, 1881),
referred to below as the 'Aberdare Report', from the name of its
chairman.

the degree of control exercised by the Established Church. The headmasters and governors of the endowed schools were invariably Anglican and, although no religious test was imposed on pupils admitted to the schools, it was not until the 1860s that the children of Nonconformist parents could gain exemption from the Anglican religious instruction included in their curricula. The need for endowed secondary schools for girls, to modify the exclusively male provision made by the traditional grammar schools, was also beginning to be recognized after about 1850. Behind these reforms lay the overwhelming demographic fact of the massive increase in population following rapid industrialization, particularly in south Wales. By 1861, the Census figures gave Wales a total population of 1.3 million, with nearly half of this total in Glamorgan, Monmouthshire and Carmarthenshire. Yet, while there were endowed grammar schools at Monmouth, with a population of 5,783, and Abergavenny with 4,621, there was none at Newport with 23,249 inhabitants. In Glamorgan, although Swansea (with a population of 41,606 in 1861) had its old-established grammar school, the only other endowed grammar school in the county was at Cowbridge (population 1,094), and none existed at Merthyr Tydfil (49,119), Cardiff (32,954) or Aberdare (32,299).

It was hardly to be expected that the complicated and often obsolete statutes of the endowed schools could be rapidly revised, and certainly not quickly enough to keep pace with the enormous growth of population which was taking place. The developing middle classes were inevitably thrown on to their own resources and there was an unprecedented increase in the number of 'private-adventure' schools, which was the contemporary term for fee-paying schools unconnected with an endowment. In contrast to the endowed schools, the private schools are poorly documented: though collectively of great importance, individually they were often transitory and small-scale. They could readily respond to the needs of the market and were not restricted by legal formularies concerning the curriculum or religious instruction; nor, of course, were they limited to boys.

The most useful sources of information about the private schools patronized by the middle classes are the trade and other directories which began to appear in the earlier part of the nineteenth century, and which often listed schools and 'academies'; advertisements in local newspapers and in the extensive Welsh and English periodical press also provide useful details. From the point of view of the development of school architecture and planning, which is the principal focus of the present study, the results are meagre because, at any rate for the first half of the century, private schools met in the teachers' houses or in the other pre-existing buildings, and no purpose-built private schools appear to have survived from before the 1850s. A sample analysis of the private boarding schools mentioned in Pigot's commercial directory of 1835, shown in Table VIII, will serve to illustrate the pattern which was emerging. Although some of these schools also took day pupils, middle--class schools which limited themselves to day pupils were viable only in the larger towns, and probably depended on word-of-mouth recommendations rather than printed advertisements. It will be seen from the Table that the number of private boarding schools was considerably larger in the south, and, given the exclusion of girls from the endowed grammar schools, it is not surprising that in Wales as a whole there were nearly twice as many schools for girls as boys. Another interesting, though not unexpected, feature is that very few of these schools were situated in the industrial areas themselves and, when they were located in the larger towns, they will usually be found to have occupied houses in what were at that date the socially more exclusive streets.

Returning to the development of the grammar schools, there was only one new foundation in the early nineteenth century. This was the grammar school founded at Lampeter in Cardiganshire in 1805 by Eliezer Williams, the vicar of the parish.[2] This school prepared some of its pupils for the

---

[2] On this school, see *SIC*, XX, 73-6 and 132-3, and J. Davies, *Lampeter School. A Catalogue of the Library* (Lampeter, 1866), introduction.

TABLE VIII — PRIVATE BOARDING SCHOOLS IN 1835

Source: Pigot & Co's, *National Commercial Directory* (London, 1835)

County	Place	Girls' Schools	Boys' Schools	Total
North Wales				
Anglesey	Beaumaris ...	1	—	1
Caernarfon	Bangor	1	—	1
	Caernarfon*	2	1	3
	Pwllheli ...	1	1	2
Denbigh	Wrexham*	4	2	6
Flint	Flint	2	—	2
	Hawarden ...	1	—	1
	Holywell ...	1	1	2
	Mold	2	—	2
Merioneth	Aberdovey ...	1	1	2
Totals	....	16	6	22
Mid Wales				
Brecon	Crickhowell	2	1	3
	Hay-on-Wye	2	1	3
Cardigan	Aberystwyth*	3	1	4
	Cardigan ...	1	—	1
Montgomery	Newtown ...	1	—	1
	Welshpool ...	1	1	2
Radnorshire	None	—	—	0
Totals	....	10	4	14
South Wales				
Carmarthen	Carmarthen*	3	1	4
	Laugharne ...	1	—	1
	Llandeilo ...	1	1	2
	Llandovery ...	2	—	2
Glamorgan	Cardiff*	1	1	2
	Cowbridge ...	1	2	3
	Neath	1	—	1
	Swansea* ...	4	4	8
Monmouth	Abergavenny*	1	2	3
	Chepstow ...	1	1	2
	Monmouth*	2	2	4
	Newport* ...	5	4	9
	Pontypool ...	2	1	3
	Usk	1	—	1
Pembroke	Haverfordwest*	6	1	7
	Milford Haven	—	2	2
	Narberth ...	1	—	1
	Pembroke ...	2	—	2
	Tenby	2	1	3
Totals	....	37	23	60
TOTALS FOR WALES		63	33	96

* Grade I towns in 1835, as classified by H. Carter in *The Towns of Wales* (1966), p.53.

Anglican ministry and achieved a considerable reputation (Sir Walter Scott, for example, sent his son to it); as a result, it was later classified as an endowed school, even though the endowment consisted only of the school building. His successor as headmaster was the Reverend John Williams, who moved from Lampeter to become the rector of Edinburgh Academy and was later appointed the first warden of Llandovery College. Lampeter grammar school, together with other grammar schools in south Wales, declined in importance once St David's College, Lampeter, had opened with the avowed object of concentrating preparation for the Anglican ministry in the diocese in one institution. An exception to this statement was the school at Ystradmeurig, mentioned in a previous chapter. Here, even as late as 1867, there were 127 pupils, mostly boarded in local farmhouses. About a quarter of the pupils at this date were receiving a purely elementary education, but the building also housed a classical school for the sons of Cardiganshire farmers, especially those who wished to learn Latin before going on to Lampeter College, or to theological colleges at St Bees, Birmingham, or St Aidan's, Birkenhead.[3] Ystradmeurig was also a prime example of what the Schools Inquiry Commission called the 'Welsh custom' of arranging for grammar school pupils to sleep and eat in private houses in the locality. Schools in remote country areas like Ystradmeurig, or Botwnnog in Caernarfonshire, could not otherwise have survived. Even in the towns, this system was sometimes used: at Haverfordwest, for example, farmers with sons at the grammar school brought a weekly supply of food in their carts on market days, to be cooked by the housewives with whom the boys lodged.[4] It may be noted that pupils such as these were usually classified as day boys in official records.

In 1818, Nicholas Carlisle's *Concise Description of the Endowed Grammar Schools in England and Wales* gave a very gloomy view of the situation in Wales, and the vivid accounts of manifest abuses included in the Blue Books of

[3] *SIC*, XX, 78.
[4] *SIC*, XX, 116.

1847 have also served to blacken the reputation of the Welsh grammar schools in the first half of the nineteenth century. For Carlisle, in particular, any school which no longer taught Latin and Greek on the model of the great public schools like Winchester and Eton was beyond the pale. More recent historians have suggested that in the late eighteenth and early nineteenth centuries the need for elementary education was paramount and, since resources for any kind of education were scarce, some moribund grammar schools, for want of any alternative, taught elementary subjects. 'That they did so', writes one author, 'does not imply that they "declined" or "decayed", but rather that as always they adapted to the society in which they found themselves.'[5] The Schools Inquiry Commissioners of the 1860s were highly critical of the use of grammar school endowments for elementary education, on the grounds that this merely absolved local landowners from the responsibility of contributing to the establishment of new National schools, which, once built, would have attracted grants from the central Government. This argument, however, had less force in those areas (numerous in Wales) where landed estates were relatively small, or owned by absentee landlords.

It may, indeed, be argued that the old endowments in Wales most severely criticized by the Commissioners were in fact serving a very useful (and often a socially comprehensive) service. At Cwmdeuddwr in Radnorshire, Northop and Trelawnyd in Flintshire, and at Pembroke and Welshpool, small and inadequate grammar-school endowments were formally transferred by their trustees to new elementary schools. At Llanegryn in Merioneth, where in 1866 the master refused to complete a questionnaire and removed himself to the seaside when Bryce called on behalf of the Schools Inquiry Commission, the endowment was still providing elementary education for forty boys and twenty girls, most of it free.[6] At Deuddwr in Montgomeryshire, so severely

---

[5] J. M. Sanderson, 'The grammar school and the education of the poor, 1786-1840', in *British Journal of Educational Studies*, 11 No. 1 (1962), 42.
[6] *SIC*, XX, 232-4.

criticized by the Commissioners of 1847, the situation in 1865 was that the endowment originally established by the lord of the manor was still providing a free elementary education to all social classes on the estate, from the children of 'landowners' to those of 'cottagers' and including the children of a blacksmith, a joiner and a gatekeeper.[7] A similar picture might be given of the schools at Llandeilo Gresynni in Monmouthshire and Presteigne in Radnorshire, which, though they had given up Latin and Greek, still offered more than elementary instruction.

The fate of other old endowments was affected by the growth of Nonconformity. The severest criticism of all the nineteenth-century commissions of inquiry was reserved for the grammar school at Pwllheli in Caernarfonshire, whose building was abandoned and whose endowment had been lost. It was reported that the supporters of Church and Chapel could not agree about the appointment of a master and that the Mostyn family denied responsibility for the endowment originally invested in the school by the Vaughans. Yet it is surely significant that, as we saw in the last chapter, a new British school of imposing appearance was opened in 1857, and this was built on the actual site of the former grammar school at Pwllheli. There was a similar situation in Merioneth. At Dolgellau, the grammar school was largely ignored by the local people but the British and National schools were well supported. At Bala, the grammar school which, as we shall see, was rebuilt in 1851, did not at first attract many pupils and in 1866 it was reported that 'the British school already receives the children of the shop-keepers, farmers and better class of artisans at Bala, who are all dissenters; while others, and especially the poorer people, resort to the National school'.[8]

The general position of the endowed grammar schools in the mid-Victorian period is indicated by the statistics given in the reports of the Schools Inquiry Commission, published

[7] SIC, XX, 238-41.
[8] SIC, XX, 235.

in 1870 and summarized in Table IX.[9] These show that, despite the four schools which had become elementary schools and the six no longer teaching classical subjects, most of the ancient foundations had survived and many of these had been reformed by schemes approved by the Court of Chancery following the notorious Blue Books of 1847. In addition, an important new boys' school had been established at Llandovery, and two schools for girls had opened at Llandaff and Denbigh. The very full details given in the reports of the social class of the parents and of the curricula taught in the schools show that most social classes were represented, apart from the leading landowners and the major industrialists, who sent their sons to public schools in England, which were themselves undergoing a major transformation. The removal of the landowning class from the local grammar schools was a phenomenon common to England as well as Wales, but in Wales it contributed to the growing gulf between landlord and tenant which religious and linguistic differences were also reinforcing. As for the curricula of the schools, the move towards the teaching of modern subjects, which we noted in some of the larger schools during the eighteenth century, was now well established. Most of the schools taught mathematics, English, history, geography and French, in addition to Latin and, in some schools, Greek. By the 1860s a new emphasis was being placed by reformers on the need to teach experimental (as distinct from text-book) science, and on physical education. Little progress had yet been made in the teaching of science, except at Llandovery, and organized recreational facilities were usually limited, though at Swansea there were lessons in swimming and several school taught drill; Ruabon even claimed to have a small gymnasium.[10] It may also be noted that some day pupils

[9] The work of visiting the schools was divided between J. Bryce and H. M. Bompas. They made their visits in 1865 and 1866, and the figures which they included in their reports do not always coincide with those given in the statistical tables attached to their reports, which were based on returns made in 1864, in some cases updated to 1869.

[10] *SIC*, XX, 253. This was probably an open-air gymnasium. The first indoor gymnasium at any public school was built at Uppingham in 1859.

continued to receive free tuition in accordance with the terms of endowments and that scholarships were awarded, principally by Jesus College, Oxford, where twenty scholarships and thirty exhibitions were available from the Meyricke endowment.[11]

The rebuilding of some of the grammar schools after about 1850, particularly in south Wales, was an accurate reflection both of the reforming movement and of the conservatism inherent in corporate bodies. In north Wales, which did not, to anything like the same extent, experience the population explosion of the south, there was relatively little new building. Earlier in the century Hawarden and Ruabon schools had extended their dormitory accommodation in the hope of attracting more fee-paying boarders, and at Botwnnog, where the boarding-out system already described permitted an increase in numbers, a new schoolroom was built on an adjoining site in 1848. This building, which survives as part of the present comprehensive school, is in a curiously elongated neo-Gothic style which suggests the hand of an inexperienced architect or builder. The only major rebuilding in north Wales in the middle decades of the nineteenth century was at Bala, whose grammar school was administered by Jesus College as part of the Meyricke endowment. The College was therefore responsible for the new building of 1851, and the correspondence between the London architect employed and the College bursar, which survives in the muniment room at the College, makes interesting reading.[12]

The architectural firm chosen to rebuild the school at Bala was that of Wigg and Pownall, whose other designs included a new library at Gray's Inn (1841) and the Staple

---

[11] *SIC*, XX, 14. For the history of the Meyricke endowment, see J. N. L. Baker, 'Edmund Meyricke and his benefaction' in *Jesus College Record*, 1966, 19-28.

[12] The bundle of correspondence, identified as 'List 5' of the Meyricke (Bala) papers, includes the architect's detailed specification, but not the plans of the school, which have not been located either at the Gwynedd Record Office or Architect's Department. I am much indebted to Dr. D. A. Rees, the College Archivist, who kindly showed me this correspondence and placed the College facilities at my disposal.

TABLE IX — ENDOWED GRAMMAR SCHOOLS FOR BOYS c. 1867

County	Place	No. of boys: Boarders	Day	Curri-culum	Grade	Social Class	Endow-ment (£)
Anglesey	Beaumaris	41	12	CL	I	A	490
Brecon	Brecon	20	29	CL	II	AB	435
Caernarfon	Bangor (a)	—	40	CL	II	?	211
	Botwnnog	—	59	SC	II	ABC	181
	Pwllheli	Closed					Lost
Cardigan	Cardigan	—	19	CL	I	AB	21
	Lampeter (b)	—	20	CL	I	AB	—
	Ystradmeurig	2	125	CL	I	AB	267
Carmarthen	Carmarthen	—	18	SC	II	AB	68
	Llandovery (c)	43	10	CL	I	AB	647
Denbigh	Denbigh	6	23	SC	II	B	53
	Llanrwst	7	21	CL	I	AB	368
	Ruabon	26	24	CL	II	AB	124
	Ruthin	26	21	CL	I	AB	266
	Wrexham	5	10	SC	II	B	32
Flint	Hawarden	15	15	SC	I	B	16
	Holywell	Closed					(5)
	St Asaph	12	34	SC	II	ABC	14
	Trelawnyd	Closed*					(93)
Glamorgan	Cowbridge	24	20	CL	I	AB	50
	Swansea	10	72	CL	II	AB	561
Merioneth	Bala	2	35	SC	III	?	150
	Dolgellau	—	14	NC	II	C	38
	Llanegryn	—	40	NC	III	BC	85
Monmouth	Abergavenny	—	15	CL	II	AB	107
	Llantilio (d)	—	120	NC	III	BC	160
	Monmouth:						
	Upper school	—	25	CL	I	AB	⎰ 2914
	Lower school	—	75	NC	II	?	⎱ jointly
	Usk	5	11	SC	III	AB	110
Mont-	Deuddwr	—	30	NC	III	BC	102
gomery	Welshpool	Closed*					(9)
Pembroke	Haverfordwest	4	41	CL	I	B	174
	Pembroke	Closed*					(11)
	St David's	4	10	CL	II	?	40
Radnor	Cwmdeuddwr	Closed*					(32)
	Presteigne	—	49	NC	II	BC	140
Totals	36 endow-ments (six closed or elementary)	Boarders 252	Day 1,037	CL 16 SC 8 NC 6	I 11 II 14 III 5	n/a	£7,824†

* Endowment transferred to National school
? No information given
† After payment of repairs, rates, taxes and insurance

(a) Temporarily closed in 1867
(b) Founded in 1805
(c) The Welsh Collegiate Institution (1847)
(d) Llandeilo Gresynni

Note: The figures above are from the *Reports of the Schools Inquiry Commission*, vol. xx (1870). In the 'Curriculum' column, CL stands for Classical (subjects taught included Latin and Greek), SC for Semi-Classical (Latin but not Greek) and NC for Non-Classical. In the 'Grade' column, I indicates that at least 10% of the boys were over 16 years of age, and II that the same percentage were over 14; remaining schools graded III. 'Social Class' was designated by the Commissioners as A (upper), B (middle) and C (lower). 'Endowment' is the net annual income from the endowment.

Inn Buildings (1851), both in London.[13] The instructions given to George Pownall, the partner concerned with the project, were that 'the Building to be erected should be plain in character and in accordance with the class of boys likely to be educated there, and particularly in regard to the Master's House, that it should not be made a residence for a Clergyman taking pupils, but built for a School-master who would in all probability be selected from the Normal school [i.e. the National Society training college] of London'.[14] A London-based clerk of works was employed to supervise the building work, which was carried out by John Evans of Corwen. Evans was chosen because, the architect wrote, the local stone to be used for the building 'would be much better understood and more carefully quarried and worked by a Builder residing on the spot than by Workmen from Shrewsbury or Chester'.[15] Unfortunately, the architect later had to report that Evans's trade was in fact that of a joiner and that he 'is giving us a great deal of trouble, not intentionally we believe, but from his being utterly incompetent to carry out such a work as this'.[16] The relationship between the architect and the builder continued to deteriorate and reached breaking point soon after the building was completed, when it was discovered that the slates blew off during the first gale. Evans stated that he had used the 'best Duchess' slates specified in the contract, even though they were also the thinnest, and that he had nailed them on as specified: it was

[13] J. Orbach, *Victorian Architecture in Britain* (London, A. & C. Black, 1987), 241; and N. Pevsner, *London* (Harmondsworth, Penguin Books, 1962), I, 329.
[14] Architect to Solicitor, 2 January, 1849.
[15] Architect to Bursar, 30 April, 1849.
[16] Architect to Bursar, 18 July, 1851.

not for him to have pointed out that thicker slates, nailed on in the 'Welsh fashion', would have better withstood the high winds common in mountainous country.

The College archives also provide information about the cost of the building, which was estimated at £2,068, plus £455 professional fees paid to the surveyor of the site, the clerk of works and the architect. It was usual for architects to be paid five per cent of the contract price of a building; presumably because of the distance between London and Bala, Pownall claimed only three per cent, but charged three guineas a day when away from London. He estimated that a total of eight journeys, each taking three days, would be necessary, plus expenses of £7 10s. per journey to pay for 'coach hire etc.'. In the event, ten journeys were needed and additional time had to be spent on the site by the clerk of works, which, with a few extras on the building, brought the final cost of the school to £2,909, including £752 professional fees.

In spite of all this effort, there was only a handful of boys at the school until after 1866, when a new scheme was introduced following lengthy negotiations between Jesus College and the Master of the Rolls, during which the College commuted its annual payments for a capital sum and so ended its direct link with the school, though the College coat of arms has remained on the building to this day.[17] The new scheme permitted parents to withdraw their sons from instruction in the Church catechism, but Latin was still taught and by 1880 the majority of the boys were from Nonconformist homes. The 1851 building consisted of the master's house and a large schoolroom (now the dining room of the modern restaurant into which the school has in recent years been converted); later in the nineteenth century a laboratory was built behind the schoolroom and a dormitory was added alongside the master's house (see Plate 41.) This was the school attended by O. M. Edwards for two terms in 1874 and by T. E. Ellis, later Liberal M.P. for Merioneth from 1886 to 1899. R. T. Jenkins, the historian, was also a

[17] *Jesus College Record,* op. cit., 24.

pupil there in 1893. On the occasion of the centenary of the rebuilding, Jenkins wrote:

> To us Old Boys, the building (even granting that there is a touch of 'ye olde' about it) seems comely; and we may be thankful not only for the fact that it was built in stone, not in brick, but that this in turn compelled the use of stone for the subsequent additions. A seemly school building (and this is now a hundred years old) is no small part of a boy's education.[18]

The other grammar schools which were rebuilt during the mid-Victorian period were in south Wales. Among these, both Abergavenny and Cowbridge were constitutionally linked with Jesus College. The school at Abergavenny continued as a small school in the converted church building described in a previous chapter, but Cowbridge acquired a new set of buildings between 1849 and 1852 at a cost to Jesus College of nearly £5,000.[19] In this case, the College had the good sense to employ a locally-based architect and it did well to choose the young John Prichard, the Llandaff diocesan architect, whom we have already met in connection with the building of new National schools in the diocese. The new buildings at Cowbridge, which are now used by the junior department of the local comprehensive school, were built in what has been described as a 'picturesque and irregular' Gothic style,[20] and successfully achieved Prichard's aim of harmonizing his school building with the church on one side and the ancient town gate on the other (see Plate 42). The new school provided not only a large schoolroom but also a dormitory above it, capable of housing up to forty boys. The sub-division of the dormitory into cubicles was a novel feature, also coming into use in some of the English public schools, but in other respects the layout was traditional.

[18] R. T. Jenkins, 'A sketch of the history of Bala grammar school 1713-1893', *Journal of the Merioneth Historical Society*, 1 No. 3 (1951), 152.
[19] Details in this paragraph from Iolo Davies, *'A Certaine Schoole'* (Cowbridge, D. Brown, 1967), 73-7.
[20] P. Howell and E. Beazley, *The Companion Guide to South Wales* (London, Collins, 1977), 280. This book also contains details of churches designed and restored by Prichard.

Although Jesus College was more successful in its choice of architect than at Bala, it was not successful in retaining the services of H. D. Harper, a fellow of the College, who was appointed headmaster in 1847 but resigned in 1850 to take up the headship of Sherborne school in Dorset, which he is said to have found with two scholars and left with 350. Harper later became the principal of Jesus College and the school's historian suggests, probably correctly, that Harper objected to the fact that the College had no conception of changing the school at Cowbridge into anything different from what it had always been: 'They merely pulled down an old school-house and school-room and replaced them by a somewhat enlarged and very expensive version of what had been there already.'[21] Certainly, the Schools Inquiry Commissioners of the 1860s criticized the smallness of the boys' dining room, the lack of a sick bay, and the absence of an adequate playground. Thus Cowbridge, in spite of its fine new building, suffered the usual problem of town schools, that of a restricted site hampering future development.

A more far-seeing approach was adopted at Swansea, where the old grammar school was rebuilt on a new site between 1852 and 1869.[22] The school endowment, which consisted of a large farm near Bridgend, greatly increased in value with the discovery of reserves of coal there. A new Chancery scheme was obtained in 1850, chiefly through the efforts of G. G. Francis, the mayor of Swansea and chairman of the school trustees (feoffees). Plans for a new building were drawn up by Thomas Taylor, architect of London, and are reproduced from *The Builder* (Fig. 21 and Plate 43). The architectural style was Perpendicular Gothic or 'Tudor' and the plan shows the building divided into two by a central tower, to the left of which was a large schoolroom open to the roof and with a gallery 'for spectators at examinations'; provision was also made for some specialist teaching in three adjoining classrooms. To the right of the tower was a library, a dining hall,

---

[21] Davies, op. cit., 77.
[22] Further details in *Swansea Grammar School* (Special Number of the School magazine, 1932), 11-15. Also, *The Builder*, 1853, 72.

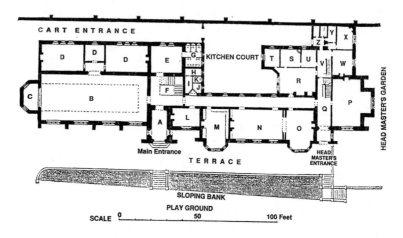

Fig. 21. Swansea, plan of new grammar school, 1853.
Thomas Taylor, architect.

Key to Letters on Plan:

A   Entrance hall
B   Schoolroom
C   Master's dais
D   Classrooms
E   Hat and cloak room
F   Main staircase
G   Water closets and urinals
H   Shoe-cleaning room
I   Shoe room
J   Wash-hand room
K   Master's water closet
L   Undermaster's sitting room
M   Library and museum
N   Boys' dining room
O   Master's dining room
P   Master's drawing room
Q   Master's staircase
R   Kitchen with hatch
S   Scullery
T   Larder
U   Coal house
V   Servants' staircase
W   Servants' hall
X   Housekeeper's room
Y   Knife and fork cleaning room
Z   Servants' entrance

and accommodation for the headmaster and undermaster, with dormitories above. The plan in fact shows a complete A to Z of a middle class school of top quality. The foundation stone of the new building was laid in 1852 and the main schoolroom opened in 1853; the rest of the building was completed (in a somewhat different form) by B. Bucknall, architect of Swansea, in 1869. When Lord Aberdare, who had been a pupil at Swansea in the 1830s, visited the school in 1880 there were sixty day boys (including twenty sons of burgesses who continued to receive free tuition) and thirteen boarders. Sixty of the seventy-three pupils were members of the Church of England. As for the later history of the building, the part designed by Taylor was destroyed by air raids during the second world war, but Bucknail's range, consisting of an elaborate, three-storey Gothic building of brown stone with dressed quoins, has survived as a listed (but derelict) building near the technical college in Mount Pleasant. The grammar school's lineal descendant is the Bishop Gore Comprehensive School at Sketty.

In Carmarthenshire, two new grammar schools built in the early Victorian period provide an interesting contrast from both the educational and architectural points of view. By the early nineteenth century, the town of Carmarthen was being outstripped in economic importance by the industrial settlement at Llanelli. (In 1861, Carmarthen had a population of 9,993, compared with Llanelli's 11,084.) As we noted in a previous chapter, there were close links between the grammar school at Carmarthen and Powell's school, which was itself closely linked with the Presbyterian interests in the town. As a result, under a new scheme of 1856, the two schools were amalgamated and the grammar school boys moved into the recently-erected Powell's school building.[23] Though the new scheme appointed trustees representing both the Anglican and Nonconformist interests, the endowment remained a

---

[23] M. Evans, *An Early History of Queen Elizabeth Grammar School, Carmarthen* (Carmarthen, n.d.), 78; also, Jasper Malcolm and Edith Lodwick, *The Story of Carmarthen* (Carmarthen, Lodwick, rev. edt. 1972), 89.

small one. Thus, at a time when grammar school masters were usually paid at least £100 a year, the endowment at Carmarthen allowed the headmaster only £20, with an adjoining house valued at £40, and no boarders were forthcoming to supplement the master's income. It was therefore not surprising that suitable masters could not be found, and in 1865, when the school was visited by Bryce on behalf of the Schools Inquiry Commission, he was struck by the 'woebegone and desolate' appearance of the schoolroom, where some twenty boys were being taught by a temporary master.[24] He reported that the townspeople desired only a commercial education and those who wanted anything more sent their sons to Llandovery College, or to England. The building occupied by the grammar school has survived at the east end of the Esplanade in Carmarthen and is, in fact, an excellent example of the earlier type of endowed school building, with some architectural distinction (see Plate 44). It has stuccoed walls and a shallow, hipped roof, still in the classical style, though apparently erected in about 1844.

The contrast between the run-down grammar school at Carmarthen and the new 'Welsh Collegiate Institution' at Llandovery could hardly have been greater. Much has been written about this bold educational venture conceived in 1847 by Thomas Phillips, a wealthy surgeon, supported by other Welsh-speaking churchmen and women.[25] The College was built on what would nowadays be called a 'green field' site, chosen because of its central position in relation to the industrial areas of south Wales and donated by Lady Llanover, who continued to support the College until her death in 1896. The generous endowment and progressive outlook of the founders were matched by the appointment as Warden of the Revd. John Williams, whom we noted earlier at Lampeter grammar school. He adopted a school curriculum which was unique in Wales for the importance which it attached to the

[24] *SIC*, XX, 83-7.
[25] See *SIC*, XX, 88-97, and W. Gareth Evans, *A History of Llandovery College* (The College, 1981), ch. 1. On the building, see *The Builder*, 1850, 9.

teaching of the Welsh language and to the teaching of science. The college buildings, illustrated on Plate 45, were first occupied in 1851 and, as at Swansea, were completed in stages. They were designed in the fashionable Tudor style by the architectural firm of Thomas Fuller and William Gingell of Bristol and the plan which was adopted, with the teaching accommodation on one side of a central tower and residential accommodation on the other, was again similar to that of the new school at Swansea and of some of the new public schools in England (e.g. Liverpool College and Cheltenham College, both built in 1843). The warden's house, which formed part of the main façade, was designed to accommodate boarders, but in 1866 it was noted that twenty-six of the forty-three boarders slept in lodgings in the locality. Williams institutionalized this traditional practice by personally approving all the lodgings and visiting them weekly: hence the boys in them were not regarded as 'day boys', as in places like Ystradmeurig and Botwnnog.

The adoption of an innovatory architectural style was not always accompanied by new educational thinking. The grammar school at Cardigan had been maintained by the corporation since the Restoration and accommodation for the school was included in a new project, completed in 1860, for bringing the open market under cover (Plate 46).[26] The inclusion of the grammar school in the project, and the choice of R. J. Withers as architect, were to the credit of the corporation, and his design has attracted the attention of architectural historians because it was one of the earliest examples of the application of the Ecclesiological (Gothic) approach to the planning of a civic building.[27] This small complex of buildings, which still stands in the centre of Cardigan, is indeed of considerable architectural interest, but from the educational point of view it is a perfect illustration of the fossilization of traditional practice, which provided the usual schoolroom but located it above the market and

---

[26] SIC, XX, 68-72, and The Builder, 1858, 114.
[27] Stefan Muthesius, The High Victorian Movement in Architecture (London, Routledge & Kegan Paul, 1972), 86-7.

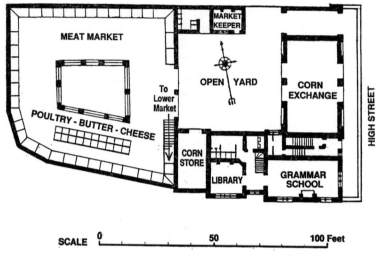

SCALE 0 _____ 50 _____ 100 Feet

Fig. 22. Cardigan, plan of market hall including a grammar school, 1859.
R. J. Withers, architect.

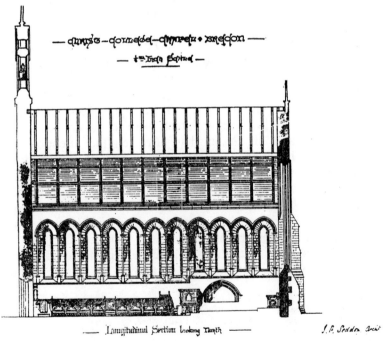

Fig. 23. Christ College Chapel, Brecon. Drawing of restored chapel by
J. P. Seddon, c.1859.

hemmed it in with spaces designed for other municipal purposes, thus imposing a stranglehold on future school development (see Fig. 22). There was no house for the headmaster or playground for the boys, and the school remained a small day school, incapable of further development on the site provided for it by the corporation.

Other venerable school foundations were being affected by the reform movement. It will be recalled that the grammar schools at Brecon and Bangor had been established after the Reformation in the former buildings of Dominican friaries. Bangor had moved into a new school building in 1789, and, although it was closed owing to financial difficulties between 1867 and 1873, its fortunes soon revived under the dynamic leadership of the Reverend Daniel Lewis Lloyd, who had already revived the school at Dolgellau and was later to take charge at Christ College, Brecon. (He is better remembered for his appointment in 1890 as the first Welsh-speaking Welshman to become Bishop of Bangor for two centuries.)[28] Well before Lloyd arrived at Brecon in 1879, considerable rebuilding had taken place.[29] The Deanery of Brecon had been abolished in the early part of Victoria's reign and its revenue allocated to the college. The friary buildings, parts of which were occupied by the school, were in a ruinous condition and were now put in order. The nave of the friary church was left as a ruin but the restoration of the former choir of the friary to make the school chapel was begun by the architect, John Seddon, in 1859 and is among his most admired works because of his scholarly understanding of medieval styles of building (see Fig. 23).[30] Then between 1861 and 1864 Seddon and Prichard restored the other parts of the friary used by the school as a schoolroom, a library and a classroom. They also built a new range to include a house for

[28] On Lloyd at Bangor, see E. W. Jones (ed.), *The Dominican Fourth Centenary Number* (1957), 69-71.
[29] *SIC*, XX, 57-67, and B. Knight, *The Story of Christ College, Brecon* (The College, 1978), 47-9.
[30] There are also superb drawings by Seddon of his adaptation of the Prior's Lodging at Monmouth as a National school in the Monmouthshire collection of building grant plans, listed in Appendix III.

the headmaster and a dining room for the boys, with four dormitories above. These were built in Venetian Gothic style and, though employing multi-coloured stone, harmonized well with the earlier buildings. Further additions were made in 1880 by the architect J. B. Fowler, and the resulting quadrangle provided a noble setting for the college.[31]

Bryce, who visited Christ College on behalf of the Schools Inquiry Commission in 1866, remarked on the architectural advantages enjoyed by the college and was surprised at the relatively small number of pupils (twenty-nine day boys and twenty boarders). He considered that the £8 annual fee paid by the day boys (apart from three boys on the foundation who were taught free) excluded all but the sons of the professional men and richer shopkeepers in the town, while the boarding fee of £50 meant that the college was competing both with privately-run schools and with some of the English public schools. In 1880, however, the Aberdare Report noted that there had been a considerable increase, with 131 boys at the school, two-thirds of them boarders.

The only other major rebuilding in south Wales during this period was at Monmouth, where the buildings so eloquently described by Nicholas Carlisle in 1818 were considerably altered after 1864 at a cost of about £5,000. This was made possible by the very large endowment accumulated by the Haberdashers' Company of London, who were the school trustees and employed their architect, W. Snooke, to do the work.[32] The old schoolroom of 1614 was pulled down to make way for a new building, which consisted of a large schoolroom with two classrooms attached to it, one for the 'upper' (classical) school and the other for the 'lower' (commercial) school. A school chapel was also built, with a library adjoining it.

In 1865, when H. M. Bompas visited Monmouth on behalf of the Schools Inquiry Commission, he reported on the long-

---

[31] Architectural description in *The Builder*, 1859, 323, and 1864, 657. See also R. Haslam, *Buildings of Wales. Powys* (Harmondsworth, Penguin Books, 1979), 293-6.
[32] *SIC*, XX, 25-32; and H. A. Ward, *Monmouth School 1614-1964* (London, Haberdashers' Company, 1964), 21-3. Also, *The Builder*, 1865, 578.

standing opposition of the townspeople to any proposal that the hundred free places available from the charity should be reduced or that the masters should be allowed to take boarders in their houses, though they had no objection to the traditional arrangement under which some of the day boys lodged in houses in the town. In the event, a new scheme of 1868 overruled these objections and the headmaster, Charles Manley Roberts, began the conversion of the school to full 'public school' status. Entry to the lower school was restricted to boys from the counties of Monmouth, Hereford and Gloucester, but the upper school was thrown open to the whole of England and Wales. Twelve free scholarships were retained, but tuition fees of £2 a year in the lower school and £6 in the upper school were introduced and the headmaster and undermaster were allowed to admit boarders, charging an annual fee of fifty guineas in the upper school and thirty guineas in the lower. Numbers rose rapidly, four new masters were appointed and three more classrooms were built. In 1871 Roberts was admitted to the Headmasters' Conference, which had been set up by Edward Thring, the headmaster of Uppingham, who had similarly transformed a local grammar school into a major public school. In 1875 the chapel was enlarged to take in the old library, and a new library and a laboratory were built. The headmaster's house and the lecturer's house in what is now Wyebridge Street were enlarged and refaced in stone, and converted into two boarding houses (Plate 47). By 1876 here were 275 boys at the school, a total not exceeded until 1941. We shall see that it later had to compete not only with public schools in England but also with the new schools set up under the Welsh Intermediate Education Act of 1889.

The changes in the endowed grammar schools described above related to the education of boys, to whom these schools were exclusively confined. It was another London Company which enabled Wales to lead the way in the provision of two purpose-built secondary schools for girls. The Howell's schools at Llandaff and Denbigh opened in 1860: the North London Collegiate Girls' School was established in 1850 but was not endowed until 1875, while Cheltenham Ladies' College was founded in 1854 but did not transfer to new buildings until 1873. The Howell's schools were financed from the charitable bequest of Thomas Howell, a sixteenth-century merchant draper of Welsh origin, who made generous provision in his will for giving dowries to orphan girls of his own lineage. In the course of time, it became impossible to trace any such descendants, and in 1852 it was agreed that the considerable amount of money accumulated by the Company of Drapers from Howell's investment in land in London should be used for the provision of two new schools for girls in Wales, especially for those who had lost one or both of their parents.[33] Thirty such girls were to be given free board and education at each of the two schools, and it was also agreed that fee-paying girls could be admitted to help pay the running costs. Both schools were designed by Herbert Williams, architect of London, in what has been called a 'free Elizabethan' style[34] and were, architecturally, virtually identical (Plate 48). They each cost about £20,000, which presumably included the cost of the site and of internal fittings and furniture.[35] The ground plan of the Llandaff school (Fig. 24) shows that excellent provision was made for the boarding side: there were day rooms for the girls when not at lessons, a large dining room and a 'convalescent room'. Upstairs, there were two dormitories over the school-room and the dining room, with twenty-five beds in each, and a third dormitory for ten girls over the library. Lavatory (i.e. washing) and toilet facilities were also provided on a generous scale. In 1868 there were thirty fee-paying boarders in each school in addition to the orphan girls, together with twenty-five day girls at Llandaff and ten at Denbigh.

[33] *SIC*, XX, 150-157 (Llandaff) and 264-5 (Denbigh). See also J. E. McCann, *Thomas Howell and the School at Llandaff* (Cowbridge, Brown, 1972) on which Fig. 24 is based; and Mollie K. Stone, 'Howell's School, Denbigh', *Denbighshire Historical Society Transactions*, 8 (1959), 157-162.

[34] E. Hubbard, *Buildings of Wales. Clwyd* (Harmondsworth, Penguin Books, 1986), 149.

[35] *SIC*, XX, 152, gives the costs as £24,000 (Llandaff) and £20,000 (Denbigh). The contract prices of the main buildings were £17,764 for Llandaff and £15,310 for the slightly smaller building at Denbigh (*The Builder*, 1858, 252).

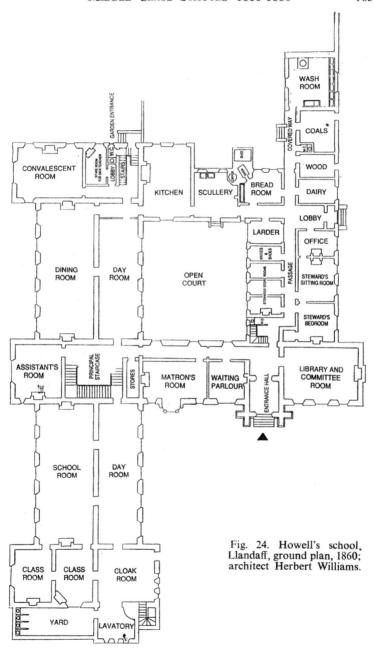

Fig. 24. Howell's school, Llandaff, ground plan, 1860; architect Herbert Williams.

There was no conception at this date that girls required a classical or scientific education, and the curriculum consisted of the principles of the Christian religion, reading, writing, arithmetic, English grammar, geography, history, music, drawing and French. Needlework was also taught, but cookery, at first included, was later omitted. When the schools were first opened, many of the girls were the daughters of small farmers and labourers, but soon afterwards the governors decided that the schools were intended for the daughters of 'gentlewomen', and the matron (headmistress) at Llandaff considered that it was 'often rather an evil than a good' to admit children 'who, after enjoying there the comforts and even luxuries of life, had to return home to labourers' cottages'.[36] The staff were required to be members of the Church of England, but the catechism was not taught to children whose parents or guardians objected. In 1880, about three-quarters of the pupils were stated to be members of the Church of England, with a slightly higher proportion at Llandaff than Denbigh.

The Nonconformists were also able to make use of an old endowment, though one considerably less valuable than that of Thomas Howell. This was Dr Williams' endowment of 1711, which had been used to support a number of elementary schools in north Wales. The trustees agreed that the passing of the Elementary Education Act of 1870 had rendered such provision unnecessary, and in 1875 the funds were re-allocated to provide, with additional voluntary subscriptions, a secondary school for girls. Both Caernarfon and Dolgellau were considered as possible locations, and Dolgellau was chosen, chiefly through the efforts of Samuel Holland (1803-92), who owned a number of slate quarries in the area and was Liberal M.P. for Merioneth from 1870 to 1885.[37] The school opened in 1878 in buildings designed in a plain and somewhat indeterminate style by a Mr Bull, about

[36] *SIC*, XX, 153.
[37] B. M. Jones, 'Dr. Williams' School, Dolgellau', *Journal of the Merioneth Historical Society*, 6 (1970), 173-6.

whom no further information has been discovered.[38] (They survive on the Barmouth road out of Dolgellau, and are now part of the college of further education.) The school syllabus appears to have been similar to that of the Howell's schools, and the fees, which in 1883 were £4 a year for day girls and £30 for boarders,[39] were also comparable with those at the Howell's schools, with the important difference that there was no provision of sixty free places for orphan children. In 1880 there were thirty-five boarders and forty-nine day girls, and three-quarters of them were stated to be from Nonconformist homes. The boarders were mainly accommodated in rented houses, some of which were of considerable historical interest.

It is essential, before concluding this chapter, to refer again to the part played by private schools, in spite of the relative lack of information about them.[40] In England in the 1830s and 1840s many 'proprietary' schools were established on the joint-stock principle, which made it possible to share the financial risks of starting new schools. In Wales, only three such schools were founded before 1880, and these were not established until the 1870s. This is probably to be accounted for by the later appearance of a well-to-do industrial middle class in Wales. The proprietary schools in Wales were established in Cardiff, Merthyr Tydfil and Neath — all, it will be noticed, in industrial areas without endowed grammar schools. The demand for middle-class secondary schools in many other parts of Wales was satisfied by enterprising individuals, who usually adapted ordinary houses for school use.

There are, however, some surviving examples of purpose-built private schools dating from the second half of the nine-

[38] The architect's surname is given in the School Minute Book for 1877 (Dolgellau Record Office, ref. Z/DBH/250).
[39] Prospectus of 1883 in Dolgellau Record Office, ref. Z/DBH/124.
[40] Volume VIII of the Report of the Schools Inquiry Commission (1868) included some information on private schools in Glamorgan, Flintshire, Denbighshire and Monmouthshire. See further, W. G. Evans, *Education and Female Emancipation* (Cardiff, University of Wales Press, 1990), 58-62,77-9. Private schools in Anglesey are listed in D. A. Pretty, *Two Centuries of Anglesey Schools* (Anglesey Antiquarian Society, 1977), Appendix N.

teenth century, notably at Welshpool and Caernarfon. (There are also good examples at Holt and Newcastle Emlyn and doubtless others elsewhere not identified by the author.)[41] The demise of the small endowed grammar school at Welshpool has previously been noted, and in 1853 William Clive, the vicar of Welshpool, built at his own expense the fine brick and stone Gothic school (now a masonic hall) which still stands in Berriew Street (Plate 49). This school was known as the 'Welshpool School' or 'Welshpool Grammar School' and was designed by George Gilbert Scott.[42] In 1880 it had twenty-five day pupils, only half of whom were members of the Church of England. Another interesting building which was still standing on the Porthmadog road into Caernarfon in 1991 (though derelict) is the former 'Carnarvon Grammar and Collegiate School', locally called 'Ysgol Jones Bach', which was built with an elaborate, ornamental side entry and ball finials reminiscent of the Skinner Street British school at Aberystwyth. The earliest reference to this school in local directories is in 1877 (though the building looks older) and the latest in 1890.[43] In 1880 it had thirty-three pupils, two-thirds of them Nonconformists. It will be recalled that the grammar school shown on Speed's map of Caernarfon in 1610 disappeared in the course of the seventeenth century, so it is not surprising to see the appearance of this 'grammar' school before 1880, when there were at least two other private schools in the town, including one for girls. At Holt in Denbighshire, the Reverend Ebenezer Powell opened a school in his house in 1855 and a few years later altered and extended it to form the 'Holt Academy', whose building still stands in Castle Street (Plate 50). In 1880 there were forty-eight boarders and six day boys and three-quarters of the pupils were from Nonconformist homes. Sir Ellis Ellis-

[41] For Holt Academy, see J. Powell, *Holt and its Records* (Denbigh, Gee, 1982), 55, and, more generally, *Denbs. Hist. Soc. Trans.*, 10 (1961), article by H. R. Evans. A small building with the inscription 'Emlyn Grammar School 1867', formerly a private school, survives in Water Street, Newcastle Emlyn, Carms.

[42] J. E. Davies, 'Three Welshpool Vicars' in *The Montgomeryshire Collections*, 76 (1988), 111.

[43] Ex inf. Deputy County Archivist, Gwynedd.

Griffith, the eminent lawyer, was a former pupil, and H. G. Wells began writing here in 1887 when he was briefly on the staff.

The Aberdare Report of 1880/81 throws much light on the private schools existing at that date. Questionnaires were sent to 290 private schools of post-elementary type, of which only about a half replied. Even so, the statistical tables published in the Report give useful information about the distribution and denominational character of both the private and endowed schools.[44] A summary of the attendance figures given for both types of school is set out in Table X.

TABLE X

POST-ELEMENTARY SCHOOLS IN WALES IN 1880
(Population: 1,570,000)

Source: *Report of the Committee to Inquire into the Condition of Intermediate and Higher Education in Wales.* (London, 1881)

Type of school	Boys	Girls	Total	
Endowed schools	27	3	30	
pupils	1,540	263	1,803	
Private schools	79	73	152	(plus 138 schools not returned)
pupils	2,287	1,871	4,158	(plus 209 pupils in proprietary schools)

The members of the Aberdare Committee were somewhat dismissive of the private schools, stressing their small average size and their low average fees, which cast doubt on the quality of the teaching provided. They may also have reacted against the pretensions of many of these schools which gave themselves such titles as 'Academies', 'Colleges' or 'Grammar Schools'. The Report was particularly concerned to show that, in what was claimed to be for the most part a Nonconformist nation, two-thirds of the boys attending the endowed grammar schools were members of the Church of England.[45]

---

[44] It should be noted that in the tables of statistics given in the Aberdare Report, it is not made clear whether a dash in a column indicates that there were no pupils in that category, or simply that the respondent had failed to supply a figure; the latter is clearly so in some cases.

[45] Aberdare Report, p. xiv.

The figures given in the Report for the religious denomination of the pupils at private schools are incomplete, but seem
to show a Nonconformist majority overall. For example,
Swansea had eleven private schools, two of which declined to
give information on religious affiliation; the percentage of
Anglican pupils in the remaining nine was thirty-seven per
cent.[46] The main point which emerges, however, is that, if one
leaves on one side the question of religious denomination
which so concerned the authors of the Aberdare Report, the
stark fact remains that two-thirds of the children receiving
some form of secondary education in Wales in 1880 were in
private schools unconnected with any public endowment.

[46] Ibid., pp. xc-xci.

CHAPTER VII

Board Schools and the County Councils, 1870-1902

The Elementary Education Act of 1870 introduced two new principles which were of the greatest importance for education in Wales no less than in England. The first was the adoption of the principle that parents could be compelled to send their children to school, and the second was the introduction of the 'dual system' by which locally-elected boards, with the power to levy a local rate, could establish non-denominational schools to 'fill the gaps' left by the voluntary schools. The principle of compulsion took thirty years to take root: the 1870 Act permitted school boards to introduce by-laws to secure compulsory attendance, but they were not at first obliged to do so. Many exemptions from school attendance were permitted and even by 1899 the minimum leaving age was only twelve. More especially, it was not until 1891 that parents were relieved of the responsibility of paying elementary-school fees.

The introduction of the board schools certainly did not mean the end of denominational education. In fact, the Church of England made strenuous efforts to build new schools before the school boards became fully established, and the Roman Catholics were wholly opposed to the non-denominational instruction given in the board schools. By contrast, the Nonconformists, particularly in Wales, were content to leave religious education to the Sunday schools, and the great majority of the British schools were handed over to the school boards. The works schools, although mainly classified as British schools, were slower to give up their voluntary status. Many of them, as we have seen, were large and well-organized schools, funded partly by Government grants and partly by deductions made from the workmen's wages. At Crewe in Cheshire, the railway company, which had established schools for its employees, was opposed to the setting up of a school board with the power to levy a rate on property (including the extensive railway property) in the town.[1] No doubt similar considerations account for the continuance of works schools in Wales until the 1890s, and the earliest surviving schools in the Valleys tend to be Edwardian in date. Nevertheless, the changes made in the provision of elementary education were fundamental. In 1869 there were 1.8 million school places in England and Wales, wholly provided by the voluntary bodies. By 1898 the number of places had risen to 5.3 million, nearly half of which (2.6 million) had been provided by the school boards.[2] The boards were especially active in the large towns: Cardiff School Board claimed as early as 1883 that it had provided 7,437 school places, compared with the 7,186 places provided by the voluntary schools when the Board had commenced work.[3]

Although the Education Act of 1870 applied equally to both England and Wales, the situation in Wales was different. Official statistics for education in the nineteenth century lump together the figures for England and Wales, and strictly comparable figures are hard to come by. The 'battle of statistics', which had begun with the Religious Census of

[1] W. H. Chaloner, *The Social and Economic Development of Crewe, 1780-1923* (Manchester University Press, 1950), 61-4, 222-48.
[2] Government statistics, quoted in more detail in C. Birchenough, *History of Elementary Education in England and Wales* (London, University Tutorial Press, 1927), 140-41.
[3] *The Builder*, 1883B, 195.

1851, continued with unabated vigour during the second half of the century in the field of education as a whole, but the partisan nature of the figures produced makes them somewhat suspect. The rate of school building gives a more reliable measure of the work of the school boards *vis-à-vis* the voluntary societies. Some indication of the position in Wales may be obtained from the survey of the dates of elementary-school buildings carried out in 1962 and published in the Gittins Report of 1967 (see Table XI).

TABLE XI

THE DATES OF PRIMARY SCHOOL BUILDINGS IN WALES AND ENGLAND (1962)

Source : Central Advisory Council for Education (Wales), *Primary Education in Wales* (London, 1967), p.458.

Age of oldest main building still in use	Wales %	England %
Pre-1875	26.7	31.25
1875-1902	35.0	28.43
1903-1918	18.7	12.26
1919-1944	8.2	11.79
1945-1962	11.4	16.26

The authors of the Gittins Report suggested that the lower percentage of pre-1875 school buildings in Wales was the result of 'fewer of the Church foundations which form a majority of the pre-1875 schools of England'. Such an interpretation fails to take account of the rural depopulation which took place in Wales in the late nineteenth and early twentieth centuries, and which was more comparable with the situation in the Highlands of Scotland than most parts of England. Many of the smaller voluntary schools in Wales, both National and British, were closed through lack of pupils. This also affected some of the rural board schools, as, for example, the school at Maestir, near Lampeter in Dyfed, which was built in 1880 and closed in 1916, and has recently been re-erected at St Fagans Folk Museum.[4] However, rural

---

[4] Described in G. D. Nash, *Victorian School-days in Wales* (Cardiff, University of Wales Press, 1991).

depopulation had an even more marked effect on the voluntary schools which, as we have seen, had been built in considerable numbers earlier in the century.

The percentages given in Table XI for the periods 1875-1902 and 1903-1918 show more significant differences between Wales and England. During these periods the movement of population from the countryside was more than counterbalanced by the further rapid growth of population in the towns. Between 1871 and 1901 the population of Wales as a whole increased from under one-and-a-half million to over two millions. During the same period, the population of Cardiff increased by 316 per cent to 164,333, while Newport increased by 149 per cent to 67,276, and Swansea by 83 per cent to 94,537. All three towns were recognized as county boroughs in 1888, with the same wide powers of self-government as those accorded to the county councils. This was also the period of the ascendancy of Liberal Nonconformity in Wales and of the development of coal production and export on an unprecedented scale. These factors explain the higher proportion of new schools built in Wales between 1875 and 1918. The subsequent decline in the rate of school building was a sad reflection of the severe economic depression of the inter-war years, which affected south Wales more acutely than most parts of England, and continued to restrict the rate of school building after the second world war. For the present purpose, it is sufficient to note that the last thirty years of the nineteenth century clearly constituted a period of major advance in elementary school provision in Wales.

The Elementary Education Act of 1870 withdrew all capital grants to voluntary societies towards the cost of new school buildings, though proposals already under consideration were permitted to continue, and grants continued to be paid towards the running costs of voluntary schools deemed to be efficient. In England, this led to a considerable burst of activity in an attempt by the churches to 'fill the gaps' before school boards had got under way and capital grants disappeared. In Wales, this provision was of little interest to

Nonconformists, who were content with the non-denominational instruction provided in the board schools. Some Anglican schools continued to be built, chiefly in the larger towns, and an architecturally distinguished National school was, for example, built in the village of Gyffin, near Conwy, as late as 1910 (this was designed by the talented local architect, H. L. North, and still survives, though no longer in use as a school). The Roman Catholics, also, continued to build schools in the urban areas. These were usually financed from the pennies of the poor, but in south Wales, as earlier in the north, wealthy patrons gave their support: thus, St Paul's Catholic school in Tyndall Street, Cardiff, was built in 1876 to the design of James and Seward, at the sole expense of the Marquis of Bute.[5]

In general, however, innovation in school architecture and design moved to the school boards, and there is some evidence of a retreat in Anglican school effort. In Anglesey, eight National or parochial schools were transferred to school boards in the 1870s and a further four in the 1880s.[6] At Bersham, near Wrexham, the National school was transferred to the school board, which converted it into an infants' school and built a new board school alongside it for the older children. The latter building survives as the Bersham Heritage Centre and is heavily Gothic in style, perhaps influenced by the architecture of the former National school, which has now been demolished. (By contrast, the purpose-built school erected by the neighbouring school board at Acrefair has the semi-circular window heads and margin panes characteristic of Nonconformist chapels in the area.) At Nantglyn, also in Denbighshire and strongly Nonconformist in character, the National school was leased to the school board; when a later rector attempted in the 1890s to cancel the lease and re-establish the National school, he was informed by the Education Department in London that, if the school board was obliged to build a new board school,

[5] *The Builder*, 1876, 1082.
[6] D. A. Pretty, *Two Centuries of Anglesey Schools* (Anglesey Antiquarian Society, 1977), 324-5.

grant would be withdrawn from the former National school, which effectively blocked the proposal.[7]

Much local research would be needed to establish how far cases of transfer such as those mentioned above were general throughout Wales, but they confirm the impression that during the late Victorian period the National schools were in an embattled position, perhaps holding their own but certainly not expanding.[8] It also appears that in many places any increase in the local child population provided the opportunity for the erection of a small board school, even when there was already a National school nearby. For example, at Cynwyd in Merioneth, the National school of 1864 was largely made redundant by the building of a board school in the same village in 1889; similarly, at Llanarth in Cardiganshire, the Gothic school designed in 1859 by R. J. Withers, which we noted in a previous chapter, soon had as its rival a new board school (still in use), erected directly opposite it in 1884. Other examples could be given of new board schools erected close to earlier National schools, and in most cases the National schools have been closed while the board schools were later taken over by the local education authority and are still in use.

The sources available for the study of the board school buildings in Wales are relatively plentiful. School boards were not given capital grants by the Government to erect new schools, but were able, subject to the approval of the Education Department in London, to take out loans from the Public Works Loan Board, which were then repaid over a lengthy period from the local rate and Government revenue grant.[9] Very few of the original plans have survived in county

[7] E. Griffiths, *Nantglyn* (Nantglyn Community Council, 1984), 18-23.
[8] According to the *Digest of Welsh Historical Statistics* (Welsh Office, 1985), II, 210, between 1886 and 1900 the number of board schools in Wales increased from 702 to 893, while the number of Anglican schools decreased from 705 to 687. Roman Catholic schools increased from 44 to 51 over the same period. There were also 78 unspecified voluntary schools in existence in 1900 (probably Works schools).
[9] The author has failed to locate the plans submitted by school boards in Wales to the Education Department in London, in connection with their applications for loans.

record offices, the main exceptions being the large urban schools of the 1890s whose documentation was usually passed on to the local councils which took over from the school boards in 1902; some of these plans were later passed on to local record offices or survive (usually on microfiche) in county architects' departments or the property service agencies set up under their control. Minute books of the numerous school boards also survive, somewhat patchily, in local record offices and usually give information about the financing of new schools, but only rarely describe the accommodation in detail and sometimes omit the names of the architects. Much the best sources from which to obtain an overall picture of the extensive building programmes undertaken by the school boards are the contemporary architectural journals. In particular, *The Builder,* which was the earliest and most influential of these journals, contains much information about Victorian buildings of all types, including schools.

The results of combing through the volumes of *The Builder* for references to board schools built in Wales between 1870 and 1902 are set out in Appendix IV. The coverage of Welsh schools, though certainly not complete, is probably representative. The references to rural board schools come mainly from the 1870s, since this was a new building type of wide interest to practising architects, who took full advantage of the almost universal practice adopted by school boards of inviting professional architects to design their schools; the building work was also normally put out to tender. In addition, the larger boards often organized architectural competitions for which small premiums were paid. The coverage of rural schools, especially after 1880, is inadequate and has to be supplemented by local research: for example, there appear to be no references to board schools in Pembrokeshire, where a number of notable examples survive, such as those by T. P. Reynolds at Bolton Hill, near Haverfordwest, and at Milford Haven. The journals tend to concentrate on the urban areas, where the major buildings and innovations were taking place. Glamorgan and Monmouthshire are particularly well represented in the pages of *The Builder* and of its later rival *The Building News*.

First, who were the architects who designed the new board schools in Wales? Many of them worked in a limited geographical area and achieved only a local reputation, but the great majority were trained and experienced in their profession. An exception, which perhaps proves the rule, was W. C. Williams, the chairman of the school board at Llandwrog in Caernarfonshire, who himself 'drew up the plans' for new schools at Nantlle and Penffordd. He was an agent to the Newborough Estate and his career provides a salutary warning against stereotyping Victorian Welshmen: he was a Congregationalist in religion, but he had as a boy attended both National and British schools and, besides being the chairman of the local school board, was also a manager of the National school in Llandwrog.[10] Some of the architects who designed board schools in Wales we have already met as designers of National or British schools. For example, E. H. Lingen Barker, who had a very wide practice based in Hereford, had designed several National schools in Radnorshire and later became the architect to no less than ten school boards, most of them in Wales, while Richard Owens of Liverpool, whom we noted as the designer of an Undenominational school in Flintshire, went on to design a number of board schools in Denbighshire. Owen Morris Roberts of Porthmadog, who designed British schools in Merioneth, is known from other sources to have designed the new board schools at Ffestiniog, Tanygrisiau, and elsewhere in the slate-quarrying area. On the other hand, none of the celebrated architects such as Scott or Street, who frequently designed National schools, appear to have designed board schools. Their buildings usually demanded wealthier patrons than were available among even the larger school boards, and school architecture, as we shall see, was becoming more specialized in its requirements. In addition, the great increase

---

[10] R. H. Mair, *The School Boards . . . Biographical sketches of Members of School Boards* (London, Dean & Son, 1872), 78, 112.

in the volume of building work of all kinds during the late Victorian period enabled local architects to emerge, often with extensive practices. The system of tendering brought into Wales a number of English firms. The board schools at Llanaelhaearn in Caernarfonshire and Rhydypennau in Cardiganshire (both of which survive) were designed by Walter Thomas of Liverpool, who may well have had Welsh connections. There were, however, no such connections in the case of Alexander & Henman of Stockton-on-Tees, who designed board schools at Bryn-mawr and Aberdare, or Szlumper & Aldwinckle of London, who designed the large board school which still survives at Aberystwyth and whose names, *The Builder* hoped, would be carefully spelt. Other architects, though newcomers to Wales, settled down to establish local or regional practices. One such was the leading Cardiff architect, Edwin Seward, who was born at Yeovil in Somerset and had a long professional career in south Wales. Others were born and practised in Wales, such as E. M. Bruce Vaughan, a native of Cardiff, who restored or built twenty-five churches in Wales and also designed a number of schools. E. A. Landsdowne of Newport established a very extensive school practice in Monmouthshire, and was co-architect of the town hall and municipal offices at Newport. Similarly, T. P. Martin of Swansea and George Morgan of Carmarthen developed important architectural practices in south Wales, including schools.[11] The Victorian Society has recently published a full-scale biography of John Douglas, the Chester architect, by the late Edward Hubbard,[12] and it is to be hoped that in the future there will be more detailed studies of some of the local architects who made important contributions to the built environment of Wales.

The architectural styles used for the new board schools to

---

[11] On these architects, see the Biographical Files in the RIBA Library, and T. Lloyd, 'George Morgan of Carmarthen, Architect' in *Capel Newsletter*, No. 11 (1990). See also J. B. Hilling, *Cardiff and the Valleys: Architecture and Townscape* (London, Lund Humphries, 1973).
[12] E. Hubbard, *The Work of John Douglas* (London, The Victorian Society, 1991).

some extent reflected developments in contemporary architecture as a whole. After about 1870, there was a marked reaction against Gothic forms, especially in domestic architecture. The 'battle of the styles' (Gothic versus Classical) had ended in stalemate: one finds a greater eclecticism and an exploration of many other styles, including the vernacular. G. F. Bodley and T. Garner, who were later to design the magnificent Decorated Gothic church of St German in the Splott area of Cardiff (1884), had, ten years earlier, designed a National school for the same industrial parish.[13] This building, which still survives in Metal Street, Cardiff, has recently been converted into flats (called 'St German's Court') and its design foreshadowed the simpler, non-ecclesiastical styles which later came to be used for schools and other public buildings, especially in the urbanized areas of Wales. E. R. Robson, who was appointed official architect to the London School Board on a full-time basis in 1871, advocated a return to the 'Queen Anne' style for school buildings in his classic book on *School Architecture* (1874).[14] He stressed the importance of good proportions and the use of traditional building materials (which, in the case of London, mainly comprised the local, pale yellow, stock bricks, relieved by bands of red brick); sash windows and shaped or Dutch gables were also characteristic features of his schools, which are still widely admired by architectural historians. On the other hand, Martin and Chamberlain, who were the principal architects employed by the Birmingham School Board, used Gothic forms, but in a new and, on the whole, lighter vein. Their schools were regarded by contemporaries as 'the best buildings in the neighbourhood', and are still recognized as notable works of Victorian architecture.[15]

A study of the many surviving board schools in Wales shows that some of these new ideas influenced school

[13] Plan in Glamorgan Record Office, ref. D/D PRO/EBG/19.
[14] E. R. Robson, *School Architecture* (reprinted with an introduction by Malcolm Seaborne. Leicester University Press, 1972), ch. XVI.
[15] F. W. Greenacre, *The Best Buildings in the Neighbourhood* (Birmingham, The Victorian Society, 1968).

architects in Wales but, as one would expect, in varying degrees. Most of the rural board schools were relatively small buildings without any architectural pretensions, though they often used simplified Gothic forms (as, for example, the school designed by George Morgan at Whitland in Carmarthenshire, illustrated on Plate 51). A notable characteristic of the Welsh rural schools was the continued use of stone rubble for the walls, and brick was not widely used until the 1890s. It is interesting to note that at Cwm Ffrwd in Monmouthshire, alternative tenders obtained in 1880 showed that a brick school would cost more than one built of stone, though this does not seem to have applied generally after about 1890. Similarly, at Newtown in 1873, it was found that clay tiles were more expensive than slates for roofing the new board school. None of the school boards in Wales could justify the employment of a full-time architect for their schools, but several of the larger boards entrusted their schools to a limited number of selected architects. This was not necessarily a disadvantage. In 1897 *The Builder* published a lengthy article on Cardiff, as one of a series on 'The Architecture of our Large Provincial Towns'. The writer, having noted a 'picturesque' board school, remarked that 'the size and architectural variety of the Board Schools is another characteristic of Cardiff; they are not built by an official architect on one model, but vary very much in style and appearance'.[16] The article included engravings of a board school in Severn Road, designed by Jones, Richards and Budgen, in a version of the Queen Anne style, and of a board school in Grangetown, designed and later enlarged by E. M. Bruce Vaughan with French Gothic detail. Both of these schools were still in use as primary schools in 1991, though with only about a quarter of the number of children for which they were originally designed. The school at Severn Road (c. 1895) has had its gables removed and its windows altered, but the school in Grangetown (1884-90) has retained its original external features on the St Fagans Street frontage.

---

[16] *The Builder,* 1897A, 243.

Better-preserved and, indeed, excellent examples of late Victorian board schools may still be seen in the Canton district of Cardiff, as at Radnor Road (designed by E. M. Bruce Vaughan in 1886), Landsdowne Road (between Surrey Street and Norfolk Street, designed by Veall and Sant in 1898), and at Virgil Street (Robert and Sidney Williams, 1900). The Landsdowne Road school was the largest of the Cardiff board schools and was designed for 1,484 pupils at a cost of £14,800, while the school in Virgil Street is particularly notable for the high quality of its carved stone-work. The Cardiff School Board also built schools in brick and terra-cotta, an example of which (the Roath Park School by E. W. M. Corbett, 1894-5) is illustrated on Plate 52. All these schools were built to the same plan. In each case, the infants' department was a single-storey building, and the older children were accommodated in an adjoining two-storey block, usually with the girls on the ground floor and the boys above. A detached house for the caretaker was also provided, and it may be noted that accommodation for a resident care-taker was invariably included in the larger board schools, each of which represented a considerable financial investment. This replaced the master's house, which had formed an integral part of the designs of earlier schools. The internal plan adopted for these Cardiff board schools was the so-called 'corridor plan' noted below.

At about this time, 'three-decker' schools were being built in the Swansea area, with the infants (as always) on the ground floor, the girls on the first floor, and the boys on the top floor. The most expensive of the schools noted in *The Builder* was the Manselton Board School in Manor Road, Swansea, which opened in 1902 and cost £23,500. This build-ing, which has recently been listed, was of three storeys, with additional mezzanine floors, and was built to accommodate 1,200 children. A London architect, G. E. T. Laurence, was employed to design the building, which was faced with stone (used in this case for reasons of prestige rather than for cheapness) and the style he used is described by CADW

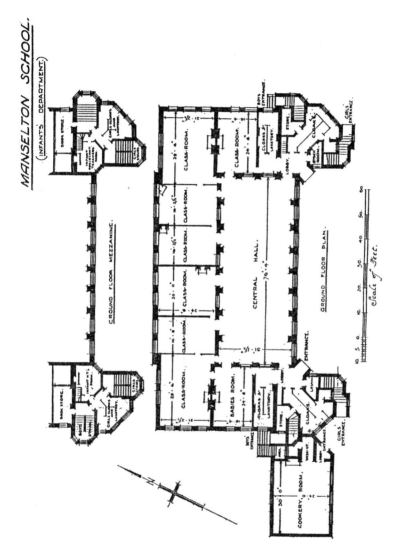

Fig. 25. Manselton Board School, Swansea, ground plan, 1900; architect G. E. T. Laurence.

(Welsh Historic Monuments) as 'Jacobethan' (see Plate 53).[17] The 'lodge' mentioned in the CADW description was the caretaker's house. The plans of the Manselton school have survived in the West Glamorgan county architect's department and the ground plan is reproduced as Fig. 25; this type of 'central-hall' plan is further discussed below. It may be added that the cost of building board schools increased from between £5 and £10 per place in the 1870s and 1880s, to between £10 and £15 in the 1890s.[18] (The Manselton school, which cost nearly £20 per place, was exceptional.) Some of this increase reflected the larger allowance permitted in the number of square feet per child, which rose from six square feet earlier in the century, to nine or ten square feet in the 1890s; inflation and better-quality building were also factors increasing the cost of schools as the century neared its close.

The internal planning and furnishing of the elementary schools showed considerable development during the last thirty years of the nineteenth century. The type of plan first recommended by the Committee of Council on Education in 1851, consisting of a schoolroom with three rows of desks arranged on the long side of the room, and with an associated galleried classroom, was still being recommended, with minor modification, in the 1870s. The initiative in school planning, however, now passed to the London School Board and its architect, E. R. Robson. He had made a thorough study of school organization both in Britain and abroad, and suggested important alterations to the standard Government plan.[19] In the first place, he considered that the long desks, arranged in three rows, should be replaced by dual desks. Each class should consist of forty children, arranged in dual desks, five deep and four wide. The dual desks, if varied in height, could be placed on the level floor, but the teacher's

---

[17] *Buildings of Special Architectural or Historic Interest: City of Swansea* (Cardiff, CADW, 1987), 66.

[18] Caution is needed in interpreting figures given for the cost of school buildings: it is not always clear whether a figure quoted is the estimated cost, the contract price, or the final cost. The cost of the site, site works, internal fittings, and furnishing are also sometimes included.

[19] Robson, *School Architecture,* op. cit., ch. IX-XI.

view of the children could, if desired, be improved by raising the two back rows of desks on blocks of wood. He also recommended that dual desks should replace galleries in the classrooms for older children. Arrangements such as these gradually spread to other schools outside London, and the steeply-raised galleries (usually without desks) were confined to the infants' schools, where they continued in use until early in the present century. Robson also recommended that more than one classroom should be provided in association with the schoolroom, but he recognized that any increase in the number of separate classrooms depended on the employment of a larger number of fully-certificated teachers, who were still in limited supply.

The period from 1870 to 1900 therefore represented a transitional phase, with the number of classrooms slowly increasing as staffing improved. The classrooms were usually separated from the schoolroom by glazed partitions, since it was considered essential for the head teacher to retain visual contact with all the classes, which were often taken by inexperienced assistant- or pupil-teachers. As very much bigger schools came to be built in the larger towns, adequate circulation space also became of vital importance. During the 1890s, some of the large board schools in Wales, as elsewhere, were planned with wide corridors from which access was gained to the classrooms. These, however, were provided by omitting or reducing the traditional schoolroom, and the corridor-plan was later replaced by plans in which the large schoolroom was restored, but used only for assembly and drill, and not, as hitherto, for normal class-teaching. The classrooms were arranged around the schoolroom, which was now called the 'central hall'. This type of plan also influenced the layout of some of the larger Sunday schools in Wales, which reached the height of their architectural development at the turn of the century.[20] It is interesting to note that school-planning, having in the present century dissolved into dispersed classrooms reached by long corridors and covered

[20] See W. B. Rees, *Chapel Building* (Cardiff Printing Works, 1903), ch. VIII on 'Sunday Schools'.

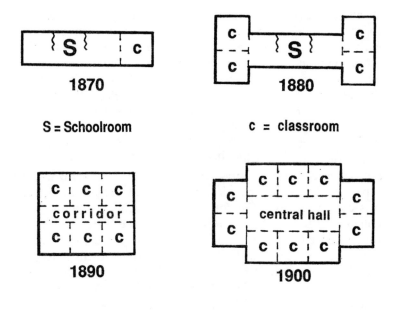

Wavy lines indicate curtains
Broken lines indicate openings or partitions

Fig. 26. Diagram showing the development of elementary school plans, 1870-1900.

ways, has more recently returned to some of the planning principles of the late Victorian board schools.[21]

These developments, which varied a great deal in the extent to which they were adopted in Wales, are summarized in diagrammatic form in Fig. 26. The actual situation was often a varied selection from all these elements, and the internal organization of the schools also depended to a considerable degree on the type of furniture provided for the children. School furniture has recently been recognized as an important part of the history of vernacular furniture, and Wales shared in its development.[22] The new board school at Aberystwyth adopted the type of dual desk used by the London School Board, which had been patented by a Mr Moss, while a new school at Hay-on-Wye ordered desks from a Mr Lewes of Ross. On the other hand, E. M. Sneyd-Kynnesley, in his account of the schools which he inspected in north Wales in the early 1870s, remarked of one of the National schools that 'there are desks for the upper standards only; the other children sit on benches with no back-rails: both desks and benches are evidently the work of the carpenter on the estate',[23] a situation closely comparable with the furnishing of the schoolroom of 1804 at Trelech a'r Betws, illustrated earlier in Fig. 5. Factory-produced furniture was now gradually introduced throughout Wales, and the products of the large English firms specializing in school furniture (such as E. J. Arnold of Leeds) penetrated into most schools. Wales itself made an important contribution to the spread of elementary education in Britain and abroad by the mass-production of writing slates, whose use had been advocated by Joseph Lancaster earlier in the century.[24] In north Wales,

---

[21] See M. Seaborne. 'The post-war revolution in primary school design', in R. Lowe (ed.), *The Changing Primary School* (London, The Falmer Press, 1987), 17-31.

[22] Christopher Gilbert, *English Vernacular Furniture 1750-1900* (New Haven and London, Yale University Press, 1991), ch. 11 on 'Schools'. He points out (p. 165) that 'most mass-produced late-Victorian school furniture evolved from traditional prototypes'.

[23] E. M. Sneyd-Kynnersley, *H.M.I. Some passages in the life of one of H.M. Inspectors of Schools* (London, Macmillan, 1910), 45.

[24] J. Lancaster, *Improvements in Education* (London, Darton & Harvey, 1805), 13 ('10 Dozen Slates, at 4s.6d. per Dozen').

the pieces of slate not suitable for splitting up into slabs were used for the making of writing slates, and a 'writing slate manufactory' at Abergynolwyn in Merioneth was described in some detail in an account of the slate quarries of north Wales published in 1873.[25]

Contemporary photographs of school interiors have survived far less commonly than those of school groups taken outside the building. A photograph of children at the former Acrefair Board School in Denbighshire, taken in 1905, shows four- or five-seater desks still in use (Plate 54); they appear to be of different heights, or are possibly on a stepped floor, and it is also likely that the children were squeezed up in the desks for the purpose of the photograph. Other Victorian photographs preserved in county record offices show the old system of five- or six-seater desks on a stepped floor (as at Frongoch school, Denbigh), while others show the later arrangement of dual desks set out in rows on a level floor (as at the new board school at Penarth, near Cardiff, erected in 1898). Plate 55 shows children and teachers at Pentre Rhondda school at the turn of the century. The long desks have been replaced by dual desks, but the stepped floor remains; the glazed partition separating the schoolroom from the classroom may also be seen.

Changes in the curriculum also influenced the design of the elementary schools. The need for greater differentiation between school classes became more apparent as attendance improved and extra subjects were taught. The Revised Code of 1862 had organized the elementary curriculum above the infant level into six standards, with reading, writing and arithmetic forming the compulsory 'class' subjects, and with other subjects (including geography, history, algebra, geometry, the natural sciences and modern languages) which could in theory be taught in the top three standards as

---

[25] M. J. T. Lewis (ed.), *The Slate Quarries of North Wales in 1873* (Snowdonia National Park Study Centre, 1987), 56. Dafydd Roberts of the Museum of the North at Llanberis informs me that several manufacturers of school slates advertised in the Bangor and Caernarfon trade directories. There was also a school slate manufactory at Pwll Fannog, on Anglesey, near the Stephenson rail bridge.

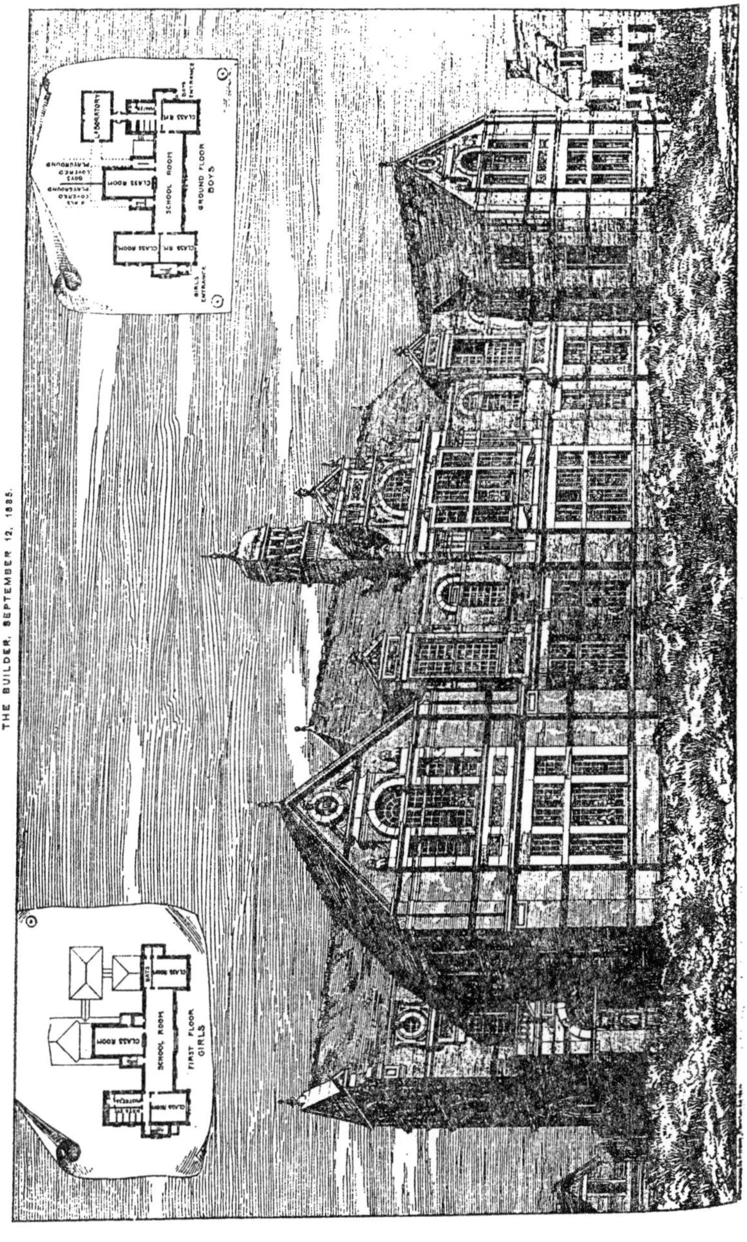

Fig. 27 Cardiff Higher Grade School. James, Seward & Thomas, 1885.

optional or 'specific' subjects. The Welsh language was recognized as a 'specific' subject in 1890, and as a 'class' subject in 1893. Technical subjects were also recognized at about the same time. A seventh standard had been added in 1882, and some schools were permitted to teach woodwork and cookery.

In some of the large towns, 'higher grade' board schools were built, which were financed partly from the rates and partly with grants from the Science and Art Department in South Kensington. *The Builder* carried reports of the building of higher grade schools at Cardiff (1885) and Llanelli (1889), while *The Building News* described and illustrated the higher grade school at Swansea (1891). The largest of these was the school for 800 boys and girls at Howard Gardens in Cardiff, designed by James, Seward and Thomas and shown in Fig. 27. This was a two-storey brick building with a schoolroom and four classrooms on the ground floor for the boys, and a schoolroom and three classrooms on the first floor for the girls. A distinctive new feature was the provision of a fully-equipped science laboratory on the ground floor. The school at Llanelli was somewhat smaller, with 640 pupils, and was a stone building in the Gothic style designed by E. H. Lingen Barker. Its main architectural feature was a central turret: this also provided the outlet for the used air from the class-rooms, which was conducted to the turret along wooden shafts (a method of ventilation used in many large board schools of this period). At Swansea, the higher grade school was also of stone, and was designed by a local architect, T. P. Martin (see Fig. 28). It was built in Dynevor Place to accommodate 480 boys, and was very well equipped. The accommodation included (in the semi-basement) two manual instruction rooms and a gymnasium, and, on the first floor, two art-rooms, a physics lecture-room, and a chemistry laboratory; the ground floor was occupied by classrooms and the offices of the school board. These schools anticipated the intermediate schools soon to be set up by county committees in all parts of Wales, but since they did not operate as county schools under the Welsh Intermediate Education Act of 1889,

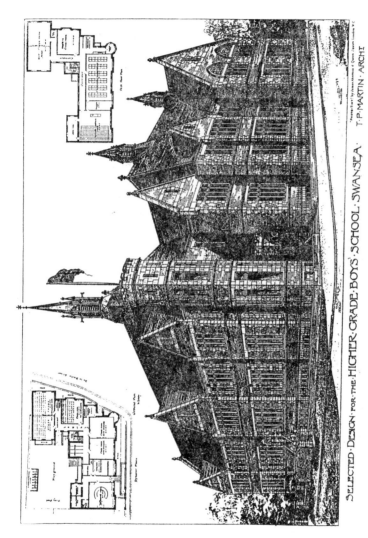

Fig. 28. Swansea Higher Grade School. T. P. Martin. 1891.

they later became municipal secondary schools. In any event, they were pioneer schools.

The days of the school boards were numbered, and the chief innovations in secondary education were made under the aegis of the new county and county borough councils, whose members were given the majority share of places on the joint education committees and county governing bodies responsible for carrying out the provisions of the Welsh Intermediate Education Act of 1889. This Act was the direct, if somewhat delayed, outcome of the Aberdare Report, and its effects on the endowed secondary schools in Wales and on the new schools established under its provisions merit a fuller treatment.

The very inadequate public provision for secondary education, which was still largely under the control of the Established Church at the time of the Aberdare Report, was mentioned at the end of the last chapter. Nonconformity in Wales was, however, now entering a period of confident consolidation of its predominant position. 'Conscience clauses' enabling the children of Nonconformist parents to opt out of Anglican religious instruction were no longer considered sufficient, and undenominational secondary schools governed by elected bodies, as already introduced for elementary education by the Education Act of 1870, were now demanded. The Aberdare Report was a real landmark in the history of education in Wales. It boldly declared that 'Wales has a distinct nationality of its own' requiring separate treatment, and Monmouthshire was firmly included within the Welsh sphere of influence. Although the educational outlook of the Aberdare Report was largely derived from the reports of the Schools Inquiry Commission of the 1860s, it was, politically, cast in a more radical mould: it affirmed that new secondary schools should be established in Wales, aided by the central government, democratically controlled, and free from denominational bias.

The recommendations of the Aberdare Report concerning the need for new university colleges in Wales were rapidly acted upon, but there was an eight-year gap before the Welsh

Intermediate Education Act was passed to reform secondary education.[26] There were two main reasons for the delay. In the first place, the Aberdare Committee had been unable to form a unanimous opinion about the new administrative framework needed to reorganize secondary education throughout Wales, and it was not until county and county borough councils were established in 1888 that a satisfactory framework became available. The second difficulty was over the question of finance. There was reluctance by the Government to authorize the levying of local rates for secondary-school purposes based on the precedent of the 1870 Act, which had authorized local rates for elementary schools only. The Welsh Intermediate Education Act of 1889 broke new ground in permitting county and county borough councils to levy a rate of a half-penny in the pound for the purpose of intermediate education, and the Technical Instruction Act of the same year, which applied to England as well as Wales, authorized the levying of a rate of a penny in the pound to sustain technical education, which could (and often did) include secondary-school provision. The Treasury was also opposed to the use of Exchequer funds for secondary-school purposes, and an important new feature of the Welsh Intermediate Education Act — and a main reason for the delay in passing it — was that it also provided for Treasury grants to be made, equal to the amounts raised by local rates. Thus, in Wales, the half-penny rate produced the equivalent of a penny rate, and Wales gained the benefit of the new emphasis on technical education at half the cost to local resources. In addition, the principle of non-denominational teaching was won, and a measure of co-ordination secured.

The Aberdare Committee considered that relatively few new schools would be needed, and the figures it produced would have resulted in very large secondary schools for that date, each of about 400 pupils; these were envisaged as of

---

[26] On the Act of 1889 and its consequences, see J. R. Webster, 'The Welsh Intermediate Education Act of 1889', *Welsh History Review*, 4 (1968-9), 273-291; and G. E. Jones, *Controls and Conflicts in Welsh Secondary Education 1889-1944* (Cardiff, University of Wales Press, 1982).

'Grade II' type, that is, semi-classical schools taking pupils up to the age of fourteen, or sixteen at the most. Although the need for secondary schools for girls was recognized, boys were to be given preference. Tuition fees were regarded as essential, and scholarships were to be provided only where endowment funds permitted. The main emphasis of the Aberdare Report was on the need to make better use of the endowments which already existed. In the event, the major endowments proved to be too firmly embedded in existing institutions to be prised away from them, and later attempts to release large endowments, such as those of Edmund Meyricke, or the Howell's endowments, or that belonging to the Welsh School (which had moved from London to Ashford in Middlesex in 1857) were largely unsuccessful. In 1898 the Charity Commissioners noted that only twelve per cent of the annual income of the newly-established intermediate schools (excluding the tuition fees paid by the parents) came from endowments, all the rest coming from the county rates, supplemented by Treasury grant and certain excise duties (the so-called 'whisky money') which became available for education throughout England and Wales in 1890.[27] Apart from the tuition fees which parents had to pay when a school actually opened, voluntary contributions were required to finance new school sites and buildings. These were forthcoming, even in those parts of Wales affected by industrial disputes (as in the slate-quarrying area of north Wales), and in rural areas suffering from the agricultural depression of the period. This was, indeed, a considerable achievement.

These developments could not, of course, have been foreseen in detail by members of the Aberdare Committee or by the framers of the Welsh Intermediate Education Act. It was much to the credit of the county and county borough councils in Wales that they all immediately agreed to adopt the Act, and great efforts were made to keep fees as low as possible and to establish scholarships on (for that time) a relatively generous scale. The Welsh Act of 1889 was, in fact, followed

[27] *The Welsh Intermediate Education Act 1889. Its Origins and Working* (London, Charity Commission, 1898), 35.

by one of the most remarkable decades in the history of secondary education in Wales. A whole network of county intermediate schools was established numbering over ninety by 1900. Some of these were still in temporary premises in 1900, but many new, purpose-built schools were erected throughout Wales. In the densely-populated areas, separate schools for boys and girls were established; elsewhere, the sexes were separated in 'dual' schools under one roof, while in the most sparsely-populated districts mixed schools were set up. It would be possible to criticize the proliferation of small schools — the largest of the schools in 1900 was the Cardiff Girls' Intermediate School with 245 pupils, and many (as in Montgomeryshire) were at first barely viable as secondary institutions. They nevertheless provided the essential nuclei for the future development of secondary education in Wales.

The endowed secondary schools which existed in 1880, and the county intermediate schools established in 1900, are listed in Table XII. In 1880 there were thirty endowed schools educating 1,540 boys and 263 girls, a total of 1,803; in 1900 there were ninety-four county schools educating 3,799 boys and 3,646 girls, a total of 7,445. It is worth considering why some of the endowed schools became county schools, which normally meant that the majority of their governors were appointed by county or county borough councils, and how others successfully resisted inclusion in county schemes. The size of the endowments was an important determining factor, but it was not the only one: the proportion of boarding pupils, the state of the buildings, and the balance of political power in the localities were also important elements in deciding the future of individual schools. The Central Welsh Board, which was set up in 1896, designated some of the county schools as 'old foundations reconstituted under the Welsh Act', and these are marked with an asterisk in Table XII. A detailed review of the situation, county by county, will enable us to draw together some of the threads from previous chapters, and to show how the complex factors affecting the development of secondary education resolved themselves in different parts of Wales.[28]

In Anglesey, the grammar school at Beaumaris was one of only five endowed schools in Wales with an annual endow-

TABLE XII — SECONDARY SCHOOL PROVISION 1880-1900

Sources: The *Aberdare Report* (1881) and *Central Welsh Board, Reports on County Schools* (1900)

In the list below, B stands for Boys, G for Girls, D for Dual (boys and girls in separate departments) and M for Mixed. An asterisk indicates a pre-existing school which became a County School.

County	Endowed Schools (1880)	County Intermediate Schools (1900)
Anglesey	Beaumaris B*	Beaumaris D*, Llangefni D.
Brecon	Brecon B	Brecon B, Brecon G, Bryn-mawr D, Builth D.
Caernarfon	Bangor B* Botwnnog B*	Bangor B*, Bangor G, Bethesda M, Botwnnog D*, Caernarfon D, Llandudno D, Pen-y-groes D, Porthmadog D, Pwllheli D.
Cardigan	Cardigan B Lampeter B Ystradmeurig B	Aberaeron D, Aberystwyth D, Cardigan D, Llandysul D, Tregaron D.
Carmarthen	Carmarthen B* Llandovery B	Carmarthen B* Carmarthen G, Llandeilo D, Llandovery G, Llanelli B, Llanelli G, Whitland D.
Denbigh	Denbigh B* Denbigh G Llanrwst B* Ruabon B* Ruthin B Wrexham B	Abergele M, Denbigh B*, Llangollen D, Llanrwst D*, Ruabon B*, Ruthin G, Wrexham B, Wrexham G.
Flint	Hawarden B St Asaph B*	Hawarden D, Holywell D, Mold D, Rhyl D, St Asaph B*.
Glamorgan	Cowbridge B Gelli-gaer B* Llandaff G Swansea B*	Aberdare D, Barry D, Bridgend D, Cardiff B, Cardiff G, Cowbridge G, Gelli-gaer B*, Gelli-gaer G, GowertonD, Merthyr D, Neath D, Penarth B, Penarth G, Pontypridd D, Port Talbot D, Porth D, Swansea B*, Swansea G, Ystalyfera D, (Howell's, Llandaff G).

[28] The figures mentioned for the number of pupils and endowment income in 1880 are taken from the 'Tabulated Returns' published as Appendix 3 in vol. I of the Aberdare Report. It should be noted that the figures of endowment income given there are gross, not net.

County	Endowed Schools (1880)	County Intermediate Schools (1900)
Merioneth	Bala B* Dolgellau B Dolgellau G*	Bala B*, Bala G, Barmouth D, Dolgellau B, Dolgellau G*, Ffestiniog D, Tywyn D.
Monmouth	Abergavenny B Monmouth B Usk B	Abergavenny G, Abertillery D, Ebbw Vale D, Newport B, Newport G, Pontypool G, Pont-y-waun D, Tredegar D.
Montgomery	Deuddwr B	Llanfair Caereinion M, Llanfyllin M, Llanidloes B, Llanidloes G, Machynlleth M, Newtown B, Newtown G, Welshpool B, Welshpool G.
Pembroke	Haverford-west B*	Fishguard M, Haverford-west B*, Haverfordwest G, Milford D, Narberth D, Pembroke Dock D, St David's M, Tenby D.
Radnor	Presteigne B*	Llandrindod Wells D, Presteigne B*.

Notes: 1. Cardiff, Swansea and Newport became county boroughs in 1888.
2. Howell's School, Llandaff, was governed by a separate Scheme.
3. Presteigne became a mixed school in 1902.

ment income of over £1,000. The other four (Christ College at Brecon, the two Howell's schools for girls at Denbigh and and Llandaff, and Monmouth School) retained their independence, and the incorporation of Beaumaris school in the Anglesey county scheme, in spite of violent protests, may be accounted for by the inadequacy of its seventeenth-century building and by the strength of local political and economic pressures, since the inhabitants of Llangefni and Holyhead were determined to obtain some share of the only major endowment on the island.[29] By contrast, in Breconshire, Christ College, with its extensive new or restored buildings and strong boarding element, was never seriously considered for incorporation in the Breconshire county scheme, and new county schools for the town of Brecon were envisaged from the start.

In Caernarfonshire, the Friars School at Bangor was unsuccessful in resisting inclusion in the county scheme. It was

[29] For a blow-by-blow account, see D. A. Pretty, *Two Centuries of Anglesey Schools,* ch. 8. A county school was opened at Llangefni in 1897 and at Holyhead in 1901 (new buildings in 1900 and 1904).

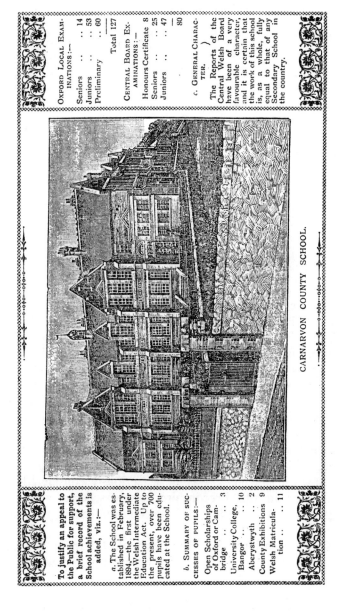

Fig. 29. Caernarfon County Intermediate School. Page of fund-raising programme, 1901.

still housed in its outdated building of 1789 and the unhealthy location of the school (which compelled it to move temporarily to Penmaen-mawr during a typhoid epidemic at Bangor in 1881) discouraged boarders. In 1888 a new school building was planned, to be built on the outskirts of the town, which would have provided up-to-date accommodation for boarders, but uncertainty about the future of the school delayed the start of the building until 1899, by which time Friars had become a county school. The only other endowed grammar school in Caernarfonshire was at Botwnnog, which, with its small endowment, could not afford the extensions required to its building of 1848: it joined the county scheme, apparently without protest. The other county schools had to start from scratch and it usually took several years to pay off the loans which had to be taken out. Typical of the fund-raising events organized was the 'Grand Chinese Bazaar' held at Caernarfon in 1901.[30] A page of the programme issued on this occasion, showing the new county school building which in 1900 replaced the temporary accommodation used by the school, is reproduced as Fig. 29.

In Cardiganshire, the Central Welsh Board did not acknowledge the new county school at Cardigan as an 'old foundation', presumably because the grammar schoolroom in the guildhall, and its miniscule endowment income of £21 a year, reverted to the corporation. The new county school opened near Victoria Gardens in Cardigan in 1898, and a photograph of the opening ceremony is reproduced as Plate 56. It shows C. Morgan-Richardson addressing the assembled company. He had been the principal organizer of the building fund, which was collected largely from church and chapel congregations. Since he was a churchman, he was not at first appointed to the school's governing body by the strongly Liberal county council, but, shortly afterwards, two of the eleven governors resigned to make way for two churchpeople, one of whom was Morgan-Richardson.[31] As for the other

[30] I am very grateful to the Associate Librarian, the Welsh Library, University College, Bangor, for drawing my attention to this programme.
[31] D. Davies in *The Cardigan and Tivy-side Advertizer*, 23 April, 1986, a reference I owe to the Senior Librarian, Public Library, Aberystwyth.

endowed schools in the county, the famous school at Ystrad-meurig, which had only thirty-two boys on the roll in 1880, refused to move to the more populous town of Lampeter, where the old grammar school had never had an endowment. Both schools were in outdated buildings, and were eventually closed, while a new county school was built at Tregaron.

In Carmarthenshire there was less party-warfare in implementing the new Act. The boys' grammar school at Carmarthen had moved to a new building in 1883, but its endowment was a very small one. Inclusion in the county scheme made it possible to enlarge the boys' school and to build a new girls' school alongside it. These buildings are now in use as a co-educational, comprehensive school (Ysgol Bro Myrddin) in Richmond Terrace. Llandovery College had, like Christ College at Brecon, a majority of boarders, all of whom were by this date accommodated on the college's excellent site. It was not pressed to join the county scheme, though it agreed to accept scholarship boys. A new county school for girls was built at Llandovery, which later became a mixed school (now Ysgol Pantycelyn in Cil-y-cwm Road). New county schools were also built at Llanelli and in other parts of the county which had not previously had any endowments.

In Denbighshire, the Howell's school for girls at Denbigh retained its independence, but the county governing body erected a new school for boys in the town. The old grammar school at Denbigh had earlier moved to a house which still survives in Park Street, and, since the proceeds of its sale went to the county council, the new county school was acknowledged as a school of old foundation. The grammar schools at Llanrwst and Ruabon were both in unsatisfactory buildings and clearly needed the help of the county committee to modernize their buildings. Only Ruthin school successfully resisted incorporation in the county scheme in 1894, but it did so only through an eleventh-hour intervention by Lord Kenyon and the Bishop of St Asaph in a House of Lords' debate. It was helped by the fact that in the previous year an excellent new building had been opened on the Mold road, financed by a public subscription and designed by the same architect (John Douglas) who had also been engaged at Bangor, but whose plan for a new school there had been shelved.[32] One curious result of the existence of an independent school for boys at Ruthin and of an independent school for girls at Denbigh was that for some years secondary-school boys from Ruthin travelled daily to Denbigh to attend the boys' county school there, while girls from Denbigh travelled daily to Ruthin, where a new county school for girls was established in a former mansion.[33] At Wrexham, the poorly-endowed grammar school had closed in 1880, and its clientele was largely being catered for by a flourishing private school, with strong Wesleyan affiliations, in Grove Park; this became the nucleus of the new county schools for boys and girls, whose continuity with the former grammar school was, quite logically, ignored by the Central Welsh Board.

In Flintshire, the grammar school at Hawarden, with a very small endowment and a seventeenth-century building housing only thirty-four boys in 1880, was unable to resist inclusion in the county scheme. The old building near the church was sold to W. E. Gladstone to house his books (it was on the site of the present St Deiniol's Library), and the school's historian claims that the revenues of the school were handed over to the county;[34] in this case, however, the Central Welsh Board declined to acknowledge that the new county school owed anything to the former grammar school. The only other endowed grammar school in Flintshire, at St Asaph, was also poorly endowed, and although it had a fine new building designed in Tudor Gothic style by R. Lloyd Williams and erected by public subscription in 1877, it failed

---

[32] Both schools organized architectural competitions in 1888 and Douglas & Fordham won both competitions. *The Builder* printed the plans of the runners-up in the competition for Ruthin (1889A,31) and Bangor (1889A, 318), but unfortunately not those by Douglas & Fordham.

[33] See *Ruthin County School for Girls 1899-1938* (Ruthin, 1988). This school was 'dualized' in 1938 and now forms part of Ysgol Brynhyfryd (Comprehensive School).

[34] W. B. Jones 'Hawarden Grammar School', *Flints. Hist. Soc. Trans.*, 6 (1916-17), 69.

to attract many boarders.[35] It was obliged, under protest, to join the county scheme, and its 1877 building now forms part of Ysgol Glan Clwyd, which in 1956 became the first bilingual secondary school to be opened in Wales, with Welsh taught as a first language.

It was in Glamorgan that the growth of industry and the increase in population threw into sharpest relief the inadequacy of the provision for secondary education. The main focus of controversy was the grammar school at Cowbridge, which was poorly endowed and occupied a cramped site in the centre of the town. It refused to join the county scheme, and its numbers continued to decline until in 1919 it was taken over from Jesus College, Oxford, by the county council. The Howell's school at Llandaff was more co-operative, and agreed to take scholarship girls and to be examined by the Central Welsh Board; it does not, however, appear to have lost control of its governing body to the county council, and its buildings were enlarged in 1900.[36] At Swansea, the old-established grammar school was housed in modern buildings and was relatively well endowed. In 1880 it had sixty day boys and thirteen boarders, and it was clear that its future lay in its further development as a day school serving the local population. The foeffees unsuccessfully appealed against its inclusion as a county school, but others connected with the school must have appreciated the value of having the resources of the new county borough behind it. In 1897 it was reported that the boarding accommodation in the grammar school building had been converted into classrooms because of the increased number of day-boys.[37]

Similar considerations influenced the outcome of the negotiations relating to the endowed school at Gelli-gaer. As we noted in a previous chapter, this school had been founded in the eighteenth century to teach purely elementary subjects. It was situated in a growing industrial area near the Mon-

---

[35] *The Flintshire Observer*, 2 November, 1877, records the official opening. The school was designed for 48 boarders and 60 day boys and cost £4000.

[36] *The Builder*, 1900B, 16 (architect G. E. Halliday, cost £5287).

[37] CWB, *Report*, 1897.

mouthshire border, and in 1851-4 was rebuilt at Pengam. The new building was designed by John Prichard, the Llandaff diocesan architect, as an elementary school for 150 boys and 100 girls, with a chapel-of-ease attached to it. However, following a new scheme of 1874, it was reorganized as a grammar school for boys only, with provision for a separate girls' school to be built at a later date. This was eventually built as a county school, which opened at Hengoed in 1900, while the boys' school also became a county school and was considerably enlarged in 1902.[38]

Continuing our examination of the situation in the remaining counties, the main disagreement in Merioneth arose at Dolgellau. The Nonconformist foundation of Dr Williams' school for girls, which had recently opened at Dolgellau, readily agreed to join the county scheme, but the boys' grammar school in the town, though poorly endowed and in an antiquated building, declined to co-operate. The school trustees refused to allow the proposed new county school for boys to make temporary use of its building, and Bishop Lloyd of Bangor, who earlier in his career had been the school's headmaster, actually demanded that the key to the building should be returned to his solicitor without delay.[39] As a result, the county school met temporarily in a room belonging to Salem Chapel, until it moved to a new building (now part of Ysgol y Gader in Aran Road) in 1897. The grammar school at Bala posed fewer problems. Jesus College, Oxford, which had rebuilt the school in 1851, seems to have lost interest in it; in 1880 all but six of the twenty-three pupils were from Nonconformist homes, and there were no boarders. It became a county school and was later extended.

Monmouthshire, on the other hand, presented a totally different picture. The William Jones endowment was much the largest in the whole of Wales, with an annual income of £3,296 in 1880. The trustees, who were mainly members of

[38] A. Wright, *The History of Lewis' School, Pengam* (Newtown, Welsh Outlook Press, 1929), 61f. for the boys' school at Pengam, and 179f. for the girls' school at Hengoed.

[39] A. M. Rees and E. Jones, 'Dr John Elis' School, Dolgellau', *Journal of Merioneth Hist. Soc.*, 5 (1966), No. 2, 125.

the Haberdashers' Company in London, co-operated with the county committee, but on their own terms. The boys' school in Monmouth had already acquired large new buildings, as noted earlier, and the Company agreed that a new secondary school for girls should be erected in Monmouth at its own expense. This was built in 1897 on a prominent site over-looking the town and was designed by the Company's architect, Henry Stock. This school, which is still in use as an independent school, is an impressive stone structure of three storeys containing numerous classrooms and a large hall at right-angles to the main building.[40] The Haberdashers' Company also responded to the criticism that the benefits of the Jones endowment should not be limited to the county town alone. In 1897, the Company financed the building of a very imposing grammar school for boys at Pontypool, called the West Monmouth School.[41] This was also designed by Henry Stock, and, though mainly of brick, cost the consider-able sum of £23,340. It was built on an elevated site in what is now Blaendare Road in Pontypool and is at present a comprehensive school for boys and girls aged from eleven to sixteen. It was originally designed for 200 day boys and 70 boarders and is U-shaped in plan. One wing consisted of a large house for the headmaster, with dormitories and day rooms for the boarders behind it; in the centre was a large hall, and in the other wing were classrooms and specialist teaching rooms. Behind the classroom block there was (and still is) a free-standing building containing a swimming pool on the ground floor and a gymnasium above. There is, surprisingly, no published history of this school, and the reasons why it did not continue as an independent boarding and day school, for which purpose it was designed, are not entirely clear. In the meantime, a county school for girls was established at Pontypool in the premises of the former Baptist

---

[40] On the reorganization of the endowment, see H. A. Ward, *Monmouth School 1614-1964* (London, Haberdashers' Company, 1964), 26. On the Monmouth Girls' School building, *The Builder*, 1897B, 502.
[41] The West Monmouth School is described in *The Builder*, 1898B, 535. I am very grateful to the Deputy Headmaster, Mr. R. Jenkins, for con-ducting me around the building.

college in Pen-y-garn Road, which is still part of the Trevethin Comprehensive School that developed from the county school. Some indication of the possible reasons for the later change in the character of the West Monmouth school is provided by the parallel, though more modest, development of the grammar school at Abergavenny, which finally moved from the town centre to the Hereford Road in 1898. The Haberdashers' Company made a grant of £3,000 towards the cost of the new building, whose total cost was £6,945, the balance coming from local subscriptions.[42] The architect was E. A. Johnson of Abergavenny, and he adopted the traditional Tudor Gothic style for his building. A 'traditional' photograph was taken as the new building neared completion and is reproduced as Plate 57. It shows (fifth from the left) the stonemason with his maul, and (on the extreme right) the carpenters with their saws. The man holding a rolled-up plan is probably not the clerk of works, who may be the only person shown in the photograph wearing both a bowler hat and a jacket, and sitting down; that person, however, might be the architect. Although the building included a chemistry laboratory, the curriculum continued to be on traditional classical lines and comparatively few pupils were attracted to it. This school was not included in the Monmouthshire county scheme, but lack of numbers resulted in financial difficulties and led to its being taken over by the county council in 1910. Similarly, at Usk, the old grammar school, which had been rebuilt in 1862, was enlarged in 1898 but later came under the control of the county council. Its two-storey, stone building survives as a community centre in Maryport Street.

The endowed grammar schools in the three remaining counties may be dealt with quite briefly. The large and increasingly depopulated county of Montgomeryshire had only the eighteenth-century grammar school building at Deuddwr mentioned in a previous chapter, and new county schools

---

[42] G. V. Nelmes, 'A history of King Henry VIII's Boys Grammar School at Abergavenny', *Gwent Local History*, No. 60 (1986), 4-6. See also *The Builder*, 1898B, 348.

were set up in six centres of population in the county. In Pembrokeshire — a much more populous county — there was only the grammar school for boys at Haverfordwest. It had moved in 1856 from a site near the parish church to a new building (now demolished) in Dew Street; in 1880 it had an endowment income of £577 and a school roll of fifty-one. This building was enlarged in 1881 and there appear to have been few difficulties in later converting it into a county school for boys.[43] The element of continuity was recognized by the Central Welsh Board, which, however, omitted to acknowledge that the new county school for girls, which was established in Haverfordwest at about the same time, benefited by the transfer to it of the elementary-school endowment made by Mary Tasker, which had previously been used to upgrade the education given to girls in the town.[44] Tasker's Girls' School, as it came to be known, had been provided with a new building in 1892, designed by T. P. Reynolds, which still stands on Tower Hill and is now used by the Little Theatre. Finally, in Radnorshire, the sixteenth-century grammar school at Presteigne had acquired a new building in 1860, but it was poorly endowed and was replaced by a new county school in 1898.[45] Another county school was built at Llandrindod Wells.

What of the brand new county schools which were built to fill some of the many gaps left by the endowed schools? It is more instructive in this case to consider their general characteristics, rather than attempt a county-by-county survey. An important general point is that most of these schools were, at first, relatively small, not only by present-day standards but also in comparison with many of the later Victorian board schools. Only nine of the ninety-four county schools (including those based on older foundations) had over 150 pupils on the roll in 1900, and all but one of these (the school at Caernarfon with 188 pupils) were in Glamorgan

[43] G. D. James, *The History of Haverfordwest Grammar School* (Haverford-west, Hammond, 1961), 23-4; *The Builder*, 1887B, 381.
[44] G. D. James, *The Town and County of Haverfordwest* (Haverfordwest, Hammond, 1958), 74f.
[45] W. H. Howse, *School and Bell* (Halesowen, Parkes, 1956), 41.

and Monmouthshire. The creation of large new secondary schools in areas with no previous experience of grammar or higher elementary education (as at Pontypool) was, owing to financial constraints, avoided. Despite their small initial size, however, the purpose-built county schools represented an important new building type. The need for a new kind of school building was clearly recognized when in 1890 the 'Tate Welsh Intermediate School Competition' was organized by a group of prominent Welshmen, who invited architects to submit model plans for the new type of school required by the Act of 1889.[46]

Three of the plans submitted to the organizers of this competition (by the architects Phillips & Holdgate of Cardiff, R. Grierson of Bangor, and T. E. Pryce of London) were specially commended, and *The Builder* printed T. E. Pryce's design for an intermediate school for one hundred boys, which is reproduced as Fig. 30. In an accompanying article, Pryce wrote that 'As the system of instruction under which knowledge is to be imparted to the pupil was — and still is — undecided, the particulars issued to architects were necessarily of a somewhat shadowy nature'.[47] However, the instructions given by the committee were clearly intended to distinguish the new county schools from the elementary schools: fifteen square feet per child were stipulated (compared with a maximum of ten square feet in the board schools), and self-contained classrooms for each class were considered to be essential, in addition to an assembly hall. The plans of schools actually built also indicate that the number of pupils in each class was expected to be lower than in the elementary schools, and the pupils were usually provided with single-locker desks. Most plans show classes of twenty-four children arranged in six rows of four desks. The cost per place was usually over £20, which was well above

[46] *The Builder*, 1890B, 211.
[47] Ibid., 1891A, 251.

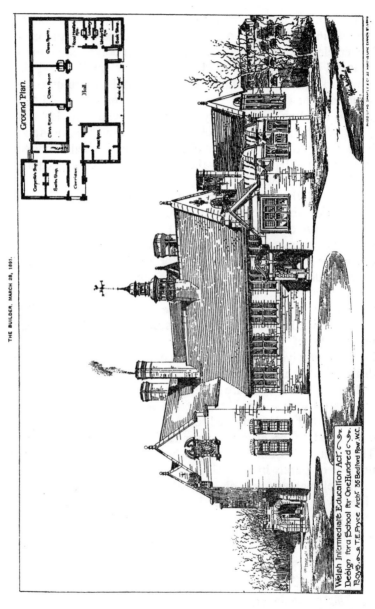

Fig. 30. Welsh Intermediate Education Act. Design for a school for one hundred boys by T. E. Pryce, 1891.

the maximum spent on elementary-school buildings at this date.[48]

The greater importance now attached to technical subjects, which had provided the main impetus behind the Technical Instruction Act of 1889 and which had also played a vital part in persuading Parliament to pass the Welsh Intermediate Education Act of the same year, had considerable influence on the designs adopted for the new county schools. Pryce's model plan included carpenter's and smith's workshops, and (a provision more usually made in girls' schools), a music room; on the first floor, an elementary science laboratory and an art room were provided. In practice, the larger schools usually had laboratories for physics and chemistry (Plate 58), and the girls' schools invariably included rooms for cookery. Indoor gymnasia were also sometimes provided. The 'practical' rooms were usually located within the main building, as on Pryce's model plan, but the smaller schools, and those in older buildings, quite often used utilitarian hutments erected elsewhere on the site. (An example of this, which was still in existence at Usk in 1990, is a former woodwork room in a lean-to annexe behind the school.) Some of the smaller, rural schools omitted the practical rooms, or acquired them several years later. Indeed, it has often been pointed out that the county schools tended to emphasize the academic rather than the technical aspects of secondary education. This, however, was a feature of the new grammar schools in England as much as in Wales, and the reasons for it are still a subject of debate.[49] Science and mathematics, Latin, French and the usual arts subjects made considerable progress, and Welsh was also taught, though only in Merioneth was it a compulsory subject.[50] In the larger towns, ambitious

[48] At Merthyr, the committee responsible for building the new intermediate school stipulated £15, then £25 per place, and the school actually cost £38 per place (*The Builder*, 1897A, 83). The cost per place elsewhere varied quite widely (see Appendix V).
[49] The lack of apprenticeships in the mainly heavy industries of Wales was stressed by the Central Advisory Council for Education (Wales), in its report *The Future of Secondary Education in Wales* (1947), 2-4.
[50] The curriculum of the schools is fully discussed in W. Davies, *The Curriculum and Organization of the County Intermediate Schools, 1880-1926* (Cardiff, University of Wales Press, 1989).

masters and mistresses often produced high academic standards, enabling some of their pupils to compete with the the leading schools in England for scholarships at Oxford and Cambridge. High standards in organized games were also achieved at some schools.

There was one aspect of the organization of the county schools in Wales which considerably simplified their design. These schools were seen as, essentially, day schools serving the local population. The desire to have schools within the reach of all who could benefit from them was the justification used for providing far more schools than the number envisaged in the Aberdare Report. Boarding education of the kind traditional in England was generally distrusted, and the headmaster of the Friars School at Bangor would not have improved his case for retaining the independence of the school, at least in the eyes of some of the local inhabitants, when he wrote in 1887 that 'Boarders are the very leaven of a school: they are the element which can be most easily manipulated', especially when he went on to commend the fact that many of his boarders came from England.[51] The new Friars School which was eventually built at Bangor was designed as a traditional boarding school, and was not of the pattern followed by most of the new county schools. There were, of course, some children who lived too far from the nearest county school to travel daily from their homes, and, for these, hostels or lodgings were provided during the week. This was a development of the much older practice in Wales (which we have noted in previous chapters) of 'boarding out' children in local houses. In 1900, of the 7,445 children attending county schools, 334 were described as 'boarding' and 816 as 'in lodgings', a total of fifteen per cent.[52] From the architectural angle, this meant that no provision for residential pupils was needed in the new school buildings, and masters' houses were only rarely included in their design.

As far as the architecture and internal planning of the new county schools are concerned, *The Builder* and *The*

[51] E. W. Jones and J. Haworth (eds.), *The Dominican* (Bangor 1957), 73.
[52] CWB, *Report,* 1900.

Building News recorded a high proportion of the schools which were being built in Wales between 1890 and 1902. The details are set out in Appendix V, together with information derived from other sources. The great majority of the architects employed were local men, and two in particular specialized on designing county schools. It will be seen from Appendix V that J. H. Phillips of Cardiff, who was one of the architects commended in the Tate Competition, designed a number of county schools in south Wales, while Harry Teather, also of Cardiff though born in Sheffield (where he had trained under C. J. Innocent, a notable local architect), designed numerous county schools, especially in mid-Wales. A rare, unspoilt example of a school designed by Teather may be seen at Llanfyllin in Montgomeryshire, which opened in 1900 and is now used as a branch library (Plate 59). This was a mixed school, where the number of pupils was too small for the school to be organized in separate departments for boys and girls. Most of the county schools in rural areas were of single-storey construction and there is an equally modest example at St David's in Pembrokeshire, which was still in use in 1990, though now much extended. In the larger towns, 'dual' or single-sex schools were more usual, but they rarely went above two storeys. Decorative detail was often confined to the main entrance of the building, as at Pwllheli (now boarded up), which had an impressive entry in the seventeenth-century manner.

A small number of Chester architects designed inter-mediate schools in north Wales. John Douglas's new building for the Friars School in Ffriddoedd Road at Bangor is shown on Plate 60. We have already seen that this school, though designed in 1888, was not actually built until 1899 and opened in the following year. The Elizabethan form of the Tudor Gothic style which Douglas employed, with a central tower such as we noted earlier at Llandovery College and elsewhere, was conventional, but he put his own stamp upon it. The result is a school building which is dignified without being pretentious. It is probable that James Hughes, the local architect chosen to build the boys' county school at Denbigh, was influenced by Douglas's design for Bangor, which had also been used in a somewhat different form at Ruthin. The Denbighshire building committee, although pressed for funds, insisted that the new county school at Denbigh should be faced with the local limestone,[53] and the result (shown on Plate 61) is an impressive pile, though it has to be admitted that the central tower has a somewhat pinched appearance. This school, which opened in 1902, is now masked by later buildings but survives as an adult education centre in Middle Lane, Denbigh.

Many of the larger intermediate school buildings were located in Glamorgan and Monmouthshire. At Swansea, the boys' grammar school was adapted for use entirely by day boys, as mentioned earlier, while the intermediate school for girls occupied a house known as Llwyn-y-Bryn in Walter Road, which had previously been a private school for middle-class girls. At Newport, however, two new intermediate schools for boys and girls were designed by B. Lawrence of Newport in 1894 and were built next to each other on a large site in Fields Road, conveniently near the railway station. These schools were illustrated in *The Building News* and were both planned on the central-hall principle which, as we saw, was also used for some of the larger board schools at this time. A similar plan was adopted by Harry Teather for his replacement of the temporary premises used by the intermediate school for boys at Newport Road in Cardiff.[54] Perhaps the most interesting building, architecturally, is that designed by George Thomas for the intermediate school for girls in The Parade at Cardiff, which is not far from the Queen Street station. This school was completed in 1900, and Thomas's drawings, which were printed in *The Building News*, are reproduced as Fig. 31. This building is now used by Coleg Glan Hafren (part of the East Cardiff Tertiary College) and its architectural detail and very attractive

[53] Minutes of County Governing Body, 166, 244 (Clwyd CRO, Ruthin).
[54] Undated plans of the permanent building in Newport Road, designed by Teather & Baldwin, survive on microfiche in the Consultant Services Division, County Hall, Atlantic Wharf, Cardiff. The building itself has been demolished, and the school has moved to the outskirts of Cardiff.

THE BUILDING NEWS. SEP. 7, 1900.

Fig. 31. Cardiff Intermediate School for Girls, 1900;
architect George Thomas.

assembly hall are, so far, intact. It may be added that many of the intermediate schools in south Wales came to be known as 'High Schools' when further secondary schools were built by the new local education authorities established after the passing of the 1902 Education Act.

There is one other outstanding feature of the county schools which should be mentioned: they were almost all built on excellent sites, and elevated positions were chosen wherever possible. This may partly have been for reasons of prestige, but considerations of health were also important. The flight of Thring's school to Borth in Cardiganshire, because of the failure of the Uppingham drains, and the more recent removal of the Friars School at Bangor to Penmaen-mawr, had created their own legends.[55] The girls' intermediate school at Bangor was for this reason sited on the hill next to the new university college (it is now the university music department), while the school at Caernarfon commands a superb view of Snowdonia and that at Holywell of the Dee estuary. The Central Welsh Board praised the school sites at, among other places, Aberdare, Merthyr and Pontypridd, and described Barry has having 'one of the most excellent sites in the country'.[56] Apart from aesthetic and health considerations, the availability of land for future expansion was of the greatest importance: it is, for example, doubtful whether comprehensive reorganization could have taken place so rapidly after the second world war without this room for expansion.

All in all, the opinion of the Welsh intermediate schools, as expressed by the Charity Commissioners in 1898, remains a valid one:

> With the establishment of the County Schemes for secondary education . . . the work of organization of secondary educa-tion may be said to have closed. It is true that much remains to be done in filling the frame-work, and in developing the system to its full capacity in the light of experience, but in

---

[55] J. H. Skrine, *Uppingham By the Sea* (Uppingham, Hawthorn, 1878; second edition, 1908).
[56] CWB, *Report,* 1897.

the main it appears that the particular machinery suited to the character of the people and to the social and industrial conditions of the country has been provided, and that henceforth attention will be more and more concentrated upon questions of curriculum and educational method.[57]

The Welsh Intermediate Education Act represented above all the triumph of rural Nonconformity. A point of criticism has been that, while in the rural areas 8,000 was taken as the minimum population of a school district, in the thickly-populated industrial areas of Glamorgan and Monmouthshire, a district frequently contained more than five times that number. The delays caused by the Cowbridge controversy meant that Glamorgan was the last county in Wales to have its scheme approved, with the power which that gave to raise a rate under the Welsh Act. As a result, recourse had to be made to the Technical Instruction Act to finance the schools which were urgently needed in the industrial areas. It must, however, be said that the rural areas of Wales had been neglected for far too long, and the industrial parts of the south could more readily afford to finance the new developments in secondary education.

The description which we have given of the reorganization of endowments and the building of new county schools explains why it is that, at the present time, although a number of other independent schools exist in Wales, there are only seven which are based on old endowments (viz. Christ College, Brecon, the Howell's Schools at Denbigh and Llandaff, Llandovery College, the Monmouth Schools for Boys and Girls, and Ruthin School). It also goes far to explain why, in 1990, of the 186,000 boys and girls in maintained secondary schools in Wales, only three per cent were in Church in Wales schools and five per cent in Roman Catholic schools; all the rest were in undenominational, comprehensive schools controlled by elected education authorities.[58] Similarly,

---

[57] *The Welsh Act . . . Its Origins and Working*, op. cit., 48.
[58] *Statistics of Education in Wales: Schools No. 4* (Cardiff, Welsh Office, 1990), 33, which gives a total of 231 secondary schools, including 6 Church in Wales and 15 Roman Catholic schools.

it was during the late Victorian period that the few large endowments devoted to elementary education were taken over for secondary school purposes, while school boards, and later county and county borough councils, became responsible for most of the provision for elementary education. In 1990, only nine per cent of the 275,000 children receiving primary education in Wales were in voluntary aided schools.[59]

A recent writer has suggested that Nonconformists demanded a state system of secular education for all because 'as a religious minority persecuted for conscience's sake they had developed a keener sense of social justice'.[60] During the relatively short period when they gained control of education in Wales, they made full use of the opportunities which presented themselves.

[59] Ibid., 29, which gives a total of 1,729 primary schools, including 58 Church aided, 124 Church controlled, and 79 Roman Catholic schools.
[60] James Musson, *The Nonconformists in Search of a Lost Culture* (London, SPCK, 1991), quoted in *The Guardian*, August 5, 1991.

Plate 1: Ruthin, Denbs., grammar school, 1574 and later.

Plate 2: Northop, Flints., grammar school, 1608; interior before restoration.
(*Reproduced by permission of the National Monuments Record for Wales*)

Plate 7: Gresford, Denbs., Strode's school (*right*) and almshouses (*left*), 1725.

Plate 8: Kerry, Mont., monument to Richard Jones, 1785.

Plate 9: A pupil at the Welsh School, London, c. 1810. (*National Library of Wales*)

Plate 10: Gwyddelwern, Mer., Ysgol Bach, c. 1800.

Plate 11: Porthkerry, Glam., the old schoolhouse, seventeenth century and later.

Plate 12: Lewis' school, Gelli-gaer, Glam., 1729 and later, shown on a modern plaque at Pengam school.

Plate 13: Llanferres, Denbs., inscription on Catherine Jones' school, 1763.

Plate 14: Cilcain, Flints., parish school, 1799.

Plate 15: Churchstoke, Mont., Downes' school, c. 1790 (*left*), with later National school (*right*).

Plate 16: Caerleon, Mon., Charles Williams' school, 1724.

Plate 17: Berriew, Mont., school in churchyard, 1819.

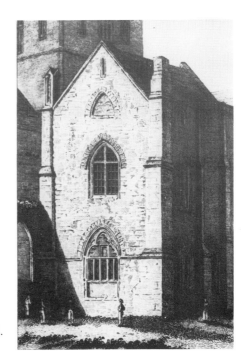

Plate 18: St. David's, Pembs.,
grammar school held in cathedral.
(*National Library of Wales*)

Plate 19: Abergavenny, Mon.,
grammar school in former church.
(*Courtesy of Gwyn Jones*)

Plate 20: Ruthin, Denbs., headmaster's house, 1742.

Plate 21: Beaumaris, Ang., grammar school (*left*) 1603, and headmaster's house (*right*), later enlarged.

Plate 22: Deuddwr, Mont., school, eighteenth/nineteenth century.

Plate 23: Llandeilo Gresynni (Llantilio Crossenny), Mon., school built in 1820 at Brynderi.

Plate 24: Wrexham, Denbs., grammar school, painting by Moses Griffith c. 1780. (*National Library of Wales*)

Plate 25. Bowl showing Edward Jones, schoolmaster, 1751. (*Copyright National Museum of Wales, Welsh Folk Museum*)

Plate 26: Amlwch, Ang., National school, 1821.

Plate 27: Nolton, Pembs., Grant's school, 1810.

Plate 28: Trelleck, Mon., endowed school, rebuilt 1820.

Plate 29: Penley, Flints., Madras school, 1811.

Plate 30: Llangasty Tal-y-llyn, Brecs., 1850, church, school and master's house designed by J. L. Pearson.

Plate 31: Chirk, Denbs., school and teacher's house designed by Thomas Penson, 1844.

Plate 32: Trelawnyd, Flints., church school designed by Lloyd Williams & Underwood, 1860.

Plate 33: Magor, Mon., church school designed by Prichard & Seddon, 1856.

Plate 34: Llangollen, Denbs., British school, 1846.

Plate 35: Aberystwyth, Skinner Street, British school, 1846 (and later?).

Plate 40: Dowlais, Glam., Lady Charlotte Guest in the school designed by Sir Charles Barry at Dowlais, Glam., 1855. (*Glamorgan Record Office*)

Plate 41: Bala, Mer., grammar school, designed by Wigg & Pownall, 1851, later extended (*right*) in similar style.

Plate 42: Cowbridge, Glam., grammar school rebuilt by John Prichard, 1849-52 (*Copyright National Museum of Wales, Welsh Folk Museum*)

Plate 43: Swansea grammar school, designed by T. Taylor, 1853. (*National Museum of Wales*)

Plate 44: Carmarthen grammar school, c. 1844. (*Reproduced by permission of the National Monuments Record for Wales*)

Plate 45: Llandovery College, designed by Fuller & Gingell, 1851 and later. (*National Library of Wales*)

Plate 46: Cardigan guild hall, including a grammar school (*ground floor, left*), designed by R. J. Withers, 1858-60.

Plate 47: Monmouth School, rebuilt to design of W. Snooke, 1865-95.
(*Monmouth Museum*)

Plate 48: Llandaff, Glam., Howell's school for girls, designed by Herbert Williams, 1860. (*Copyright National Museum of Wales, Welsh Folk Museum*)

Plate 49: Welshpool, Mont., grammar school designed by George Gilbert Scott, 1853.

Plate 50: Holt Academy, Denbs., 1855 and later.

Plate 51: Whitland, Carms., board school designed by George Morgan, 1877.

Plate 52: Roath Park Board School, Cardiff, 1894; architect, E. W. M. Corbett.

Plate 53: Manselton Board School, Swansea, 1900; architect, G. E. T. Laurence. (*Swansea City Archives*)

Plate 54: Acrefair, Denbs., board school interior, 1905. (*Clwyd County Record Office, Ruthin*)

Plate 55: Pentre Rhondda, Glam., board school interior, c. 1900.
(*Copyright National Museum of Wales, Welsh Folk Museum*)

Plate 56: Cardigan, county intermediate school, official opening ceremony, 1898.
(*Dyfed Cultural Services, Aberystwyth Public Library*)

Plate 57: Abergavenny, Mon., new grammar school building nearing completion, 1898. (*Abergavenny Museum*)

Plate 58: Carmarthen, Queen Elizabeth grammar (intermediate) school, science laboratory, c. 1909. (*Copyright National Museum of Wales, Welsh Folk Museum*)

Plate 59: Llanfyllin, Mont., county intermediate school designed by Harry Teather, 1900.

Plate 60: Bangor, Friars School, by John Douglas, 1900.

Plate 61: Denbigh, County Boys' School, by James Hughes, 1902.

Appendices

Note: It has not been practicable to include in the Index all the names of persons and places listed in these Appendices, apart from those also mentioned in the text. The names of the architects and builders listed in Appendices III, IV and V are, however, arranged alphabetically on page 251-4.

APPENDIX I (A)

NON-CLASSICAL SCHOOLS ENDOWED IN THE EIGHTEENTH CENTURY

Source: Digest of Schools and Charities for Education (London, 1842)

ANGLESEY

Aberffraw, 1735 (Sir A. Owen)
Llanbadrig, 1723 (R. Gwynne)
†Llanfihangel Ysceifiog, 1719 (Dean Jones)
‡Llantrisant, 1733 (Blanche Wynne)
†Pentraeth, 1719 (Dean Jones)

‡Llangendeirne, 1784 (Catherine Goldfrap)
Llangynog, 1721 (J. Vaughan)
‡Llansadwrn, 1731 (Letitia Cornwallis)
Mydrim, c.1729 (Not known)
Trelech-a'r-Betws, 1788 (W. Davies)

BRECON

Builth, 1752 (T. Pritchard)
‡Llanbedr, 1728 (Mary Herbert)
Llanigon, 1714 (L. Watkins)
‡Llanwrtyd, 1782 (Margaret Jones)

DENBIGH

Betws-yn-Rhos, 1722 (Subscriptions)
‡Bryneglwys, 1714 (Margaret Lloyd)
‡Denbigh, n.d. (Mrs Oldfield)
*Denbigh, 1711 (Dr Williams)
‡Gresford, 1715 (Dame Strode)
‡Llanarmon-yn-Ial, 1746 (Margaret Vaughan)
Llanfair Talhaearn, 1708 (D. Jones, etc)
‡Llanferres, 1764 (Catherine Jones)
‡Llangollen, 1732 (Jane Owen)
Llanrhaeadr-yng-Nghinmeirch, 1750 (Subscriptions)
Llanrhaeadr-ym-Mochnant, 1730 (J. Powell)
Ruabon, 1706 (G. Hughes, etc.)
‡Wrexham, 1728 (Lady Jeffreys)
‡Wrexham, 1751 (Mary Drelincourt)
*Wrexham, 1711 (Dr Williams)

CAERNARVON

†Aber, 1719 (Dean Jones)
Bodfaen, 1784 (W. Lloyd)
Bryncroes, 1784 (R. Evans)
Cricieth, 1795 (Revd D. Ellis)
†Gyffin, 1719 (Dean Jones)
†Llanllechid, 1719 (Dean Jones)
Penmachno, 1729 (R. Lloyd)

CARDIGAN

Llanbadarnfawr, 1752 (R. Richards)
Llanddewibrefi, 1780 (D. Thomas, etc.)
Llanilar, 1792 (R. Jones)

FLINT

‡Bangor Is-coed, 1728 (Lady Jeffreys)
Mold, 1744 (Revd H. Lloyd, etc.)
*Newmarket (Trelawnyd), 1711 (Dr Williams)
Whitford, 1711 (B. Jones)

CARMARTHEN

Abergwili, 1713 (G. Lloyd)
Carmarthen, 1729 (Sir T. Powell)
‡Cynwyl, 1721 (Anne Warner)
‡Llandeilo, 1721 (Anne Warner)
Llanfynydd, 1738 (Revd D. Jones)

GLAMORGAN

‡Cardiff, 1707 (Jane Herbert)
‡Eglwysilan (Caerphilly), 1729
   (Anne Alldworth)
Gelligaer, 1715 (E. Lewis)
Neath, 1719 (J. Davies)

MERIONETH

*Llanuwchllyn, 1711 (Dr Williams)
Tywyn, n.d. (V. Corbet, etc.)

MONMOUTH

†**Bedwas, 1729 (Anne Alldworth)**
Caerleon, 1717 (C. Williams)
Llanfihangel Ystum Llywern,
   1734 (Revd R. Thomas)
Matherne, 1734 (C.Pratt)

MONTGOMERY

Castle Caereinion, 1797
   (D. Thomas)
Churchstoke, 1790
   (W. Downes, etc.)
Kerry, 1785 (R. Jones, etc.)
Llanbrynmair, 1702 (M. Lloyd)
*Llanbrynmair, 1711 (Dr Williams)

‡Llanerfyl, 1728 (Priscilla Foster)
‡Llanfihangel, 1720 (Mary Vaughan)
‡Llanfyllin, 1720 (Mary Vaughan)
Llangynog, 1797 (E. Jones)
Montgomery, 1764 (J. Edwards)
Meifod, 1714 (W. Pugh)
Newtown, 1748 (St Asaph Diocese)

PEMBROKE

Amroth, 1789 (D. Rees)
Pwllcrochan, 1765 (G. Mears)
St Issells, 1712 (J. Jones)

RADNOR

Beguildy, c.1786 (Lord Wharton)
Llandegley, 1738 (S. Williams)
‡Llanelwedd, n.d. (Lady Hartstrong)
New Radnor, 1788 (J. Green)
Old Radnor, n.d. (Not known)
‡Whitton, 1703 (Dame Child)

GENERAL

Circulating schools set up under the
will of Madam Bevan (1779) not
implemented until 1807: in 1836
there were 34 of these schools in
existence, mainly in S. Wales.

---

* Dr Williams' schools;   †Dean Jones' schools;   ‡ Lady founders

APPENDIX I (B)

NON-CLASSICAL SCHOOLS ENDOWED BETWEEN 1800 AND 1835

Source: Digest of Schools and Charities for Education (London, 1842)

ANGLESEY

None

BRECON

Hay-on-Wye, 1813 (E. Goff)

CAERNARVON

*Llanystumdwy, 1819
(D. E. Nanney)

CARDIGAN

Llanbadarnfawr, 1808
(L. Jones)

CARMARTHEN

None

DENBIGH

Chirk, 1830 (Mrs M. Biddulph)
*Eglwysbach, 1835
(Revd H. Edwards)
*Llanfair Talhaearn, 1835
(R. W. Wynne)

FLINT

*Northop, 1823 (Transfer of
O. Jones's charity)

GLAMORGAN

Coychurch, 1830 (Elizabeth Davies)

MERIONETH

*Gwyddelwern, 1806 (H. Roberts)
Llanbedr, 1817 (M. Parry)
Llanenddwyn, 1801
(Ellin Humphreys)
*Llangelynnin, 1831 (Transfer of
E. Morgan's charity)

MONMOUTH

*Grosmont, 1810 (Ann George)
Michaelston-y-Fedw, 1819
(B. Tate)
Raglan, 1813 (E. Goff)

MONTGOMERY

Machynlleth, 1830 (J. Jones)

PEMBROKE

Narberth, 1832 (G. Devonald)
*Nolton, 1806 (J. Grant)
Roch, 1806 (J. Grant)
Stainton, 1832 (Martha Devonald)

RADNOR

None

* indicates that the original school building has survived

APPENDIX II

SURVIVING PAROCHIAL AND NATIONAL SCHOOL BUILDINGS 1800-1840

Notes:

1. Only purpose-built schools which retain some original features are included.

2. The name of the original parish has been added in brackets in appropriate cases. Places where the schools are still in use as schools are shown in italics. Dates shown in italics indicate the presence of original dated plaques.

3. References to CCR are to the *Reports of the Charity Commissioners* and give the number and year of the report, and the relevant page number.

4. References to SEW are to the *Reports of the Commissioners on the State of Education in Wales* (1847), and give the volume number and the page numbers of the relevant entries in the appendices and tables. It should be noted that the dates of 'establishment' given in the Reports do not necessarily coincide with the dates of surviving buildings.

County and Place	Date	Location	Comment	References
ANGLESEY				
Llandyfrydog	1815	Near church	First National school in Anglesey	SEW III, 11, 170
Beaumaris (Llandegfan)	1816	Steeple Lane	Now private dwellings	SEW III, 10, 166
Amlwch	*1821*	Bull Bay Rd.	See Plate 26	SEW III, 4, 166
Llandegfan	*1832*	Near church	Supported by Duchess of Kent	SEW III, 9, 166

County and Place	Date	Location	Comment	References
BRECON				
Defynnog	*1811/55*	Prospect Row	Old charity school rebuilt	CCR 32(1837), 350 SEW II, 128, 210
Felindre (Llanfihangel Cwm Du)	1833?	Near the bridge in Cwm Du	Built by **Revd. T. Price**	SEW II, 137, 214
CAERNARFON				
Llandygai	*1810/16*	Near church	Founded by Baroness Penrhyn	SEW III, 36, 186
Llanystumdwy	1812?	Near church	Later the master's house	CCR 28(1834), **517** SEW III, **42**, 186
Llanrhos (Eglwys-rhos)	1822	Opp. church on Conwy Rd.	Founded by Frances Mostyn	SEW III, 30, 182
Llandwrog	1833?	1-3 School Cottages	Possibly Lord Newborough's school	SEW III, 38, 186
Mynytho (Llangian)	1833	At foot of Foel Gron	Y-tracery windows	SEW III, 40, 186
Llannor	*1834/55*	Near church	Disused	SEW III, 41, 186
Caernarfon (Llanbeblig)	1836?	Lôn Ysgol	Former infant school inscribed 'Feed my lambs'	SEW III, 34, 182
Conwy	1838	Rose Hill St.	Now a visitors' centre	SEW III, 25, 178

County and Place	Date	Location	Comment	References
CARDIGAN				
Llanrhystud	1806?	On edge of churchyard	Now a parish room	SEW II, 169, 230
Lampeter	1826?	Church St.	Round-headed windows	SEW II, 150, 222
Llanddeiniol	1827	Near church	Attached to former vicarage	SEW II, 160, 226
Llandre (Llanfihangel Genau'r-glyn)	c.1830?	Up steep lane off B4353	Disused	SEW II, 164, 226
Llangoedmor	1834?	Near church	Two-storey, Tudoresque, may be of later date	SEW II, 166, 226
CARMARTHEN				
Kidwelly	1833	On edge of churchyard	Now St Mary's parish room	SEW I, 22, 278
Llanedi	1839	Opposite St Edith's church	Windows in rounded-headed recesses	SEW I, 2, 209
Marros	1840	Near church	Roofless	SEW I, 18, 260
DENBIGH				
Clocaenog	1817?	Near church	Much altered	SEW III, 49, 194
Llanddoged	1827	Part of present school	Date-stone inside	SEW III, 58, 198

County and Place	Date	Location	Comment	References
DENBIGH—*Continued*				
Eglwysbach	1835	In main street	Y tracery	CCR 32(1837), **52** SEW III, 52, 194
Llangollen	1840	On A5 next to Hand hotel	See Fig. 11	SEW III, 64, **202**
FLINT				
Penley (Ellesmere)	1811	On main road	See Plate 29	SEW III, 90, 214
Ysceifiog	1817/51	Centre of village	Village hall	SEW III, 114, 230
Northop	1823	The Green on old A55	Grammar endow't transferred	CCR 32(1837), 192 SEW III, 108, 226
Rhuddlan	1829	Castle St.	Walls of large limestone blocks	SEW III, 110, 230
Hawarden	1834	Gladstone Way	Later re-faced?	SEW III, 94, 218
Connah's Quay (Northop)	1837	Opp. church of St Mark	Designed by J. Lloyd of Mold	SEW III, 108, 226
Gwernaffield (Mold)	1838	Behind church	J. Lloyd of Mold	SEW III, 105, 226
Bagillt (Holywell)	1840	On road below church	J. Lloyd of Mold	SEW III, 98, 222
GLAMORGAN				
Merthyr Mawr	c.1837	Main street	Thatched	SEW I, 74, 358

County and Place	Date	Location	Comment	References
MERIONETH				
Gwyddelwern	pre-1806	On edge of churchyard	See Plate 10	CCR 28(1834), 547
Llandderfel	1828	Centre of village	Altered 1852	SEW III, 121, 234 SEW III, 124, 234
Ffestiniog	1829	Below church on B4391	Later home of Bertrand Russell	SEW III, 120, 234
Llwyngwril (Llangelynnin)	1831	On the Tywyn road	Enlarged 1923	CCR 28(1834), 570 SEW III, 130, 238
Maentwrog	1837	On Gellilydan road	Supported by Oakeley family	SEW III, 135, 238
Llanycil	1838	Opposite church on A494	House and school under one roof	SEW III, 132, 238
MONMOUTH				
Grosmont	c.1810	Main street	Private house	CCR 27(1833), 427 Not covered by SEW
Blaenafon (Llanover)	1816	Church Road	First ironworks school in Wales	SEW II, 307, 316
Trelleck	1820	Opposite church	See Plate 28	See Plate 38 CCR 27(1833), 422 Not covered by SEW
Penallt	1834	Attached to later church of St Mary	Now the village hall	CCR 27(1833), 419 Not covered by SEW

County and Place	Date	Location	Comment	References
MONTGOMERY				
Guilsfield	1812?	Near church	Altered	SEW III, 144, 246
Berriew	1819	On edge of churchyard	See Plate 17	CCR 32(1837), 298 / SEW III, 139, 246
Llanfyllin	1826	Attached to nave of church	Regency windows	CCR 32(1837), 265 / SEW III, 151, 250
Llanwrin	c.1830?	Near church	No school known until 1863 — used an older building or an outdated style?	No reference in CCR or SEW
Llanfechain	1832	Centre of village	Now the village shop	SEW III, 150, 250
Buttington	1839?	On edge of churchyard	Altered	SEW III, 140, 246
Belan (Welshpool)	1840	Nr. Belan Lock, S. of Welshpool	Apse added in 1868	SEW III, 164, 262
PEMBROKE				
Newport	c.1800?	1-2 College Square	Former training school of Madam Bevan	CCR 32(1837), 479 / SEW I, 110, 415
Nolton	1810	On edge of churchyard	See Plate 27	CCR 28(1834), 740 / SEW I, 122, 448
Cresselly (Jeffreyston)	1835	On A4075 road	Pointed windows on rear of schoolroom	SEW I, 114, 426

County and Place	Date	Location	Comment	References
RADNOR				
Whitton (also serves Pilleth)	1834	Centre of village	Old charity school rebuilt	CCR 32(1837), 446 SEW II, 185, 238

ACKNOWLEDGEMENTS

The author was helped in his search for early school buildings by the provisional lists of buildings of architectural or historic interest issued by the Welsh Office, with copies in the offices of the Royal Commission on Ancient Monuments in Wales at Aberystwyth, to whose staff he is particularly grateful. These lists, though useful, have many gaps and are in process of revision by CADW. The above list does not claim to be complete. (Most of these buildings are now private houses, community centres, or empty.)

APPENDIX III

VOLUNTARY SCHOOL BUILDING GRANT PLANS 1840-1875

Notes:

1. The School Building Grant Plans are now housed in County Record Offices (CROs), or the National Library of Wales (NLW), as detailed below.

2. The spelling of place-names follows that given on the plans. The names of the designers of the schools, where given on the plans, are shown in italics; some of these were laymen, surveyors or builders rather than architects. Dates, when stated on the plans, are included; n.d. indicates that no date is stated. Additional information, when available from other sources, is given in brackets.

3. Where the original buildings are known to have survived, an asterisk precedes the place-name. The number of askerisks would undoubtedly be increased by further local investigations.

4. Other surviving schools built during this period but not included in the Grant Plans have been added under their respective counties; again, these supplementary listings are not intended to be exhaustive.

ANGLESEY (Gwynedd CRO, Llangefni, ref. WA/13)

National schools
*Aberffraw, *John Lloyd,* 1858; Bodedern, *Lloyd Williams & Underwood,* 1865 (*The Builder,* 1867, 596); Gaerwen, *Henry Kennedy,* 1848; *Holyhead (Church Terrace), *Henry Kennedy,* 1859; Llandysilio (Menai Bridge), *Henry Kennedy,* 1852; Llanfihangel-yn-howyn, (*Henry Kennedy*), 1858 (*The Builder,* 1858, 183); *Llangefni (Penrallt), *Henry Kennedy,* 1851 (*The Builder,* 1852, 641); *Llangristiolus, *John Lloyd,* 1840 (date-stone 1841); Penmon, n.d.; Pentraeth, 1863; *Rhosneigr (Llanfaelog), 1847 (virtually rebuilt 1872); Trefdraeth, *Henry Kennedy,* 1859; Trewalchmai (Gwalchmai), n.d. (Total 13)

British schools
*Amlwch, *George Northcroft,* n.d.; Cemaes Bay, n.d. (1846); *Holyhead (Cambria St.), *Owen Thomas,* 1847/58 (now flats); Llanddona, n.d.; Llandysilio (Menai Bridge), *William Haslam,* 1862; *Llangefni (Stryd-y-bont), *William Dew,* n.d.; Llangeinwen, n.d.; Llanrhyddlad, *Hugh Griffiths,* n.d.; *Newborough, *John Thomas,* 1867; Pentraeth, 1863; Rhosybol, n.d.; Trewalchmai (Gwalchmai), *Thomas Owen,* n.d. (Total 12) *See also:* *Marianglas, 1845.

BRECONSHIRE (NLW, Greg. Box 17)

National schools

Brecon, Boys' school by *Frederick R. Kempson*, 1867, and Girls' school by *William Williams*, 1871; Bronllys, *J. Lewis*, 1875; *Devynnock, Davy's Endowed School, alterations, *William Williams*, n.d.; *Hay-on-Wye, master's house, *Thomas Nicholson*, 1868; Llanafan Fawr, *William Williams*, n.d.; Llanfaelog Fach, master's house, *C. Buckeridge*, n.d., and new schoolroom, *F. R. Kempson*, 1874; Llandefalle, *William Williams*, 1874; *Llanelly (at Gilwern), n.d. (1846); Llanfihangel Nant Bran, n.d.; Llanfrynach, 1855; Lanhamlach, *John Bacon Fowler*, 1876; Llanthew (Llanddew), *William Williams*, 1868; Llanspythid, *William Williams*, 1860 (*The Builder*, 1861, 361); Llanwrtyd, *William Williams*, 1865; Llyswen, *J. Daniels*, 1872; *Llywel (at Trecastle), *William Williams*, 1862 (*The Builder*, 1864, 400); Pentrevelyn, *William Williams*, 1871; *Talybont, *William Williams*, 1860 (*The Builder*, 1861, 469); Trallong, *William Jones*, n.d.; *Vaynor, *William Williams*, 1861; Ystradgynlais, additions, 1868. (Total 21) *See also:* *Llanfihangel Cwm Du, 1873; *Llanfihangel Tal-y-llyn, c. 1860; *Llangasty Tal-y-llyn, *J. L. Pearson*, 1850.

British schools

Aberwessin (Abergwesyn), *George Mair*, 1848; Brynmawr, alterations, *James Walters*, 1854; Castle Madoc, *William Williams*, n.d.; Crickhowell, *John Richards*, 1866; Talgarth, n.d.; Yniscedwyn Ironworks, 1842 and later. (Total 6)

CAERNARFONSHIRE (Gwynedd CRO, Caernarfon, ref M/901)

National schools

*Bangor (Garth Road, façade only survives), *Kennedy & O'Donoghue*, 1867 (*The Builder*, 1868, 219); Beddgelert, *Henry Kennedy*, 1857; *Bodfaen, 1841/2; Bron-y-foel, *G. Hedley*, n.d.; Caernarvon, model school, *John Lloyd*, 1842, and alterations 1851; Caernarvon, training college, additions, *Henry Kennedy*, 1856 (*The Builder*, 1858, 359); Clynnog Fawr, *Henry Kennedy*, n.d.; *Conway (1838), additions, n.d.; Dinorwic, *John Lloyd*, 1854; *Edern (1845), alterations, *Thomas Roberts*, 1871; Glan Ogwen, *Henry Kennedy*, 1851; *Llandudno, *Henry Kennedy*, 1844, and extension 1853; *Llandwrog, *Henry Kennedy*, n.d. (1853); *Llanengan, *Hugh Jones*, 1845; Llanfairfechan, *Geo. & J. R. Shaw*, n.d.; Llanfairisgaer, *Kennedy & Rogers*, 1860; Llangwynadl, 1854/7; Llaniestyn (1843), alterations, n.d.; Llanllechid (1828), alterations by *Henry Kennedy* 1846, *T. H. Wyatt* (c. 1851), and *Kennedy & O'Donoghue*, 1868 (*The Builder*, 1870, 811); *Llannor (1834), alterations, 1854; *Llanystumdwy (1812?), alterations, *Henry Kennedy*, 1851; *Llysfaen (now in Clwyd), *George Edmund Street*, 1869; *Nevin, alterations, *William Pritchard*, n.d.; Pantglas, Upper Clynnog, *Henry Kennedy*, 1857; Penmachno, n.d.; Portmadoc, 1855; *Pwllheli

(Penlleiniau) 1843, alterations, n.d. (by *Roberts & Morrow, The Builder,* 1872, 754); Vaynol, n.d. (Total 28)
See also: *Aber-erch, *Henry Kennedy,* c. 1875; *Llandygai, school financed by Hon. Col. Douglas Pennant, 1843; *Llangelynnin, Henryd, 1844; *Trefriw, Lord Willoughby's school?, 1843, now part of later school.

British schools
*Bangor (The Garth, 1848), alterations, 1854; *Bangor, St Paul's Wesleyan (Sackville Rd.) *John Lloyd,* 1857; *Bangor (Normal) college, *John Barnett,* 1862 (*The Builder,* 1858, 314, and 1859, 322); Beddgelert (1850), additions, 1865; *Carnarvon (South Penrallt) *John Lloyd,* 1856; Deiniolen, *George Northcroft,* 1854; Gorsbach Undenominational, n.d.; Llanengan, 1844/5; *Llanllyfni, n.d. (1863); Llanrug, n.d.; Nant Peris, *John Lloyd,* 1856; *Nevin, *George Northcroft,* n.d. (c. 1860); *Portmadoc (Chapel St., by *O. M. Roberts*) n.d. (1869), (*The Builder,* 1868, 596); *Pwllheli (Troed yr Allt), *Wehnert & Ashdown,* 1855 (part only survives); Tremadoc and Penmorfa, *Owen Morris Roberts,* n.d. (c. 1870). (Total 15)

CARDIGANSHIRE (NLW, Greg. Box 18)

National schools
Aberaeron, *Jenkin Pugh,* 1848; Aberbank, *Charles Davies,* 1848; Aberporth, *Charles Davies,* 1852; Bangor (Teifi), *R. Williams,* n.d.; *Cardigan, St Mary's, *G. G. Scott and W. B. Moffat,* n.d. (c. 1850); *Lampeter (Church St.), W. B. Moffat, 1849; *Llancynfelin (at Tre Taliesin on A487) (1856), new classroom, *David Rees,* 1870; *Llanarth, *R. J. Withers,* 1859 (*The Builder,* 1859, 783), and additions, 1871; Llandyssul, n.d.; *Penbryn, *R. J. Withers,* 1857 (*The Builder,* 1858, 200); *Penparcau (1846), alterations, *J. H. Thomas,* 1869. (Total 11)
See also: *Borth, 1842; *Dihewid, Ysgoldy a Stabl, 1855; *Llangwyryfon, 1861.

British schools
Llwyndafydd, 1845; Talybont, n.d. (Total 2)
See also: *Aberystwyth, Skinner Street, 1846.

CARMARTHENSHIRE (Dyfed CRO, Carmarthen, ref. Educ. 245-282)

National schools
*Abergwili, *R. J. Withers* 1864/5 (*The Builder,* 1866, 588); *Carmarthen (St Catherine's St.), St Davids model school (1848), additions, *Henry Clutton,* 1856; *Carmarthen, Welsh Training School (now Trinity College), *Henry Clutton,* 1847 and additions, 1860 (*The Builder,* 1847, 163 and 1848, 358); Cenarth, restoration, *Charles Davies,* 1856; Cil y Cwm, Berrisbrook, n.d.; Cil y Cwm, Llandilo, 1865; Conwil Caio, Llandilo, 1867; Cwmdwr, n.d.; *Ferryside, *R. K. Penson,* 1855 (*The Builder,* 1856, 486); *Llandybie

n.d. (c. 1850); Llandefeilog, *William W. Jenkins*, 1852 and *S. Bartley*, 1853; *Llandovery (Garden Lane), *Ed. Haycock*, 1845; Llanfihangel Uwch Gwile, n.d.; Llangeler, 1874; Llangennech, 1856, enlarged 1860; Llanllwch, *R. Barrett*, 1850; *Llannon, n.d. (1841 and later); Merthyr (village), *T. W. A. Thompson*, 1870; *Newcastle Emlyn, n.d. (1846), and additions by *Charles Davies*, 1856; Rhandirmwyn, 1858; Trap, Llandilofawr, n.d.; Tremoilet, *A. Ritchie*, 1875. (Total 22)
See also: *Carmarthen, Priory St., *R. K. Penson*, 1869/70; *Golden Grove (Llanfihangel-Aberbythych), 1848; *Llandeilo, Carmarthen Street, *W. M. Teulon* (*The Builder*, 1860, 328).

British schools
Bankyfelin (Llanfihangel Abercowyn), *T. W. A. Thompson*, 1870; Carmarthen (Pentrepoeth), *Wm. W. Jenkins*, 1849, 1853 and 1859; Conwil Elvet, n.d.; Felinfoel, new classroom, 1861; *Kidwelly (Castle St.), *Daniel Davies*, 1858; Llandefeiliog Idole, *John Lewis*, 1862, and another headed 'Idole', 1867; *Llandovery (Victoria Crescent), 1848; Llanelly (Market St.), *James Wilson*, n.d. (1847), and additions by *Henry Rogers*, 1855; Llanelly Bryn, enlarged, *D. Davies*, n.d.; Llanelly, Five Roads, *D. Davies*, 1862; Llanelly, New Dock, *Lander & Bedells*, 1867; Llanelly, Prospect Place, n.d.; Llangadock, n.d.; Llanllawddog, n.d.; Llanpumpsaint, *J. L. Collard*, 1861; Llwynhendy, *Henry Thomas*, 1868. (Total 16)
See also: *Llansadwrn, 1858 and later.

DENBIGHSHIRE (Clwyd CRO, Ruthin, ref. ED/SBD)
National schools
Bersham, *E. Williams*, 1855; *Bettws yn Rhos, *R. Lloyd Williams*, 1859, and *Lloyd Williams & Underwood*, 1861; *Brymbo, *R. K. Penson*, 1849 (*The Builder*, 1849, 561), and additions, 1868; *Brymbo and Minera (at Minera, very well restored 1991), *R. K. Penson*, 1849 (*The Builder*, 1849, 235); *Burton, teacher's house, n.d. (1862); *Cerrig y Drudion, *W. Jones*, 1868; *Chirk (on A5), *Thomas Penson*, 1844; *Denbigh (Lenten Pool), *Henry Kennedy*, 1845/6; *Derwen, *R. Lloyd Williams*, 1858; *Gwersyllt, *Thomas Penson*, 1850, and additions, 1857; *Gyffylliog, *Thomas Roberts*, 1855; *Llanbedr Dyffryn Clwyd, *R. Lloyd Williams*, 1874; *Llandyrnog (1834), alterations, n.d.; *Llanferres (1847), *John Lloyd*, additions, n.d.; *Llangollen, *Ellis Davies*, n.d. (1840); *Llanrhaiadr yn Kinmerch, n.d. (1871); *Llanrhaiadr ym Mochnant, n.d. (1858); *Llanrwst (Y Berllan), *Henry Kennedy*, 1844; Llansantffraid Glyn Ceiriog, *Wm Morris*, 1858; Llansantffraid Glan Conwy, *Henry Kennedy*, 1856; *Llansannan, *R. Lloyd Williams*, n.d. (1856); *Llantysilio, n.d. (1858); *Llanychan, *Lloyd Williams & Underwood*, 1865 (*The Builder*, 1867, 596); (Llysfaen, see under Caernarfonshire); *Nantglyn, *R Lloyd Williams*, 1858; Rhosllannerchrugog (1844), alterations, 1856; Ruabon, alterations, *J. R. Gummon*, 1855; Ruabon Penycae, *William Turner*, n.d. (1864);

Ruthin, school in converted barn (1817) and new school* in Borthyn by *Richard Cash*, 1847; *Trefnant, *George Gilbert Scott*, n.d. (1860); Trevor, *William Turner*, 1864; Wrexham (1804), alterations, *Edward Welch*, n.d. (c. 1835?); Ysbytty (Ysbyty Ifan), n.d. (1857). (Total 32)
See also: *Abergele, *G. E. Street*, 1870; *Acton, Wrexham, *B. Ferrey* (*The Builder*, 1868, 457); *Bylchau, c. 1856; *Gresford (Church St.), *Edward Jones*, 1874; *Llandegla, 1874; *Llanefydd, *Lloyd Williams & Underwood*, 1866; *Llanfair Dyffryn Clwyd, *Lloyd Williams & Underwood*, 1859; *Llangernyw, 1852; *Llangollen (on A5), 1871; *Pentrefoelas, 1852; *St George, 1848 (occupies former Independent chapel); *Tywyn (on A548), *G. E. Street*, 1871.

British schools
*Adwy and Coedpoeth (at Coedpoeth), *W. Cruickshank*, 1865; Blaenau Llangerniew, n.d.; Brymbo and Broughton, *T. M. Penson*, 1859; *Denbigh (Love Lane), *T. Jones*, 1844; *Gwytherin, n.d.; *Llangollen (Brook Street, 1846), refurnishing, *Morris Roberts*, n.d. (c. 1850); *Llanrwst (Nebo Rd.), n.d. (c. 1860); Rhosllannerchrugog, *John Pritchard*, 1864; *Ruthin (Rhos St.), *Richard Cash*, 1846; Vron, Llangollen, n.d. (Total 10)
See also: *Gellifor, nr. Denbigh, 1868; *Llangwm (free-standing in centre of village), c. 1850?; *Wrexham, Brook Street, *Thomas Penson*, 1844.

FLINTSHIRE (Clwyd CRO, Hawarden, ref. ED/SBD)
National schools
*Bagillt, *John Lloyd*, n.d. (1840); *Bistre, *John Lloyd*, n.d. (1842); *Bodvari, *H. John Fairclough*, 1858; *Buckley, St Matthew's Infants (Church Rd.), *James Harrison*, n.d. (1857); *Connah's Quay, St Mark's, (1837), alterations (*J. Lloyd*) 1845/53; Flint, *T. M. Penson*, n.d. (1859); *Gorsedd, *T. H. Wyatt*, n.d. (1853); *Gwernaffield, *John Lloyd*, n.d. (1838); *Higher Kinnerton, *Kelly & Edwards*, 1872; Holywell, alterations, 1851; *Leeswood (Eaton Place), *E. Bate*, 1858; *Llanasa, *H. John Fairclough*, 1857; *Meliden, 1841, and alterations, 1855; Mold, *John Lloyd*, n.d. (1849); *Rhosesmor, *James Harrison*, 1858; *Rhuddlan (1829), new floor, n.d.; *Rhydymwyn, *T. H. Wyatt*, n.d. (1868); Rhyl, Clwyd St., *T. M. Penson*, n.d. (1842) and *R. Lloyd Williams*, 1855; *St Asaph (Upper Denbigh Rd.), *H. John Fairclough*, 1862; Treuddyn (1845), alterations, n.d.; *Worthenbury (Church Rd.), *T. M. Penson*, n.d. (1862); *Ysceifiog (1817), alterations, *John Lloyd*, n.d. (1851). (Total 22)
See also: *Bodelwyddan, *John Gibson*, 1857; *Bronington, 1864; *Brynford. *T. H. Wyatt* (*The Builder*, 1852, 487); *Cilcain, 1842; *Dyserth, 1863; *Gwernymynydd, *Lloyd Williams & Underwood* (*The Builder*, 1867, 596); *Halkyn, 1849; *Mostyn, Glan-y-don, *Ambrose Poynter*, 1845; *Llanfynydd, 1845; *Overton, 1848; *Pentrobin, 1844; *Rhyd-y-goleu, c. 1870; *Trelawnyd, *Lloyd Williams & Underwood*, 1861; *Tremeirchion, 1865.

British schools
*Ffynnongroew, Non-denominational (Well Lane), *Richard Owens,* 1869;
*Holywell (Halkyn Rd.) *Robert Scrivener,* 1863/4; *Lixwm, n.d. (1847);
*Mold (Glanrafon Rd.), 1844/56; Rhyl, *F. D. Johnson,* n.d. (*The Builder,*
1862, 807, 1864, 139 and 1869, 234). (Total 5)
See also: *Carmel, 1862; *Gronant, 1871 (in former chapel); *Rhuallt,
1863.

Roman Catholic school
*Llanasa, Talacre, *J. Spencer,* n.d. (1857). (Total 1)

GLAMORGAN (Glamorgan CRO, Cardiff, ref. D/D PRO/EBG; the
plans with WG in brackets in the list below are housed in the West
Glamorgan Record Office, County Hall, Swansea)

National schools
Aberavon (WG), *R. G. Thomas* (1854); Abercanaid, *G. E. Robinson*
(1868); Aberdare, St Fagans, *C. E. Bernard,* 1856, 1857, 1870; Aberdare,
Town, *W. P. James,* n.d.; Bridgend, *Prichard & Seddon* (1862); Briton
Ferry (WG), *S. S. Teulon,* 1855; Bryncethin, (*Evan David,* 1860); Bryn-
coch (WG), *Geo. Truefitt,* 1857/8 (*The Builder,* 1858, 66); Cadoxton-
juxta-Neath (WG), *R. Chaunders* (1849) and *W. Richards* (1857); Caer-
philly, *W. P. James,* 1867; Cardiff, Canton, *Prichard & Seddon,* 1858 and
W. P. James, (1874); Cardiff, Cathays, *W. P. James* (1869, 1872); Cardiff,
Grangetown, *C. E. Bernard,* 1860, and *H. Snell,* 1877; Cardiff, Maindy,
(*J. P. Seddon*) 1859; *Cardiff, Roath, Metal St. (now St German's Court),
G. F. Bodley & T .Garner, 1874; Cardiff, St John's, *G. E. Robinson,* 1867;
Cardiff, St. John's, Tredegarville, *W. G. Habershon & Pite,* 1870/71;
Cardiff, St Mary's, *G. Clinton* (1848/9) and *G. E. Chittenden,* 1860;
Cheriton (WG), *B. Bucknall* (1876); Clydach (WG), *W. Richards,* 1862;
Cowbridge, *Wm James* (1855); Crynant (WG), (*W. Richards*), 1857;
Cwmbach, *Andrew Moseley* (1850), (*The Builder,* 1850, 557); Cymysgwydd-
gwyn (Gelligaer), *C. Buckeridge* (1866); Cyfarthfa (c. 1855), (*The Builder,*
1857, 266, by *J. S. Benest*); Cymmer, *Prichard & Seddon,* 1857; Fochrhiw,
C. Buckeridge, 1863 (*The Builder,* 1863, 337, 831); Glyntaff, *C. E. Bernard,*
1857; Graigberthlwyd (Llanfabon), n.d.; Llandaff, *Prichard & Seddon,*
1854/60 (demolished) (*The Building News,* 1867, 510); Llandeilo Talybont
(WG) (Pontardulais, 1846); Llandough (near Cardiff), *Wm Burnett,* 1870;
Llanfabon, *J. Prichard* (1850); Llantrisant, *W. P. James* (1868); Llanwonno,
C. E. Bernard, 1853 (*The Builder,* 1852, 726); Loughor (WG), (*Henry
Morris,* 1854); Marcross, (*D. Vaughan* 1872); Merthyr Tydfil, St David's,
W. S. Clark, n.d., *Wyatt & Brandon,* n.d., and *S. O. Harpur,* 1868;
Mountain Ash, *E. Brigden,* 1860/68/69; Mountain Ash, Duffryn, *J. Norton*
(1857); Neath (WG), (Orchard St.), Alderman Davies' Charity, *E. Moxham*
(1858), (*The Builder,* 1857, 41 and 1858, 487); Neath Abbey, Skewen (WG),
M. Reynolds, 1867/8; Neath Higher (WG), *G. Truefitt,* 1859; Newton

Nottage, n.d. (1848); Penclawdd (WG), n.d. (1843); Pentyrch, n.d.; Pont-ardawe, Llanguick (WG), *Ashpitel & Whichern*, 1856; Pontlottyn, (*Evan Evans*, 1868); Rudry, n.d. (1844); St Bridge's Major, *Rees John*, 1844; Swansea (WG) *Thomas, Watkins & Jenkins* (c. 1845) and *Wyatt & Brandon* (c. 1865); Swansea, St Peter's (WG), *R. K. Penson* (1858), (*The Builder*, 1857, 679); Tonypandy, *G. E. Robinson*, (c. 1871); Treherbert, (*E. Moxham*, c. 1861); Treorchy, *G. E. Robinson*, 1870; Walnut Tree Bridge (Eglwysilan), *W. P. James*, 1868; Whitchurch, (*W. Evans*, 1861). (Total 57) *See also:* *Cadoxton near Barry (Coldbrook Rd. East), 1847; *Llandough near Cowbridge, *J. Prichard* (*The Building News*, 1867, 340, 343, 513); *Parkmill, Gower, 1876 (*The Builder*, 1876, 819); *Penmark, Vale, 1847; *St Fagans, Cardiff Rd., 1852 (*The Builder*, 1851, 482).

British schools
Aberaman, (*Jn. Griffiths*, 1872); Aberdare (Park School, now Ysgol y Comin, Hirwaun Rd., Trecynon), (*Evan Griffiths*, 1866); Cwmaman, (*Evan Griffiths*, 1867), additions 1870/78; Dinas Colliery (Llantrisant), additions (*Jas. Jones*, 1862); Llwynypia Colliery, *J. Rees*, 1870/92; Merthyr Tydfil, *Jn. Williams*, 1866/7 (*The Builder*, 1866, 331); Morriston (Llangyfelach) (WG), (*Jn. Humphreys*) 1865 (*The Builder*, 1868, 457); Neath (WG), (*Thos. Thomas*, 1858); Neath Abbey (WG), (*Wm. Davies*, 1860); Swansea, Goat Street (WG), extension, *R. K. Penson*, 1861; Swansea, Queen Street (WG), (1858); Ynysbwl, (*Evan Griffiths*, 1871). (Total 12)

Roman Catholic schools
Bridgend, St Mary's House, *Benj. Bucknall*, n.d.; Cardiff, David Street, *Chas. Hansom*, 1853 and alterations by *W. P. James*, 1870 (demolished); Dowlais, St Mary's, *E. Brigden*, 1861/4; Swansea (WG), St Davids, *Benj. Bucknall*, 1859. (Total 4)

MERIONETH (Gwynedd CRO, Dolgellau, ref. A/18)

National schools
Aberdovey, alterations, n.d.; *Bala, *B. Ferrey*, 1870 (*The Builder*, 1873, 393); Barmouth (1841), alterations, 1854; *Corwen (on A5), *S. Pountney Smith*, 1867; Ffestiniog, *Griffith Owen*, 1853; Llanfrothen, *Henry Kennedy*, 1854; *Llansantffraid Glyndyfrdwy (at Carrog), *R. Lloyd Williams*, n.d. (1858); Mallwyd, *John Baggaley*, n.d.; Trawsfynydd (1844), alterations, n.d. (Total 9)
See also: *Cynwyd, 1864; *Glan-yr-afon, 1867 (on A494 opp. church by *G. G. Scott*); *Llanuwchllyn, Wynn's school, 1841; *Llanuwchllyn, *B. Ferrey*, 1866 (*The Builder*, 1880, 282), opp. Wynn's school.

British schools
*Bala, *Ebenezer Thomas*, 1854 (now a visitors' centre); *Corris, Talyllyn, *Owen Morris Roberts*, 1870 (now a youth hostel); *Corwen, *George*

Northcroft, n.d. (c. 1860); *Dolgelley (Aran Rd.), n.d. (c. 1860); Dyffryn,
Llanenddwyn, *Ellis Williams*, n.d.; Ffestiniog, Slate Quarries, 1849; *Glyndyfrdwy, *John Evans*, n.d. (now a garage); *Llandrillo, *Edward Jones*,
1846 (still in use); *Llanuwchllyn, 1867 (near chapel); *Penrhyndeudraeth,
additions, *Owen Morris Roberts*, n.d. (*The Builder*, 1878, 1080); *Talsarnau,
William Lloyd, n.d.; Tanygrisiau, Ffestiniog, n.d.; Trawsfynydd, *Owen
Morris Roberts*, n.d. (c. 1870); Tywyn, n.d. (Total 14)
See also: *Glan-yr-afon (Llawrbetws), c. 1850; *Llandderfel (near chapel,
now a workshop), 1872?

MONMOUTHSHIRE (Gwent CRO, Cwmbran, ref. D527)

National schools
Aberbeeg (Llanhileth), *Habershon, Pite & Fawckner*, n.d.; Abergavenny
Boys, *Henry Clutton* (model school), 1847 (*The Builder*, 1848, 131);
Abergavenny Girls and Infants (Castle St.), 1866; *Abersychan Works
School (later British) — plans of 1856 missing; Abertillery, *J. Norton*,
1853 (*The Builder*, 1854, 322); *Blaenavon Infants, 1847; *Blaenavon
Boys, 1859; Crumlin, *Graham & Lawrence*, 1863; Cwmbran (Pontnewedd),
Prichard & Seddon, 1858 (demolished); Cwmcarvan, n.d.; *Cwmyoy, *J.
H. Evins*, 1855 (*The Builder*, 1855, 498); Goytrey, *Wyatt & Brandon*, n.d.;
*Gwehelog, *J. Daniels*, 1872; *Llanarth, *D. Roberts*, 1858; *Llanddewi
Rhydderch, 1867; Llandevaud, *Prichard & Seddon*, additions, 1856; *Llan-
ellan, *Prichard & Seddon*, n.d. (1862); Llanfihangel Crucorney, *J. Nevill*,
1874; Llanfoist Lower, n.d. (*The Builder*, 1872, 251, by *J. Nevill*);
*Llangwm, *J. P. Seddon*, 1870; *Llantilio Pertholey, 1871; *Llantrisant,
J. H. Evins, n.d.; *Llanvair Kilgeddin, 1871; Llanwenarth Cintra, n.d.;
Llanwenarth Ultra (1843), additions, *Wyatt & Burgoyne*, 1861; Maindee,
Christchurch, *Habershon & Pite*, 1866; *Magor, *Prichard & Seddon*, 1856;
*Mamhilad, 1856; *Marshfield, *Prichard & Seddon*, 1857; *Monmouth,
(Priory St.), *Prichard & Seddon*, alterations, 1854 and *J. P. Seddon*, 1870;
Monmouth, St Thomas, Overmonnow, 1866; Newport (1840), extensions,
W. G. & E. Habershon, 1857; Newport, St Woolo's (St Mary's St.),
A. O. Watkins, 1870 (later Undenominational); Newport, Tredegar Wharf
(Charlotte St.) *A. O. Watkins*, 1871 (later Undenominational); Panteg,
Wern Sebastopol, *R. G. Thomas*, 1859; Penrhos, *G. J. J. Mair*, 1867, (*The
Builder*, 1889, 104); Pontnewynydd (Trevethin) n.d.; Pontymoel, Pontypool
Iron Works School, *R. G. Thomas*, 1857 (*The Builder*, 1857, 600); Pont-
ypool Charity (Crane St.) school of 1836 extended by *J. F. Williams*,
1849; St Arvan's, nr. Chepstow, n.d.; *Shirenewton, Earlswood, *J. Norton*,
1860; *Skenfrith (1843), alterations, n.d.; *Trostrey, 1870; Whitson,
W. Williams, 1870; *Wyesham, *J. P. Seddon*, 1871. (Total 45)

British schools
Blackwood, *C. Thomas*, 1846; Goytrey, *W. P. James*, 1869; *Llanddewi
Rhydderch, Mount Pleasant, n.d. (1867). (Total 3)

See also: *Mynydd Islwyn, New Bethel, 1847 (not 1817 — see Rees, T. and Thomas, J., Hanes Eglwysi Annibynol Cymru (Liverpool, 1871), 93.)

Roman Catholic school
*Newport, Catholic Infants School (Stow Hill), J. & C. Hansom, 1857. (Total 1)

MONTGOMERYSHIRE (NLW, Greg. Box 20)

National schools
*Bwlch y Cibau, Thomas Ricketts, 1853; *Churchstoke, alterations, 1867; *Dolfor, William White, 1864; Dylife, n.d.; *Guilsfield, Pool Quay (on A483), John Baggaley, n.d. (1861); Llanbrynmair, John Baggaley, 1856; Llandrinio, master's house, J. W. Porteous, 1854; Llanfair Caereinion, n.d.; Llanfyllin, n.d.; Llangadfan, n.d.; *Llanidloes, n.d. (classroom added to original school of 1845); Llanwnog, Thomas Penson, 1850; Llanwyddllan, 1857; Machynlleth, (D. Owen) n.d. (The Builder, 1853, 234); Newtown, Thomas Penson, 1850; *Penybontfawr, John Morris, 1857; Sarn, n.d.; *Welshpool (Berriew St.), infant school (added to original school of 1821, now demolished), n.d. (Total 18)
See also: *Castle Caereinion, 1852; *Kerry, Walker & Poundley (The Builder, 1868, 791); *Llandysilio; *Llandyssil, T. H. Wyatt (The Builder, 1863, 729); *Llanllwchairn, 1857 (now Powys Theatre); *Llansantffraid-ym-Mechain, 1878 (by Hurst, The Builder, 1878, 1026); *Tregynon, 1872 (concrete walls, now rendered).

British schools
Caersws, Edward Jones, 1867; Carno, Edward Jones, 1867; Cemmaes, new fittings, n.d.; Llanbrynmair, James Lloyd, n.d.; Llanfair Caereinion, n.d.; Llanfyllin, n.d.; *Llanrhaiadr ym Mochnant, n.d. (c. 1865, next to chapel); Newtown (1847), refurnishing, n.d. (Total 8)
See also: *Llanidloes (Glandwr Rd.), 1865.

PEMBROKESHIRE (Dyfed CRO, Haverfordwest, ref. TSE/1)

National schools
*Amroth, Edward M. Goodwin, n.d. (1858?); Brawdy (Tancredston), John Watts, n.d.; *Carew, K. W. Ladd n.d.; Cilgerran, n.d. (1845?); *Cosheston, Prichard & Seddon, 1859 (renovation of old school); Crunwear, Henry Hitchings, n.d.; *Hubberstone, Hakin, W. H. Lindsey, 1855 (The Builder, 1855, 498); *Llandeloy, Joseph Jenkins, n.d.; Llangwm, Goode & Owen, 1869; *Llanrhian, Joseph Jenkins, n.d. (1850?); Llanwhaden, George Child. n.d. (c. 1860?); Manorbier, n.d.; *Martletwy, T. E. Owen, 1852; Mathry, n.d.; Pembroke Dock, W. Edge, 1841; Puncheston, James James, 1853; Rhydberth, n.d.; *Robeston Wathen, n.d. (plaque of 1872); *St Brides and Marloes, E. H. Lingen Barker, 1872 (at Marloes, The Builder, 1872, 654); St Florence, J. Rogers, 1857; St Ishmaels, George S. Harvey, 1871; Spittal,

Joseph Jenkins, n.d.; Tenby, *Daniel Birkett* 1872; *Tenby, New Hedges,
J. Rogers, 1852; Walton West and Talbenny, n.d. (Total 25)
See also: *Haverfordwest, model school (Barn St.) (*The Builder,* 1848,
461; *Fishguard, Hamilton St. (mid-19C. and porch dated 1886); *Pembroke,
Main St. (date-stone 1861); *St. Davids, Quickwell Hill (c. 1870);
*Templeton, c. 1860; *Uzmaston, 1847 plaque.

British schools
Dinas Undenominational, 1869; Moilgrove, n.d.; Monkton Orielton Un-
denominational, *K. W. Ladd,* n.d.; Pembroke, *K. W. Ladd,* n.d.; Pembroke
Dock, 1846 and ?1855; St Dogmells, n.d.; *St Issels, Saundersfoot, *W.
Griffiths,* 1867/8. (Total 7)

RADNORSHIRE (NLW, Greg. Box 20)
National schools
Beguildy, *E. H. Lingen Barker,* n.d. (*The Builder,* 1875, 742); Beguildy
Crugybyther, *E. H. Lingen Barker,* n.d. (*The Builder,* ibid.); *Cascob,
Thomas Nicholson 1856; Cefnllys and Llandrindod, 1878; *Clyro, *Thomas
Nicholson,* 1859; Disserth Penkerrig, *John Norton,* 1865; *Glan Ithon,
Henry Lote, 1859; Glasbury Ffynnongynyd, *E. P. Vulliamy,* n.d.; Heyope,
Henry Lote, 1857 and *Thomas Nicholson,* 1863 (*The Builder,* 1865, 770);
*Knighton, *Thomas Nicholson,* 1862; Llanbedr Painscastle, *Thomas
Nicholson,* 1872; Llandilo Graban, *Thomas Nicholson,* 1874; Nantmel,
John Wilding, n.d. and *Thomas Nicholson,* 1863; Presteigne, *Henry
Curzon,* 1868; St. Harmons, n.d. (*E. H. Lingen Barker, The Builder,* 1867,
634), (Total 15)
See also: *Abbey Cwmhir, 1857; *Aberedw, *J. L. Pearson,* 1870; *Llan-
deglau, *E. H. Lingen Barker* (*The Builder,* 1871, 275 and 1873, 414);
*Llanfihangel Rhydithon, octagonal tollhouse converted to school (plaque
dated 1848); *Newbridge-on-Wye, 1866 (master's house only, schoolroom
demolished); *Old Radnor, c. 1848.

British schools
None included in Radnorshire collection, or *The Builder.*

Acknowledgements
My thanks are due to the staff of the various record offices, who
courteously produced the plans for inspection. In locating school buildings
still in existence, I was helped by the published work of Edward Hubbard
on Clwyd and Richard Haslam on Powys. Thomas Lloyd and Julian
Orbach generously gave me information on schools in Dyfed and J. Freer
on schools in Gwent. I owe most of the references from *The Builder* to
Vernon Hughes, who kindly lent me his index of Welsh buildings referred
to in that journal from 1843 to 1890.

APPENDIX IV

WELSH BOARD SCHOOLS MENTIONED IN 'THE BUILDER'
1870-1902

Notes:

1. In the list below, the place where the school was built is followed by the name of the architect in brackets, and by the year and page number of *The Builder*. The references usually give the cost of the building and the number of pupils for which it was designed. The internal layout and other details are sometimes included, especially after 1890.

2. The spelling of place-names follows that given in *The Builder*. From 1880 there are two volumes of *The Builder* each year, shown below as A (January to June) and B (July to December). An asterisk indicates that an illustration is included.

3. Most of these buildings have survived and many are still in use as schools.

ANGLESEY
Beaumaris (E. G. Thomas) 1879, 1299
Brynsiencyn (R. Davies) 1898B, 156
Penmynydd (R. G. Thomas) 1875, 1050

BRECON
Brecon (W. Williams) 1875, 94
Brecon, Mount St. (E. H. Lingen Barker) 1892A, 364
Brynmawr (Alexander & Henman) 1873, 171, 1874, 818

CAERNARFON
Bronyfoel (R. L. Jones) 1898A, 283
Carnarvon, North Penrallt (R. L. Jones) 1898A, 283
Llanaelhaiarn (W. W. Thomas) 1872, 810, 1873, 114, 1874, 182
Nantlle (W. C. Williams) 1873, 841
Penffordd (W. C. Williams) 1873, 841

CARDIGAN
Aberystwyth, nr. station (Szlumper & Aldwinckle) 1872, 303, 1872, 574, 1874, 734
Llanychaiarn (Szlumper & Aldwinckle) 1875, 561
Rhydypenau (W. W. Thomas) 1875, 379

CARMARTHEN
Bynea (J. B. Morgan) 1894A, 445
Llanelly (J. B. Morgan) 1894A, 257

Llanelly Dock (J. B. Morgan) 1892B, 147
Llanelly, Higher Grade (E. H. Lingen Barker, 1889A, 457, 1889B, 35, 1891A, 255
Llanelly, Lakefield (E. H. Lingen Barker) 1884B, 641, 1886A, 358, 1888B, 129

DENBIGH
Bersham (W. Turner) 1874, 361
Broughton (W. Turner) 1875, 1158
Llangollen East St. (R. Owens) 1874, 924
Llangollen, Garth (R. Owens) 1875, 936
Penygelli, Tabor Hill (W. Turner) 1874, 361, 1875, 604
Wrexham, Victoria Rd. (W. Moss) 1901A, 66

FLINT
Bagillt (Hill, Grylls & Wilcocks) 1875, 425, 1876, 1036, 1878, 1025

GLAMORGAN
Aberdare, Clifton St. (Alexander & Henman) 1875, 672
Aberdare Junction (A. O. Evans) 1896A, 259
Abernant (E. H. Lingen Barker) 1876, 1206
Barry Dock (Seward & Thomas) 1890B, 374
Barry, Hannah St. (Jones, Richards & Budgen) 1900A, 245
Blaengwawr (E. H. Lingen Barker) 1880B, 172
Bridgend (H. C. Harris) 1875, 760
Brynhyfryd (G. Harmain) 1875, 738
Cadoxton, Barry Rd. (H. Budgen) 1898A, 304
Cadoxton Common (Seward & Thomas) 1891A, 438
Cardiff, Adamsdown, System St. (W. D. Blessley) 1878, 26
Cardiff, Albany Rd. (A. Llewellyn Batchelor) 1887B, 790
Cardiff, Court Rd. (J. P. Jones) 1891A, 176
Cardiff, Grangetown, Holmesdale St. (E. M. Bruce Vaughan) 1884A, 43 1890B, 468, 1897A, 242*
Cardiff, Higher Grade, Howard Gardens (James, Seward & Thomas) 1885B 356*
Cardiff, Lansdowne Rd. (Veall & Sant) 1898A, 161
Cardiff, Marlborough Rd. (Habershon, Fawckner & Groves) 1900A, 67
Cardiff, Marshes Rd. (W. G. Habershon & Fawckner) 1879, 34
Cardiff, Moorland Rd. (W. G. Habershon & Fawckner) 1891A, 54
Cardiff, Radnor Rd. (E. M. Bruce Vaughan) 1886B, 543
Cardiff, Roath Park, Penywain Rd. (E. W. M. Corbett) 1895A, 52
Cardiff, Rutland St. (Jones, Richards & Budgen) 1893B, 162
Cardiff, Severn Rd. (Jones, Richards & Budgen) 1897A, 242*
Cardiff, Virgil St., Ninian Park (Robert and Sidney Williams) 1900B, 548
Cogan (H. Snell) 1882B, 798

Glyn Neath (J. C. Rees) 1901B, 63
Gorseinon (J. B. Morgan) 1891B, 317, 1893B, 17
Gwaelod-y-Garth (Bruce Vaughan) 1898B, 511
Llangyfelach (T. H. Jones) 1897B, 476
Llansamlet (Rees Llewellyn) 1889B, 162
Maesteg Uchaf (E. W. Burnett) 1897A, 445
Neath (J. C. Rees) 1898B, 107
Oystermouth (Mr. Thomas) 1878, 1000
Oystermouth (J. B. Wilson) 1884A, 219
Penarth (H. C. Harris) 1875, 480
Penarth, Cornerswell (J. H. Phillips) 1897B, 32, 1898B, 63
Pontfaen (H. A. Goodman) 1878, 976
Pontnewydd (J. Williams) 1890B, 97
Pontycymmer (Seddon & Carter) 1887A, 170
St George's-super-Ely (Blessley & Vaughan) 1881A, 392
Swansea, Brynmill (G. E. T. Laurence) 1896B, 256
Swansea, Edward St. (G. E. T. Laurence) 1900A, 120
Swansea, Higher Grade, Dynevor Place (T. P. Martin) 1891B, 490
Swansea, Manselton Rd. (G. E. T. Laurence) 1902A, 117

MERIONETH
Gwyddelwern (R. Owens) 1873, 671

MONMOUTH
Abercarn (A. D. Edwards) 1890B, 137, 197, 277
Abersychan (E. A. Lansdowne) 1882A, 90
Abertillery (W. D. Blessley) 1886B, 897
Blaenavon (E. A. Lansdowne) 1882B, 292
Blaina (W. D. Blessley) 1882B, 385
Chepstow (W. Evill) 1877, 1089
Clytha (Habershon, Fawckner & Groves) 1901A, 471
Cross Keys (Watkins & Sons) 1879, 700
Crumlin (E. A. Lansdowne) 1884B, 73, 344, 1885B, 276
Cwmbran (E. A. Lansdowne) 1874, 484
Cwmffrwdoer (E. A. Lansdowne) 1880A, 208
Garndiffaith (E. A. Lansdowne) 1875, 608
Glascoed (E. A. Lansdowne) 1879, 1141, 1880B, 712
Griffithstown (E. A. Lansdowne) 1874, 813
Grosmont (E. H. Lingen Barker) 1876, 1059
Llangattock-nigh-Usk (Haddon Bros.) 1875, 830
Llanvrechva (E. A. Lansdowne) 1874, 718
Machen (E. A. Lansdowne) 1883B, 506
Monmouth (Lawrence & Goodman) 1876, 180
Newbridge (Watkins & Sons) 1875, 380
New Inn (E. H. Lingen Barker) 1876, 1059

Newport, Bolt St. (E. A. Lansdowne) 1884B, 73
Newport, Chepstow Rd., additions (W. B. Gardner) 1897B, 190
Newport, Duke St. (E. A. Lansdowne) 1885B, 242
Newport, Durham Rd. (A. Swash) 1894A, 76
Newport, Powell's Place (Lawrence & Goodman) 1872, 781, 1873, 951
Newport, Spring Gardens (E. A. Lansdowne) 1888B, 347, 1890B, 214
Norton's Cross (E. H. Lingen Barker) 1877, 48
Panteg (E. A. Lansdowne) 1886A, 428
Pantygasseg (E. A. Lansdowne) 1883A, 694
Pontypool (E. A. Lansdowne) 1882B, 98, 1895A, 317
Trevethin (E. A. Lansdowne) 1879, 1147
Tydu (E. A. Lansdowne) 1875, 1006, 1888A, 347
Upper Cwmbran (E. A. Lansdowne) 1890B, 157, 197

MONTGOMERY
Llydiarth-y-waen (Powell & Swettenham) 1872, 274
Newtown (B. Lay) 1873, 771, 1875, 130

PEMBROKE
No references located

RADNOR
Genfron, Nantmel (Haddon Bros.) 1876, 940
Llanbister (Haddon Bros) 1875, 698
Llanfihangel Rhydithon (Haddon Bros.) 1875, 698

ADDENDUM

The following Board schools are described and illustrated in *The Building News:*

DENBIGH
Llanrwst (Grierson & Bellis) 1896A, 931*

GLAMORGAN
Cardiff, Albany Rd. (A. Llewellyn Batchelor) 1888A, 180*
Pencoed (H. C. Harris) 1881B, 526*
Swansea, Higher Grade (T. P. Martin) 1891A, 804*

MONMOUTH
Newport, Bolt St. (E. A. Lansdowne) 1889A, 66*

ACKNOWLEDGEMENTS

There is a complete run of *The Builder,* and of the other architectural journals, in the British Architectural Library, 66 Portland Place, London. I am very grateful to the staff of that Library, and to the staff of Newport Central Library, which also has a complete set of *The Builder,* for answering numerous queries. I was also greatly helped in the initial stages of compiling this list by the manuscript index of Welsh buildings kindly lent to me by Vernon Hughes of Abergele.

APPENDIX V

WELSH INTERMEDIATE SCHOOL BUILDINGS RECORDED IN JOURNALS 1890-1902

Notes:

1. All the references in the first column are to the year and page of *The Builder*. An asterisk indicates a reference to the official opening of the school.

2. Additional references have been added in brackets under 'Name of Architect'. *BN* stands for *The Building News*, and *CB* for *Contemporary Biographies*, ed. W. T. Pike (1907).

3. In the 'Type of school' column, **B** stands for Boys, **G** for Girls, **D** for Dual and **M** for Mixed.

4. In the 'Number of pupils' column, the 'planned' figures are those given in *The Builder*, with a dash indicating that no such figures are mentioned, and the 'actual' figures are those contained in the *Reports* of the Central Welsh Board for 1900. A letter **T** denotes that temporary premises were still in use at that date.

5. In the 'Cost' column, a dash indicates that no figure is available.

Reference	County and place	Name of architect	Type of school	No. of pupils Planned	No. of pupils Actual	Cost
	ANGLESEY					
—	Llangefni	H. Teather of Cardiff (*CB*,314)	D	—	106	—
	BRECON					
1898B, 511*	Bryn-mawr	J. H. Phillips of Cardiff	D	100	44	£ 1,883
1899A, 529*	Builth Wells	S. W. Williams of Rhayader	D	120	46	—
1901B, 63*	Brecon	Phillips & Baldwin of Cardiff & Abergavenny	B	100	87T	£ 6,715
			G	80	61T	

Reference	County and place	Name of architect	Type of school	No. of pupils Planned	No. of pupils Actual	Cost
1896A, 259	CAERNARFON Caernarfon	Rowland L. Jones of Caernarfon	D	175?	188	—
1897A, 324 } 1897B, 332*	Bangor	J. H. Phillips of Cardiff	G	100	92	£ 2,320
1897A, 426* 1898A, 304	Porthmadog Llanberis	W. H. D. Caple of Cardiff Rowland L. Jones of Caernarfon	D D?	120? —	62 —	£ 2,676 —
1899A, 396	Bangor (Friars)	Douglas & Minshull of Chester	B	—	57	—
1899B, 280*	Botwnnog (extension)	Rowland L. Jones of Caernarfon	D	75	30	£ 1,500
—	Pwllheli	Rowland L. Jones (Opened 1903) (Cambrian News, 30.10.1903)	D	—	68T	—
1898B, 296*	CARDIGAN Aberaeron	Ll. Bankes Price of Lampeter	D	—	56	—
1898B, 297*	Cardigan	Morgan & Son of Carmarthen	D	—	97	£ 3,500
1899B, 420*	Aberystwyth (extension to private school)	T. E. Morgan of Aberystwyth	D	—	145	—

Reference	County and place	Name of architect	Type of school	No. of pupils Planned	Actual	Cost
	CARDIGAN—*Continued*					
—	Llandysul	J. H. Phillips of Cardiff (*Who's Who in Wales*, 1922) (Opened 1898)	D	—	80	—
—	Tregaron	Ll. Bankes Price of Lampeter (*Carmarthen Journal*, 7.1.98)	D	—	67	—
	CARMARTHEN					
1896B, 360*	Llandeilo	David Jenkins	D	130	103	—
1896B, 409	Llanelli	W. H. D. Caple of Cardiff	B	—	69	£ 5,000
			G	—	67	
			G	—	79	
—	Carmarthen	G. Morgan of Carmarthen (*The Welshman*, 28.3.91) (Opened 1899)				
—	Llandovery	J. H. Phillips of Cardiff (*Who's Who in Wales*, 1922) (Opened 1897)	G	—	41	—
—	Whitland	Griffiths of Tonypandy (*Carmarthen Journal* 18.1.95 and 10.4.95)	D	—	41	£ 1,875

Reference	County and place	Name of architect	Type of school	No. of pupils Planned	Actual	Cost
	DENBIGH					
1897A, 405	Llanrwst (extension of old school)	H. Teather of Cardiff	D	—	57	—
1897B, 265	Llangollen	H. Teather of Cardiff	D	—	62	£ 4,790
1899B, 328*	Ruthin (conversion of mansion)	James Hughes	G	—	40	—
—	Denbigh	James Hughes (County Governing Body minutes) (Opened 1902)	B	—	51T	£ 2,945
	FLINT					
1898B, 389	Rhyl	F. H. Shayler of Welshpool	D	166	81T	—
1899A, 529*	Hawarden	Grayson & Ould of Liverpool and Chester	D	98	81	£ 2,450
	GLAMORGAN					
1891B, 79	Ystalyfera	J. B. Wilson & G. Moxham of Swansea	D	—	102	—
1892B, 399 1893B, 143 1896B, 341*	Aberdare	J. H. Phillips of Cardiff	D	180	166	£ 5,000

Reference	County and place	Name of architect	Type of school	No. of pupils Planned	No. of pupils Actual	Cost
	GLAMORGAN—*Continued*					
1893A, 354	Port Talbot	T. P. Martin of Swansea	D	140	104	£ 3,293
1893B, 267 } 1895A, 418* }	Barry	W. D. H. Caple of Cardiff	D	100 (extensions under construction)	197	£ 2,700
1894A, 142 } 1896B, 276* } 1894A, 411	Porth	Jacob Rees of Pentre	D	180	181	£ 5,000
	Bridgend	Lambert & Rees of Bridgend	D	120	103	£ 3,500
1897A, 83*	Merthyr (Penydarren)	E. Lingen Barker of Hereford	D	180	99	£ 6,918
1897A, 105*	Penarth	H. Snell (of Penarth)	B G	120 80	56 } 38 }	£ 8,000
1897A, 445	Cardiff (Newport Rd)	Temporary premises (later rebuilt by Teather & Wilson)	B	(300 eventually)	184T	—
1897B, 427	Cardiff (The Parade)	George Thomas of Cardiff (see also *B.N*, 1900B, 323, illus.)	G	(435 eventually)	245	£14,000 so far
1898A, 278	Gowerton	T. P. Martin of Swansea	D	120	99	£ 5,000

References	County and place	Name of architect	Type of school	No. of pupils Planned	Acutal	Cost
	GLAMORGAN—*Continued*					
1900B, 449*	Hengoed (Gelli-gaer)	James & Morgan of Cardiff	G	80	50T	£ 3,800
—	Neath	D. M. Jenkins of Neath (Plans dated 1894 in C.R.O., Swansea)	D	—	119	—
	MERIONETH					
1899A, 529	Ffestiniog	Willink & Thickness of Liverpool	D	—	79T	£ 6,000
—	Dolgellau	T. M. Lockwood & Sons of Chester (*Journal of Merioneth Hist. Soc.,* V, 2, 125-6) (Opened 1897)	B	—	26	—
	MONMOUTH					
1898A, 113	Abertillery	Swash & Bain of Newport	D	—	98	£ 2,430
1898B, 348	Abergavenny	E. A. Johnson of Abergavenny	G	70	78	£ 1,700
1899B, 309*	Ebbw Vale	J. H. Phillips of Cardiff, and F. Baldwin of Brecon	D	100	81	—

References	County and place	Name of architect	Type of school	No. of pupils Planned	Actual	Cost
	MONMOUTH—*Continued*					
—	Newport (Fields Rd)	B. Lawrence of Newport (see *BN*, 1894B, 177, Illus.)	B G	— —	138 108	— —
	MONTGOMERY					
1898A, 618*	Welshpool	Frank H. Shayler	B G	75 75	51 43	— —
1898B, 130*	Newtown	H. Teather of Cardiff and Shrewsbury	B G	72 56	53⎫ 47⎭	£ 3,000
1900A, 524*	Llanfyllin	H. Teather	M	—	42	—
—	Llanfair Caereinion	H. Teather (*CB*, 314) (Opened 1900)	M	—	25	—
—	Llanidloes	H. Teather (*CB*, 314) (Opened 1900)	M	—	42	—
	PEMBROKE					
1902B, 304*	St David's	D. E. Thomas of Haverfordwest	M	—	38T	£ 1,800
—	Narberth	J. M. Thomas of Narberth (*Carmarthen Journal*, 27.9.95)	D	—	40	—

References	County and place	Name of architect	Type of school	No. of pupils Planned	Acutal	Cost
	RADNOR					
1897B, 155	Llandrindod Wells	H. Teather	D	90	72	—
1899A, 396*	Presteigne	H. Teather	B	54	22	—

Acknowledgement

I am very grateful to Thomas Lloyd for some of the references to schools in Dyfed.

NAMES OF ARCHITECTS AND BUILDERS LISTED IN THE APPENDICES WHO DESIGNED SCHOOLS IN WALES

Note

In the list below, A3 stands for Appendix III, A4 for Appendix IV and A5 for Appendix V.

Alexander & Henman, A4 Brecs., Glam.
Ashpitel & Whichern, A3 Glam.

Baggaley, J., A3 Mer., Mont.
Barker, E. H., Lingen,
A3 Pembs., Rads.
A4 Brecs., Carms., Glam., Mon.
A5 Glam.
Barnett, J., A3 Caerns.
Barrett, R., A3 Carms.
Bartley, S., A3 Carms.
Batchelor, A. L., A4 Glam.
Bate, E., A3 Flints.
Benest, J. S., A3 Glam.
Bernard, C. E., A3 Glam.
Birkett, D., A3 Pembs.
Blessley, W. D., A4 Glam., Mon.
Blessley & Vaughan, A4 Glam.
Bodley & Garner, A3 Glam.
Brigden, E., A3 Glam.
Buckeridge, C., A3 Brecs., Glam.
Bucknall, B., A3 Glam.
Budgen, H., A4 Glam.
Burnett, E. W., A4 Glam.
Burnett, W., A3 Glam.

Caple, W. H. D., A5 Caerns., Carms., Glam.
Cash, R., A3 Denbs.
Chaunders, R., A3 Glam.
Child, G., A3 Pembs.

Chittenden, G. E., A3 Glam.
Clark, W. S., A3 Glam.
Clinton, G., A3 Carms., Mon.
Clutton, H., A3 Carms., Mon.
Collard, J. L., A3 Carms.
Corbett, E. W. M., A4 Glam.
Cruickshank, W., A3 Denbs.
Curzon, H., A3 Rads.

Daniels, J., A3 Brecs., Mon.
David, E., A3 Glam.
Davies, C., A3 Cards., Carms.
Davies, Daniel, A3 Carms.
Davies, David, A3 Carms.
Davies, E., A3 Denbs.
Davies, R., A4 Ang.
Davies, W., A3 Glam.
Dew, W., A3 Ang.
Douglas & Minshall, A5 Caerns.

Edge, W., A3 Pembs.
Edwards, A. D., A4 Mon.
Evans, A. O., A4 Glam.
Evans, E., A3 Glam.
Evans, J., A3 Mer.
Evans, W., A3 Glam.
Evill, W., A4 Mon.
Evins, J. H., A3 Mon.

Fairclough, H. J., A3 Flints.
Ferrey, B., A3 Denbs., Mer.
Fowler, J. B., A3 Brecs.

Gardner, W. B., A4 Mon.
Gibson, J., A3 Flints.
Goode & Owen, A3 Pembs.
Goodman, H. A., A4 Glam.
Goodwin, E. M., A3 Pembs.
Graham & Lawrence, A3 Mon.
Grayson & Ould, A5 Flints.
Grierson & Bellis, A4 Denbs.
Griffith, H., A3 Ang.
Griffiths, E., A3 Glam.
Griffiths, J., A3 Glam.
Griffiths, W., A3 Pembs.
Griffiths, —, A5 Carms.
Gummon, J. R., A3 Denbs.

Habershon, W. G. & E., A3 Mon.
Habershon & Fawckner, A4 Glam.
Habershon, Fawckner & Groves,
    A4 Glam., Mon.
Habershon & Pite, A3 Glam.,
    Mon.
Habershon, Pite & Fawckner,
    A3 Mon.
Haddon Bros., A4 Mon., Rads.
Hansom, J. & C., A3 Glam., Mon.
Harmain, G., A4 Glam.
Harpur, S. O., A3 Glam.
Harris, H. C., A4 Glam.
Harrison, J., A3 Flints.
Harvey, G. S., A3 Pembs.
Haslam, W., A3 Ang.
Haycock, E., A3 Carms.
Hedley, G., A3 Caerns.
Hill, Grylls & Wilcocks, A4 Flints.
Hitchings, H., A3 Pembs.
Hughes, J., A5 Denbs.
Humphreys, J., A3 Glam.
Hurst, —, A3 Mont.

James, J., A3 Pembs.
James, W. P., A3 Glam., Mon.
James & Morgan, A5 Glam.
James, Seward & Thomas,
    A4 Glam.
Jenkins, D., A5 Carms., Glam.

Jenkins, J., A3 Pembs.
Jenkins, W. W., A3 Carms.
John, R., A3 Glam.
Johnson, E. A., A5 Mon.
Johnson, F. D., A3 Flints.
Jones, E., A3 Denbs., Mer.,
    Mont.
Jones, H., A3 Carms.
Jones, J., A3 Glam.
Jones, J. P., A4 Glam.
Jones, R. L., A4 Caerns.,
    A5 Caerns.
Jones, T., A3 Denbs.
Jones, T. H., A4 Glam.
Jones, W., A3 Brecs., Denbs.
Jones, Richards & Budgen,
    A4 Glam.

Kelly & Edwards, A3 Flints.
Kempson, F. R., A3 Brecs.
Kennedy, H., A3 Ang., Caerns.
    Denbs., Mer.
Kennedy & O'Donoghue,
    A3 Caerns.
Kennedy & Rogers, A3 Caerns.

Ladd, K. W., A3 Pembs.
Lambert & Rees, A5 Glam.
Lander & Bedells, A3 Carms.
Landsdowne, E. A., A4 Mon.
Laurence, G. E. T., A4 Glam.
Lawrence, B., A5 Mon.
Lawrence & Goodman, A4 Mon.
Lay, B., A4 Mont.
Lewis, J., A3 Carms.
Lewis, J. & Son, A3 Brecs.
Lewis, T. L., A3 Rads.
Lindsey, W. H., A3 Pembs.
Llewellyn, R., A4 Glam.
Lloyd, James, A3 Mont.
Lloyd, John, A3 Ang., Caerns.,
    Denbs., Flints.
Lloyd, W., A3 Mer.
Lockwood, T. M., A5 Mer.
Lote, H., A3 Rads.

Mair, G., A3 Brecs., Mon.
Martin, T. P., A4 Glam.,
    A5 Glam.
Moffat, W. B., A3 Cards.
Morgan, G., A5 Carms.
Morgan, J. B., A4 Carms.,
    Glam.
Morgan, T. E., A5 Cards.
Morgan & Son, A5 Cards.
Morris, H., A3 Glam.
Morris, J., A3 Mont.
Morris, W., A3 Denbs.
Moseley, A., A3 Glam.
Moss, W., A4 Denbs.
Moxham, E., A3 Glam.

Nevill, J., A3 Mon.
Nicholson, T., A3 Brecs., Rads.
Northcroft, G., A3 Ang., Caerns.,
    Mer.
Norton, J., A3 Glam., Mon.,
    Rads.

Owen, D., A3 Mont.
Owen, G., A3 Mer.
Owen, T., A3 Ang.
Owen, T. E., A3 Pembs.
Owens, R, A3 Flints., A4 Denbs.,
    Mer.

Pearson, J. L., A3 Brecs., Rads.
Penson, R. K., A3 Carms., Denbs.,
    Glam.
Penson, T., A3 Denbs., Mont.
Penson, T. M., A3 Denbs., Flints.
Phillips, J. H., A4 Glam.,
    A5 Brecs., Caerns., Cards.,
    Carms., Glam.
Phillips & Baldwin, A5 Brecs.,
    Mon.
Porteous, J. W., A3 Mont.
Powell & Swettenham, A4 Mont.
Poynter, A., A3 Flints.
Price, L. B., A5 Cards.
Prichard, J., A3 Glam.

Prichard & Seddon, A3 Glam.,
    Mon., Pembs.
Pritchard, J., A3 Denbs.
Pritchard, W., A3 Caerns.
Pugh, J., A3 Cards.

Rees, D., A3 Cards.
Rees, J., A3 Glam.
Rees, Jacob, A5 Glam.
Rees, J. C., A4 Glam.
Reynolds, M., A3 Glam.
Richards, J., A3 Brecs.
Richards, W., A3 Glam.
Ricketts, T., A3 Mont.
Ritchie, A., A3 Carms.
Roberts, D., A3 Mon.
Roberts & Morrow, A3 Caerns.
Roberts, M., A3 Denbs.
Roberts, O. M., A3 Caerns., Mer.
Roberts, T., A3 Caerns., Denbs.
Robinson, G. E., A3 Glam.
Rogers, H., A3 Carms.
Rogers, J., A3 Pembs.

Scott, G. G., A3 Cards., Denbs.,
    Mer.
Scrivener, R., A3 Flints.
Seddon, J. P., A3 Glam., Mon.
Seddon & Carter, A4 Glam.
Seward & Thomas, A4 Glam.
Shaw, G., A3 Caerns.
Shayler, F. H., A5 Flints., Mont.
Smith, S. P., A3 Mer.
Snell, H., A3 Glam., A4 Glam.,
    A5 Glam.
Spencer, J., A3 Flints.
Street, G. E., A3 Caerns., Denbs.
Swash, A., A4 Mon.
Swash & Bain, A5 Mon.
Szlumper & Aldwinckle, A4 Cards

Teather, H., A5 Ang., Denbs.,
    Mont., Rads.
Teather & Wilson, A5 Glam.
Teulon, S. S., A3 Glam.

Teulon, W. M., A3 Carms.
Thomas, C., A3 Mon.
Thomas, D. E., A5 Pembs.
Thomas, E., A3 Mer.
Thomas, E. G., A4 Ang.
Thomas, G., A5 Glam.
Thomas, H., A3 Carms.
Thomas, J., A3 Ang.
Thomas, J. H., A3 Cards.
Thomas, J. M., A5 Pembs.
Thomas, O., A3 Ang.
Thomas, R. C., A3 Glam.
Thomas, R. G., A3 Glam., Mon.,
    A4 Ang.
Thomas, T., A3 Glam.
Thomas, W. W., A4 Caerns.,
    Cards.
Thomas, Watkins & Jenkins,
    A3 Glam.
Thomas, —, A4 Glam.
Thompson, T. W. A., A3 Carms,
Truefitt, G., A3 Glam.
Turner, W., A3 Denbs., A4 Denbs.

Vaughan, D., A3 Glam.
Vaughan, E. M. B., A4 Glam.
Veall & Sant, A4 Glam.
Vulliamy, E., A3 Rads.

Walker & Poundley, A3 Mont.
Walters, J., A3 Brecs.

Watkins, A. O., A3 Mon.
Watkins & Jenkins, A3 Glam.
Watkins & Sons, A4 Mon.
Watts, J., A3 Pembs.
Wehnert & Ashdown, A3 Caerns.
Welch, E., A3 Denbs.
White, W., A3 Mont.
Wilding, J., A3 Rads.
Williams, E., A3 Denbs., Mer.
Williams, Ellis, A3 Mer.
Williams, J., A3 Glam., A4 Glam.
Williams, J. F., A3 Mon.
Williams, R., A3 Cards.
Williams, R. L., A3 Denbs.,
    Flints., Mer.
Williams & Underwood,
    A3 Ang., Denbs., Flints.
Williams, R. & S., A4 Glam.
Williams, S. W., A5 Brecs.
Williams, W., A3 Brecs., Mon.,
    A4 Brecs.
Williams, W. C., A4 Caerns.
Willink & Thickness, A5 Mer.
Wilson, J., A3 Caerns.
Wilson, J. B., A4 Glam.
Wilson & Moxham, A5 Glam.
Withers, R. J., A3 Cards., Carms.
Wyatt, T. H., A3 Caerns., Flints.,
    Mont.
Wyatt & Brandon, A3 Glam.,
    Mon.
Wyatt & Burgoyne, A3 Mon.

SELECT BIBLIOGRAPHY

Full details of the general works consulted are given in the foot-notes, and this bibliography is limited to published histories of individual schools and of education in specific areas before 1900. It has not been possible to include more than a small selection of the 'in-house' school histories published anonymously to celebrate centenaries, or of town histories which sometimes include chapters on education. I am very grateful to the Associate Librarian, The Welsh Library, University College of North Wales, and to the staff of a number of county record offices and libraries for their help in compiling this list.

ANGLESEY

(*TAAS* stands for *Transactions of the Anglesey Antiquarian Society*)

CARR, A. D., 'The Free Grammar School of Beaumaris', *TAAS* (1962).

DAVIES, B. L., 'Anglesey and the reports of . . . 1847', *TAAS* (1981).

JONES, E. M., 'The Free Grammar School of Beaumaris', *TAAS* (1922).

MORGAN, John, *David Hughes: Founder of Beaumaris Free School* (Caernarvon, 1883).

NOTTINGHAM, Lucie, 'Llandegfan, 1727-1972: the education of a parish', *TAAS* (1986).

OWEN, Hugh, 'Gruffydd Jones's circulating schools in Anglesey', *TAAS* (1936).

PRETTY, D. A., *Two Centuries of Anglesey Schools* [1700-1900] (Anglesey Antiquarian Society, 1977).

WALKER, T. G., *Hanes Ysgol Henblas, 1841-1943* (Llangefni, 1943).

WILIAM, D. W., 'Hanes addysg yn ardal Bodedern', *TAAS* (1964-5).

————— *Addysg ym Modedern* (1990).

WILLIAMS, John, *David Hughes and his Free Grammar School at Beaumaris* (1864, reprinted with additions by Vaughan Bowen, Leeds, 1933).

WILLIAMS, W. M., 'Anglesey schools a century ago', *TAAS* (1946).

BRECONSHIRE

ANON., *Christ's College, Brecon. Its past history and present capabilities* (London, 1853).

DAVIES, Dewi, *Brecknock Historian* (Brecon, 1977) [includes a chapter on education].

DAVIES, P. V., *The College of Christ of Brecknock 1538-1811* (Brecon, 1968).

EVANS, J. and HARRIS, T. J. B., *School and play in the parish of Vaynor from 1650 to the present* (Cowbridge, 1983).

KNIGHT, B., *The story of Christ College, Brecon* (Brecon, 1978).

POWELL, G., 'Hanes Plwyf Crai. History of the parish of Cray', [including schools] *Brycheiniog*, 10 (1964).

CAERNARFONSHIRE
(*TCHS* stands for *Transactions of the Caernarvonshire Historical Society*)

BARBER, H. and LEWIS, H., *The History of Friars Schools, Bangor* (Bangor, 1901).

CLARIDGE, S. A., 'The first of the county schools' [Caernarfon] *TCHS*, 19 (1958).

CLARKE, M. L., 'The Elizabethan statutes of Friars School, Bangor', *TCHS*, 16 (1955).

DAVIES, J. Ifor, *The Caernarvon County School. A History* (Caernarfon, 1989).

EVANS, G. J., 'Dyddlyfrau Ysgol Bethel', *TCHS*, 11 (1950).

———— *The entrance scholarship examination in Caernarvonshire 1897-1961* (Caernarvon Historical Society, 1966).

EVANS, L. W., 'Bron-y-foel School, Caernarvonshire', *TCHS*, 16 (1955).

GRESHAM, C. A., 'The Botwnnog Free Grammar School', *Archaeologia Cambrensis*, 116 (1967).

HUGHES, D. G. L., 'Ysgol Ramadeg rad Pwllheli', *TCHS*, 40 (1979).

JONES, Geraint, *Canmlwyddiant Ysgol Trefor* (Trefor, 1978).

JONES, Leslie, *Ysgol Waunfawr 1876-1976* (Caernarfon, 1976).

OWEN, P. E., 'The beginnings of the county schools in Caernarvonshire', *TCHS*, 18 (1957).

PARRY, Gruffydd, 'Hanes Ysgol Botwnnog', *Transactions of the Honourable Society of Cymmrodorion* (1957).

PRITCHARD, M., *Tros Bont Penllyn i Ysgol Sir Brynrefail* (Caernarfon, 1975).

RICHARDS, G., 'The early story of the schools of Dyffryn Nantlle', *TCHS*, 24 (1963).

ROBERTS, D. J., 'The early history of Penmaenmawr National School', *Gwynedd Archives Service Bulletin*, 1 (1974).

ROBERTS, Glyn, et al., 'A history of Friars School, Bangor, 1557-1957', *The Dominican* [school magazine] (1957).

ROBERTS, Nesta, *St. Winifred's Llanfairfechan, 1887-1937* [independent girls' school] (Shrewsbury, 1937).

THOMAS, Ifor, 'Braslun o hanes addysg ym mhlwyf Dolwyddelan', *TCHS*, 33 (1972).

WEBSTER, J. R., 'Botwnnog grammar school in 1833', *Transactions of the Honourable Society of Cymmrodorion* (1960).

WHELDON, W. P., *St. Paul's* [Wesleyan] *School, Bangor* (Bangor, 1936).

WILLIAMS, H. G., 'Lloyd George and Catholic education in Caernarvon', *Caernarvonshire Record Office Bulletin*, 6 (1973).

———— 'William George, schoolmaster' [father of Lloyd George], *Gwynedd Archive Service Bulletin*, 3 (1976).

———— 'The Kynnersley educational returns for Caernarfonshire', *Welsh History Review*, 13 (1986-87).

———— 'The school board movement in Caernarfonshire, 1870-1880', *TCHS*, 50 (1989).

CARDIGANSHIRE

BUNDOCK, D. W., *Crwydro Dyffryn Clettwr . . . Ysgol Pontsian 1879-1979* (Llandysul, 1979).

DAVIES, D. J., 'Ysgol Llanwnen', *Yr Ymofynnydd*, 54 (1954).

DAVIES, Donald, 'Cardigan Intermediate School', *Cardigan & Tivy-side Advertiser*, 11.4.86, 18.4.86, 25.4.86, 2.5.86.

DAVIES, G. G., 'Addysg Elfennol yn Sir Aberteifi, 1870-1902', *Ceredigion*, 4 (1960-63).

DAVIES, Kate, *Ysgol Tregroes 1878-1978* (1978).

DAVIES, M. H., *Ysgol Rhydlewis 1877-1977* (1977).

DAVIS, J., *Lampeter* [Grammar] *School. A catalogue of the Library* (Lampeter, 1866) [has an historical introduction].

DONALDSON, M. C., 'Edward Richard of Ystrad Meurig', *Ceredigion*, 5 (1964-7).

EVANS, Lyn, *Portrait of a pioneer: a biography of Howell Thomas Evans* [of Aberaeron Intermediate School] (Landybie, 1982).

EVANS, W. G., 'The Aberdare Report and Cardiganshire', *Ceredigion*, 9 (1980-83).

GRIFFITHS, R. S., 'The Welsh Intermediate Education Act and Cardiganshire', *Ceredigion*, 8 (1976-79).

JONES, J. R., *Ysgol Llangynfelyn 1876-1976* (1976).

JONES, S. E., *Ysgol Ysbyty Ystwyth 1878-1978* (Llandysul, 1978).

LLEWELYN, W. D., *Crynodeb o Hanes Cribyn . . . Ysgol Gynradd Cribyn 1877-1977* (1977).

OSBORNE-JONES, D. G., *Edward Richard of Ystradmeurig, with the story of his school . . . 1734-1934* (Carmarthen, 1934).

REES, J. R., *Ysgol Penuwch 1879-1979* (Llandysul, 1979).

SAMUEL, D., *Some Old Schools and Schoolmasters of Aberystwyth* (Aberystwyth, 1901).

———— *History of Lampeter Grammar School* (Aberystwyth, 1909).

THOMAS, D. W., 'Addysg yng Ngheredigion, 1800-1850', *Ceredigion*, 6 (1968-71).

THOMAS, Owen, 'Log books of Cardiganshire schools', *Transactions of the Cardiganshie Antiquarian Society*, 13 (1938).

TROTT, A. L., 'Aberystwyth school board and board school, 1870-1902', *Ceredigion*, 2 (1952).

——————— 'Church day schools in Aberystwyth during the nineteenth century', *Ceredigion*, 2 (1953).

——————— 'Elementary day schools for children of the working classes in Cardiganshire in 1847', *Ceredigion*, 2 (1954).

——————— 'The implementation of the 1870 Elementary Education Act in Cardiganshire', *Ceredigion*, 3 (1956-59).

——————— 'Educational charities in Cardiganshire 1833-35', *Ceredigion*, 4, (1960-63).

CARMARTHENSHIRE

BAKER, Barbara, *The story of Pentrepoeth* [British/Board school] (Carmarthen, 1988).

COMMINS, Nigel, *The story of the Model School, Carmarthen* (Carmarthen, 1987).

DAVIES, Jacob, *Hanes Ysgol Nantcwmrhys* (Pencader, 1957).

——————— *Hanes Pedair Ysgol* [Pen-y-bont, Tre-lech, Alma, Penrhiwlas] (Llandysul, 1975).

EVANS, G. E., 'Carmarthenshire schools', *Transactions of the Carmarthenshire Antiquarian Society*, 2 (1906-7), 16 (1923), 22 (1929-31), 23 (1932).

EVANS, Martin, *An Early History of Queen Elizabeth Grammar School, Carmarthen, 1576-1800* (Carmarthen n.d.).

EVANS, W. Gareth, *A History of Llandovery College* (The College, 1981).

——————— *Educational Development in a Victorian Community* [Carmarthenshire] (Aberystwyth, 1990).

GIBBARD, Noel, 'Llanelli Schools 1800-1870', *Carmarthenshire Historian*, 5 (1968).

HAMER, W. B., 'Thomas Phillips, founder of the Collegiate Institution at Llandovery', *Transactions of the Radnorshire Society*, 14 (1944).

JENKINS, D. E. A., 'The log books of Ferryside School 1889-1937', *Carmarthen Antiquary*, 6 (1970).

JONES, Eluned, *Eu Ceiniogau Prin. Ysgol Heol y Farchnad, Llanelli* (Llandybie, 1982).

JONES, J. F., 'The schools of Llanboidy', *Transactions of the Carmarthenshire Antiquarian Society*, 28 (1937-8).

KNIGHT, L. S., 'The grammar schools of Carmarthen to 1576', *Transactions of the Carmarthenshire Antiquarian Society*, 13 (1919).

LEWIS, P. (ed.), *Hanes Ysgol Bancffosfelen, 1877-1977* (Llandysul, 1978).

MORRIS, W. H., 'Two Carmarthenshire schoolmasters', *Carmarthen Antiquary*, 4 (1962-3).

PRYS-JONES, A. G., 'Queen Elizabeth School, Carmarthen', *Carmarthenshire Local History Magazine*, 2 (1962).

RANDALL, A. B., 'The education of young ladies' [private adventure schools in Carmarthen 1810-40], *Carmarthenshire Historian*, 16 (1979) and 18 (1981).

SAMUEL, David, 'Ysgol Llanymddyfri [Llandovery College], *Cymru*, 40 (1911).

WALTERS, Huw, *Hanes Ysgol Glanamman* (1983).

WARD, A. H., 'The beginnings of intermediate technical education for boys in Llanelli', *Carmarthen Antiquary*, 8 (1972).

WILLIAMS, Glanmor, 'Thomas Lloyd his skole: Carmarthen's first Tudor grammar school', *Carmarthen Antiquary*, 10 (1974).

WILLIAMS, M. E. *Hanes Ysgol Esgerdawe* [1877-1982] (Llandysul, 1982).

DENBIGHSHIRE

(*TDHS* stands for *Transactions of the Denbighshire Historical Society*)

ANON., 'The History of the Denbigh Grammar School', *Y Bych* [school magazine] (1954).

————— *Ruthin County School for Girls 1899-1938* (Ruthin, 1988).

————— *Rydal* [independent school]: *the First Hundred Years* (Colwyn Bay, 1985).

DAVIES, J. C., *Bwlchgwyn* [Board] *School 1875-1975*, (Bwlchgwyn, 1975).

DODD, Charles, *Wrexham Schools and Scholars* (Wrexham, 1924).

DODD, A. H., 'Keeping school in Victorian Wrexham' [based on diary of author's father], *TDHS*, 21 (1972).

EDWARDS, Ifor, 'Log book of the Brymbo and Broughton British School', *TDHS*, 23 (1974).

————— *Acrefair County Primary School Centenary 1877-1977* (Mold, 1977).

EVANS, H. R., 'Ebenezer Morris Powell, founder and headmaster of Holt Academy, 1820-76', *TDHS*, 10 (1961).

JONES, E. K., *The Story of . . . the schools of Cefnmawr, 1786-1933* (Cefnmawr, 1933).

GRIFFITHS, G. M., 'Ruabon grammar school', *NLW Journal*, 9 (1955-6).

KEARNS, Clifford, *The National School, Lenten Pool, Denbigh, 1846-1976* (Denbigh, 1976).

MATTHEWS, E. G., *Ysgol yr Eglwys: Llanrhaeadr Church School* (1986).

MORRIS, G. H., 'Meeting held for . . . erecting a new National school in Lenten Pool, Denbigh', *TDHS*, 19 (1970).

PARRY, R. J. and JONES, H. P., *Llanrwst Grammar School, 1610-1960* (Llanrwst, 1961).

PRITCHARD, T. W., *Llanferres Endowed School 1763-1976* (Mold 1976).

————— 'A history of the old endowed grammar school, Ruabon, 1618-1896', *TDHS*, 20 (1971).

ROBERTS, E., *Braslun o Hanes Ysgol Ty'n-y-Felin, Glasfryn, 1874-1974* (1974).

ROBERTS, S. T., *Ysgol Eglwysbach 1835-1985* (Caernarfon, 1985).

SEABORNE, M., 'Day Schools and Sunday Schools in mid-nineteenth century Denbighshire', *TDHS*, 39 (1990).

STONE, M. K., 'Howell's School, Denbigh', *TDHS*, 8 (1959).

THOMAS, A. M., 'Grove Park [private] School, Wrexham 1823-94', *TDHS*, 30 (1981).

————— 'Wrexham County School for Girls, 1896-1925', *TDHS*, 31 (1982).

THOMPSON, K. M., *Ruthin School: The First Seven Centuries* (The School, 1974).

VAUGHAN, B. C., 'The log book of Llansannan School', *TDHS*, 6 (1957).

WILLIAMS, A. H., 'The origins of the old endowed grammar schools of Denbighshire', *TDHS*, 2 (1953).

————— 'Education controversy at Gellifor a century ago', *TDHS*, 24 (1975).

FLINTSHIRE
(*FHSJ* stands for *Flintshire Historical Society Journal*)

EDWARDS, J. G., '[Education in] Flintshire one hundred years ago', *FHSJ*, 17 (1957).

GRIFFITHS, G. M., 'Education in the diocese of St. Asaph 1729-30', *NLW Journal*, 6 (1949-50) and 7 (1951-2).

————— 'Educational activity in the diocese of St Asaph, 1500-1650', *Journal of the Historical Society of the Church in Wales*, 3 (1953).

HAVARD, W. T., 'The educational and religious movement in the diocese of St. Asaph in the eighteenth century', *NLW Journal*, 4 (1945-6).

JONES, J. C., *St. Matthew's School, Buckley, 1849-1949* (Buckley, 1949).

————— 'A history of the schools and education in Buckley', *Flintshire Historical Society Publications*, 15 (1954-5).

JONES, W. B., 'The Hawarden grammar school', ibid, 6 (1916-17).

PRITCHARD, T. W., 'Northop Grammar School', *FHSJ*, 29 (1979-80).

SEABORNE, M., 'Education and school building in Flintshire during the early Victorian period', *FHSJ*, 33 (1992).

GLAMORGAN

ANON., *Aberdare Intermediate Schools 1896-1946* (Aberdare, 1946).

————— *Cardiff High School* [for Boys] *Magazine, Jubilee Number, 1898-1948* (Cardiff, 1949).

————— *Gowerton Intermediate School 1896-1946* (Gowerton, 1946).

————— *Port Talbot County School 1896-1946* (Port Talbot, 1946).

————— *Swansea* [Llwyn-y-bryn] *High School for Girls 1888-1948* (Swansea, 1948).

BENNETT, G. (ed.), *Something Attempted, Something Done* [Gowerton Grammar School] (Llandybie, 1973).

BROWN, R. L., 'The early history of education in the Glyncorrwg area', *Afan Uchaf*, 6 (1983).

————— 'Education in the Upper Afan 1869-1885', *Afan Uchaf*, 7 (1984).

————— 'The Glyncorrwg School Board 1884-1903', *Afan Uchaf*, 8 (1985).

CARR, Catherine, *The Spinning Wheel: City of Cardiff High School for Girls, 1895-1955* (Cardiff, 1955).

COOKE, S. P., 'A history of Blaengwawr schools in the early years', *Old Aberdare*, 2 (1982).

CRONIN, J. M., 'Catholic education in Cardiff 1836-47', *St. Peter's Magazine* (1922).

CUMMINGS, Ronald, 'The log books of a Rhondda school, 1864-1910', *Glamorgan Historian*, 11 (1975).

DAVIES, E. T. 'Glamorgan and the Treachery of the Blue Books', *Glamorgan Historian*, 11 (1975).

DAVIES, Iolo, '*A Certaine Schoole'. A History of Cowbridge Grammar School* (Cowbridge, 1967).

DAVIES, W. E., *The National Schools, Oxford Street, Swansea, 1848-1948* (Swansea, 1948).

ENOCH, D. G., 'They That Sow in Tears. A Hindsight into Victorian Education in Llantrisant', *Morgannwg*, 29 (1985).

EVANS, L. W., 'Sir John and Lady Charlotte Guest's educational scheme at Dowlais', *NLW Journal*, 9 (1955-6).

EVANS, Thomas, *History of the Navigation school, Aberycynon, 1875-1945* (Cardiff, 1946).

FRANCIS, G. G., *The Free Grammar School, Swansea* (Swansea, 1849).

GILCHRIST, W. J. M., 'Unwillingly to school' [absenteeism c. 1860-1900], *Gower*, 27 (1976).

HARDWICK, G. H., *Pengam School Board* (Risca, 1980).

HOPKINS, K. S. (ed.), Chapter on Education 1870-1923 by John Davies in *Rhondda Past and Present* (Rhondda, 1975).

HOWELL, B, *The County Grammar School for Boys, Pontypridd 1896-1946* (Pontypridd, 1946).

HOWELLS, W. J., *Rhondda County School for Boys 1896-1946* (Tonypandy, 1946).

IMPEY, A. C., 'Board School versus Intermediate School . . . in Cardiff, 1880-1914', *Morgannwg*, 25 (1981).

JONES, Eben, 'The birth, life and death of the Aberavon Unsectarian Schools 1885-1977', *Transactions of the Port Talbot Historical Society*, 3, (1984).

McCANN, J. E., *Thomas Howell and the School at Llandaff 1860-1890* (Cowbridge, 1972).

MORGAN, Prys (ed.), 'Educational developments in Glamorgan, 1780-1980', ch. XIV by G. E. Jones in *Glamorgan County History*, Vol. VI (Cardiff, 1988).

O'BRIEN A. M., *The County School for Boys, Pontypridd, 1896-1973* (Pontypridd, 1989).

OWEN-JONES, S. M., 'Religious influence and educational progress in Glamorgan, 1800-33', *Welsh History Review*, 13 (1986-87).

POWELL, Glan, 'Seventy-five years of Dynevor [Higher Grade] School [Swansea], *South Wales Evening Post*, 22 May, 1958.

PRICE, W. W., *Park* [British] *Schools Centenary* (Aberdare, 1948).

SIMONS, Henry, 'The Caerphilly National Schools', *Caerphilly*, 1 (1968).
———— 'The Ann Allworth charity school endowment 1729-1971', *Caerphilly*, 2 (1971).
———— 'The Eglwysilan Board Schools', *Caerphilly*, 4 (1977).
———— 'Early education in Gower', *Gower*, 22-25 (1971-4).

STEAD, P. P., 'Schools and Society in Glamorgan before 1914', *Morgannwg*, 19 (1975).

THOMAS, D. J. (ed.), *Swansea Grammar School, 1682-1932*, special number of school magazine (1932).

THOMAS, Jack, *Alderman Davies' Church in Wales School, Neath, 1858-1958* (Neath, 1958).

THOMAS, N. L., *A Hundred Years in School: St. Helen's 1874-1974* (Swansea, 1974).

WILLIAMS, A. H., 'The Wesleyan Day School, Pontypridd', *Bathafarn*, 5 (1950).

WILLIAMS, Glanmor (ed.), 'Religion and Education in Glamorgan, 1660-1775', chapter IX of *Glamorgan County History*, Vol. IV (Cardiff, 1974).

WILLIAMS, W. G., *A Brief History of the Hafod Copperworks School* (Swansea, 1905).

WRIGHT, Arthur, *The History of Lewis' School, Pengam . . . with a chapter upon Hengoed School* (Newtown, 1929).

MERIONETH
    (*JMHS* stands for *Journal of the Merioneth Historical Society*)

ELLIS, Tecwyn, 'Educational Charities in Merioneth before 1837', *JMHS*, 7 (1973-6).

EVANS, W. G.. 'The Aberdare Report and education in Merioneth 1881', *JMHS*, 9 (1981-84).
———— 'Canmlwyddiant . . . Ysgol Cynwyd 1886-89', *JMHS*, 10 (1985-88).
———— 'The . . . Welsh Intermediate Education Act, 1889, and the location of the intermediate schools in Merioneth', *JMHS*, 10 (1989).
———— 'T. E. Ellis and the Welsh Intermediate Act in Merioneth' *JMHS*, 11 (1990).

HARRIS, M. C.. 'Cwm School, Llanfachreth', *JMHS*, 8 (1977-80).

JENKINS, R. T., 'A sketch of the history of Bala grammar school, 1713-1893', *JMHS*, 1 (1951) and 2 (1953).

JONES, B. M., 'Dr. Williams' School, Dolgellau', *JMHS*, 6 (1970).

JONES-ROBERTS, K. W., 'Education in the parish of Ffestiniog', *JMHS*, 2 (1956).

REES, A. M. and JONES, E., 'Dr. John Elis' School, Dolgellau, and its successors, 1665-1965', *JMHS*, 5 (1966).

ROBERTS, R. F., 'A Merioneth School book' [Dr. Williams' School, Llanuwchllyn], *NLW Journal*, 11 (1959-60).

WILLIAMS, Ffestin, *Brief outline history of Penrhyndeudraeth* [British] *School 1834-1984* (Penrhyndeudraeth, 1984).

MONMOUTHSHIRE
(*GLH* stands for *Gwent Local History*)

ALLSOBROOK, D. I., 'Aspects of the history of Monmouthshire grammar schools in the nineteenth century', *GLH*, 55 (1983).

ANON., *Abertillery County School 1896-1946* (Newport, 1946).

———— *Ebbw Vale County School 1897-1947* (Ebbw Vale, 1947).

———— *The History of the County School for Girls, Pontypool, 1897-1947* (Pontypool, 1947).

———— *Pontypool Town School, 1838-1938* (Pontypool, 1938).

BRADNEY, J. A., *A History of the Free Grammar School in the parish of Llantilio-Crossenny* (London, 1924).

CLARK, Arthur, 'The Treason of the Blue Books', *Presenting Monmouthshire* 13 (1962).

CORTEN, A., 'Aspects of the history of the grammar schools in Monmouthshire during the nineteenth century', *GLH*, 53 (1982) and 54 (1983).

DAVIES, Eileen, 'Aspects of nineteenth century education in Cwmbran', *Presenting Monmouthshire*, 32 (1971).

DAVIES, E. T., *Monmouthshire Schools and Education to 1870* (Newport, 1957).

GLOVER, E. P., *The First Sixty Years 1896-1956* [Newport High School for Boys] (Newport, 1957).

GRAHAM, J. D. P., 'Schooling in Ewyas', *GLH*, 65 (1988).

JONES, R. T., 'State education comes to the Blackwood area' [1873-4], *Presenting Monmouthshire*, 31 (1971).

KISSACK, Keith, 'Education', chapter V of *Monmouth. The Making of a County Town* (Chichester, 1975).

MORGAN, T. M., *Caerleon Endowed Schools, 1724-1983* (Risca, 1983).

MORGAN Trevor, *Monmouthshire Education 1889-1974* (Cwmbran, 1988).

———— 'The Blue Books and Monmouthshire', *GLH*, 70 (1991).

NELMES, G. V., 'A History of King Henry VIII's Boys Grammar School at Abergavenny', *GLH*, 59 (1985) and 60 (1986).

PHILLIPS, Roger, 'Religion . . . and education at Castleton and Wentloog moors in the nineteenth century', *GLH*, 57 (1984).

ROBERTS, Idris, *Early Beginnings of Workschools in Monmouthshire* (1973).

SHEEN, I. D., 'Elementary education in Abergavenny 1869-1902', *GLH*, 48 (1980).

THOMAS, D. G., 'Gelligaer Village School log books 1875-1894', *Gelligaer*, 2 (1965).

THOMPSON, E. C., 'The Grammar School of Abergavenny', *Jesus College Record* (Oxford, 1966).

VERRIER, Ursula, *Llanddewi Rhydderch School 1867-1967* (Abertillery, 1967).

WARD, H. A., *Monmouth School 1614-1964* (London, 1964).

WARLOW, W. M., *A History of the Charities of William Jones at Monmouth* (Bristol, 1899).

WATERS, Ivor, 'Chepstow Schools, 1605-1902', *Presenting Monmouthshire*, 17 (1964).

WILKS, F. E., 'James Davies — an old Monmouthshire schoolmaster'. *GLH*, 45 (1978).

MONTGOMERYSHIRE

(MC stands for Montgomeryshire Collections)

CAMPBELL, M. C., 'Some records of the free grammar school at Deythur in the county of Montgomery, 1690-1900', *Y Cymmrodor*, 43 (1932).

CARR, H., *A Survey of Schools in the Administrative County of Montgomery* [by the County Architect] (Welshpool, 1944).

DAVIES, D. W., *A History of Education in Machynlleth* (Machynlleth, 1986).

DAVIES, J. A., *Education in a Welsh Rural County, 1870-1973* [Montgomeryshire] (Cardiff, 1973).

EVANS, M. J., 'Elementary education in Montgomeryshire 1850-1900', *MC*, 63 (1973-4).

MORRIS, E. R., 'The Vaughan and Strangways Charity and the Llanfyllin Charity Schools', *MC*, 66 (1978).

OLIVER, H. N., *A History of Llanllwchaiarn Church Schools* (Newtown, n.d.).

PEATE, David, *Manafon School 1833-1983* (Welshpool. 1983).

PHILLIPS, R. J., *Church and State: Hereford Diocesan Schools* (Hereford 1986) [includes schools in Mont. and Rads.].

THOMAS, O., 'Berriew Road [National] School, Welshpool, 1821-1967', *MC*, 60 (1967-68).

WILLIAMS, A. J. B., 'Education in Montgomeryshire in the late nineteenth century', *MC*, 52 (1951-2).

WILLIAMS, L. H., 'Beginnings of intermediate education in Montgomeryshire', *NLW Journal*, 16 (1969-70).

PEMBROKESHIRE

DAVIES, Wynford, 'Narberth County Intermediate School, 1895-1924', *NLW Journal*, 23 (1983-84).

————— 'Aspects of change in secondary education in Pembroke-shire, 1880-1930', *Journal of the Pembrokeshire Historical Society,* 1, (1985).

HARRISON, Wilfred, *Greenhill School, Tenby 1896-1964* (Cardiff, 1979).

HOWELLS, B. (ed.), 'Religion and Education in early modern Pembroke-shire, 1536-1815', chapter by R. Brinkley in *Religion and Education* (Haverfordwest, Pembrokeshire Historical Society, 1987).

HUGHES, W. O., 'The Barham Memorial School, Trecwn', *Bathafarn,* 3 (1948).

JAMES, G. D., 'The Schools of the Town' in *The Town and County of Haverfordwest and its History* (Haverfordwest, 1958).

————— *The History of Haverfordwest Grammar School* (Haverford-west, 1961).

JONES, A. J., *John Morgan, first headmaster of Narberth County School* (Llandysul, 1939).

RICHARDS, W . L., *The Schoolmaster Abroad. A History of education in Camrose parish* (West Wales Guardian, 1985).

SALMON, David, *A brief history of education in Pembrokeshire* (Carmarthen, 1926).

RADNORSHIRE

(*TRS* stands for *Transactions of the Radnorshire Society*)

HOWSE, W. H., *School and Bell: Four Hundred Years of a Welsh Grammar School* [Presteigne], (Halesowen, 1956).

JONES, P. A., 'The use of pupil-teachers at Newbridge-on-Wye school 1872-1907', *TRS,* 56 (1986).

MOSTYN, John, 'Radnorshire school log books', *TRS,* 2-9 (1932-39).

————— 'Radnorshire schools in 1902', *TRS,* 22 (1952).

OLIVER, R. C. B., 'The Hartstonges and Radnorshire', *TRS,* 43 (1973).

PHILLIPS, H. D. and DAVIES, D. S., 'Pioneers of education in Radnor-shire', *TRS,* 17 (1947).

WATKINS, W., 'Education in Llanfihangel Rhydithon and district', *TRS,* 6, (1936).

Index

267